Cavendish
Publishing
Limited

# INTELLECTUAL PROPERTY

## WITH COMPETITION LAW AND PRACTICE

**London Guildhall-Cavendish
Legal Practice Course Companion Series**

**LONDON GUILDHALL**
**UNIVERSITY**

# TITLES IN THE SERIES

Assessment of Skills

Business Law & Practice

Civil Litigation

Commercial Law & Practice

Conveyancing Law & Practice

Corporate Insolvency Law & Practice

Criminal Litigation

Employment Law & Practice

Evidence

Family Law & Practice

Immigration & Nationality Law & Practice

Intellectual Property with Competition Law & Practice

Introduction to the Legal Practice Course

Pervasive Subjects

Wills, Probate & Administration

Cavendish
Publishing
Limited

# INTELLECTUAL PROPERTY

## WITH COMPETITION LAW AND PRACTICE

**Peter Groves, LLB, MA, PhD**

**Solicitor**

## London Guildhall-Cavendish
## Legal Practice Course Companion Series

**LONDON GUILDHALL**

**UNIVERSITY**

First published in Great Britain 1994 by Cavendish Publishing Limited, The Glass House, Wharton Street, London WC1X 9PX.

Telephone: 071-278 8000  Facsimile: 071-278 8080

**British Library Cataloguing in Publication Data**

London Guildhall University
Intellectual Property with Competition Law & Practice - (LPC Series)
I Title II Series
344.10648

ISBN 1-874241-54-6
Printed and bound in Great Britain

# Outline contents

# Contents

## 13 Intellectual property protection

## 14 Unfair competition and passing off

# Table of cases

# Table of statutes

# Chapter 1

## Identifying intellectual property rights

### What is intellectual property?                    1.1

Intellectual property – universally abbreviated to 'IP' – is a type of intangible personal property comprising (broadly) matter created by the exercise of the human intellect. Statute provides a definition, although in a rather strange place: s.72(5), Supreme Court Act 1982 (as amended by the Copyright, Designs and Patents Act 1988) provides that:

intellectual property means any patent, trademark, copyright, design right, registered design, technical or commercial information or other intellectual property ...

Intellectual property is – except for patents – enforceable as a chose in action, enforceable not by possession (for there is nothing which you can physically possess) but by action.

---

*Note*

By s.30(1), Patents Act 1977 a patent is *not* a chose in action; however, that Act provides for *assignments* of patents, so the difference is academic.

---

The law grants rights in this type of property according to the nature of the property involved, IP rights are said to 'subsist' in the property they protect. Inventions are protected by patents, designs by registration as registered designs or by unregistered design right, original works by copyright. The word 'subsist' (as opposed to 'exist', for example) implies that the rights are sustained by the property they protect.

### Intellectual property and industrial property        1.1.1

The expression 'industrial property' is sometimes heard. Formerly, this was understood to mean patents, trademarks and designs (the subject matter of the Paris Convention on Industrial Property 1883 (*see* Chapter 4); trademarks (which protect reputations) were often considered not to be intellectual property. Now, particularly since the subject matter of copyright has come to include 'small coin' works, for example computer programs, intellectual property and industrial property should be considered synonymous. (*See* also *Musik-Vertrieb Membran v GEMA* (1981) where the European Court of Justice (ECJ) decided that copyright could fairly be described as commercial and was therefore industrial or commercial property within the meaning of Article 36, Treaty of Rome 1957: and *see* Chapter 7.)

1.1.2        **Registered and unregistered rights**

The most important *distinction* to draw between the different intellectual property rights is between those which are registered and those which are not.

*Registered rights* – including patents, trademarks and registered designs – are granted after an examination procedure and their existence is a matter of public record. They can therefore be readily identified by *searching the appropriate register* and because they are recorded in a public register it is reasonable to accord them *monopoly protection*.

Rights which come into existence without the need to register such as copyright and unregistered design right, give protection only against copying; *independent* creation is a defence to an infringement action.

1.1.3        **Related areas**

Intellectual property is also often taken to include confidential information and know how (which may be the same thing). Passing off, an action to protect a trade reputation (and therefore to protect unregistered trademarks), is also considered an area of intellectual property law.

The law which protects these matters does not invest the person who may enforce them with property rights, so, strictly speaking, they do not belong to the world of intellectual property. However, for practical reasons we shall treat them as being part of the subject, as a comprehensive knowledge of IP law requires familiarity with these subjects.

1.1.4        **Intellectual property as a business asset**

Intellectual property rights may be among the most valuable assets owned by a business. For many individuals – inventors, designers, writers, composers, artists, computer programmers – they are a means to earn a living (sometimes a very good one). Publishing companies depend on owning copyright (or licences granted by copyright owners); many pharmaceutical companies rely for their profitability on their patents; consumer goods manufacturers spend a great deal of money on the design of their products; and most businesses use trademarks to identify their goods or their business to their customers.

*Note*

This Companion is primarily about intellectual property as a business asset – how it comes into existence, how it can be protected, how the law places restrictions on the exercise of IP rights, and how it may be communicated.

## Ownership and use of intellectual property            1.2

### Ownership            1.2.1

The laws which govern the different types of intellectual property lay down rules on who is entitled to use them. Special rules deal with inventions, designs and copyright works which are created by employees.

### Exploitation            1.2.2

The owners of intellectual property rights may earn value from it in different ways. First and foremost, they may use it themselves – by making a product which incorporates an invention, for example, or publishing a book. They may also sell it outright or permit others to use it.

#### Assignment

If intellectual property is sold outright, it is assigned to the new owner. The consideration may be a lump sum but is more likely to be a periodic royalty payment based on what the assignee earns from the rights transferred.

#### Licence

Permission to use intellectual property rights is known as a licence and an IP licence may be a complicated document. It may also be quite informal or may be assumed from the conduct of the parties. Licences may be sole or exclusive, or non-exclusive. (A sole licence differs from an exclusive licence in that the former does not preclude the owner of the rights exploiting them itself, whereas under the latter an exclusive licensee becomes the only person entitled to do the things covered by the licence agreement.)

#### Mortgage

Intellectual property can also be used as security for an advance, in a similar way to real property.

## Common features of IP rights            1.3

### IP rights are divisible            1.3.1

Intellectual property is highly divisible, and a particular right may be divided by function.

*Example*

An author may sell the right to publish a literary work to one person, the right to make a play from it to another, the right to translate it into French to another, and the right to make a film from it to yet another. All these rights form part of the bundle of rights called copyright.

Similarly, a trademark owner may give the right to use it on one type of product to one person and the right to apply it to something else to another. Note, however, that in the nature of trademark law there are limits to the extent to which this is possible.

### 1.3.2     IP rights are territorial

Intellectual property is by nature national, so these rights may be assigned or licensed to different people in different countries. They may also be split up between different parts of the same country.

*Note*

The competition rules of the Treaty of Rome may prohibit anything which might amount to partitioning the common market (*see* Chapter 8) or which is an abuse of a 'dominant position' (*see* Chapter 9). The Treaty will also prohibit restrictions on the free movement of goods (*see* Chapter 20).

### 1.3.3     IP rights are quite independent of each other

The different types of intellectual property exist without reference to each other.

Intellectual property rights protect different subject matter, which might all co-exist in the same article.

*Example*

A computer may embody patented technology and the appearance of the machine may be a registered design. It is likely to be sold under a trademark, and to have in its memory programs protected by copyright. The layout of the semiconductor chip which lies at the heart of the machine will also have protection, under a special intellectual property right known as 'topography right'.

Similarly, an act which infringes one right may have no implications for any of the other rights involved. The rights will also last for different periods of time and they may be assigned or licensed independently of each other.

In short, there is *little or no co-ordination* of different IP rights.

### 1.3.4     IP rights can be bought and sold

The fact that IP rights are tradeable is what gives them value. It can also mean that they can become vested in a variety of different people (natural and legal). As nothing can be deduced about the ownership of IP from possession (since there is nothing for the owner to possess) ownership may be difficult to establish, and legal and beneficial ownership may be split.

Where rights are registered, the task seems easier, as the register shows the name of the registered owner, but beneficial ownership may be different and there may be an assignment which has not been registered (perhaps simply because it was overlooked).

IP rights can also be exploited by granting others licences to use them.

### IP rights are anti-competitive                    1.3.5

The basic principle of all IP law is to create limited monopolies. In patent, design and copyright law, this serves to give an incentive to inventiveness or creativity, but this incentive has to be balanced against the consequences of giving someone exclusive rights.

As we shall see, in patent law this balance is struck by requiring comprehensive public disclosure of the invention; in copyright, the monopoly is carefully limited in scope so only the author's own expression and not the underlying idea enjoys protection. However, the law abhors monopolies, even when they are granted for good reasons, and IP law is therefore on a collision course with competition law.

### IP rights are at best only provisional            1.3.6

Even rights which are registered are not absolutely sound. Registered rights are capable of being challenged if they have been wrongly granted.

*Example*

1   A registered trademark which has not been used on goods for which it is registered for five years may be cancelled.

2   If it later becomes apparent that an invention was not novel, any patent granted on it may be cancelled.

### Putting IP in the right place                     1.3.7

IP rights do not conveniently conform to corporate structures and lawyers must sometimes indulge in a little legal engineering to make sure that ownership vests in the right place. This problem might arise in a joint venture, where one party develops a new invention but the other party, which might have provided all the finance, should own the rights in it. And the IP ramifications of partnerships are endless.

Tax savings can be achieved by moving IP portfolios around. The tax treatment of trademarks, for example, is particularly generous in the Netherlands. Putting rights into a Dutch holding company can be advantageous.

## 1.4    Intellectual property professionals

Intellectual property professionals fall into three broad categories, those concerned with:

- *Protecting* IP;
- Its *exploitation*; and
- *Valuing* the property rights.

The same professionals may deal with more than one of these functions.

Protecting IP involves several stages and different professionals have different roles to play.

### 1.4.1    Patent agents

Patent agents are concerned with securing protection for registered intellectual property rights, including registered designs and plant variety rights. They may, however, specialise in particular areas; some may confine their patent drafting activities to particular technical areas, some do no trademark work.

> *Note*
>
> Trademark agents are a separate profession (though many patent agents are also trademark agents). Registration of the different rights requires detailed knowledge of complicated rules and procedures and the special expertise of practitioners in the field is needed.

In the UK, the patent agents' profession is regulated by the Chartered Institute of Patent Agents which maintains the register of patent agents. Qualification is by:

- Degree or equivalent qualification in a scientific or technical field;
- Examination, touching upon knowledge of the whole of IP law (not just patents) and practical skills; and
- A four year training contract.

Only a duly qualified and registered patent agent or a solicitor (*see* 1.4.4) may act for reward as a patent agent.

### 1.4.2    Trademark agents

Trademark agents qualify in a similar way, obtaining membership of the Institute of Trademark Agents. Only registered trademark agents (who are usually but not always members of the Institute) may describe themselves as such.

However, the title 'trademark agent' remains free for anyone to use.

*Note* _____

The government, in the course of the passage of the Copyright, Designs and Patents Act 1988 (which regulates the profession) expressed the view that the protection of consumers did not require the same rigorous approach in the case of trademark agents as it did in the case of patent agents. Solicitors with appropriate experience may become registered as trademark agents relatively easily.

### European patent attorneys                              1.4.3

European patent attorneys are qualified to practice before the European Patent Office. They have passed different examinations and have demonstrated ability in foreign languages.

In this country they are usually also UK patent agents, but there is a growing tendency for patent agents to rely on the European qualification alone.

### Solicitors and barristers                              1.4.4

Solicitors are entitled to do the same work as patent agents, but rarely do. This is largely due to the technical nature of the patent agent's work. Solicitors also deal with transfers and licences of intellectual property rights and with infringement actions.

Barristers provide specialist advice on IP law (and for this purpose patent and trademark agents have direct access) and appear in the Courts and before the tribunals on IP matters.

### IP training and expertise                              1.4.5

Despite the growth during the 1980s in the number of courses in IP law offered at both undergraduate and postgraduate level, relatively few lawyers qualify with much knowledge of IP law. (We are about to change that!) It is still a speciality found in a small proportion of law firms (particularly the big ones) and in a few specialist sets of chambers.

### Rights of audience                                     1.4.6

In the Patent Office, the Designs Registry and the Trademarks Registry, patent and trademark agents (as appropriate) can and usually do appear on their clients' behalf. So too may solicitors, and counsel may also be instructed to appear.

Patent and trademark agents (and, at the time of writing, solicitors) enjoy no rights of audience in the High Court. However, many patent and design matters are now within the jurisdiction of the Patents County Court (*see* Chapter 8), where patent agents and solicitors may appear.

### 1.4.7 Exploitation brokers and technology transfer consultants

Many patent agents also offer clients advice on exploiting inventions. There are also professional brokers who put inventors in touch with potential industrial partners or financial backers. Patent and know-how licensing is all about technology transfer and a new breed of consultant in this activity has also come into being.

### 1.4.8 Valuers

Intellectual property valuation is a relatively new and uncharted area. There have been some well-publicised recent instances of intellectual property being grossly over-valued as a result.

The Institute of Chartered Accountants in England and Wales has now prohibited auditors from performing specialist valuations, including IP valuations. This should see an end to some of the worst cases of optimistic valuations, making it necessary to have an expert determine the value to be included in the balance sheet.

### 1.4.9 Brand creation

The creation of brand names is largely a matter of inspiration followed by a rigorous sifting process based on a sound knowledge of trademark law. Computer programs are available to generate names, but the same result can be achieved by a small roomful of people and several bottles of wine, though this is not recommended for the second part of the process.

## Self-assessment questions

1  What are the four main types of intellectual property?
2  What types of property does the Paris Convention cover?
3  Why is monopoly protection usually accorded only to registered IP rights?
4  What type of property is protected by a patent?
5  What protection does a trademark have if it is not registered?
6  What possible consequences of the exercise of IP rights will the Treaty of Rome control?
7  How can the owner of intellectual property make money from it?
8  Who may file and prosecute UK patent applications for reward?

# Chapter 2

# Competition and the law

## Introduction                                    2.1

This chapter and the two following will give you a basic knowledge of competition law. This chapter:

- Explains the purpose of competition law; and
- Describes very briefly the oldest competition law system in the world, that of the USA.

## Rationale for competition law                    2.2

The purpose of competition, or antitrust, laws is to:

- Promote competition;
- Prohibit monopoly; and
- Preserve the free enterprise system.

These laws are designed to protect both consumers and businesses from unfair, anti-competitive and predatory business practices. As the US Supreme Court has observed:

Antitrust laws are the Magna Carta of free enterprises. They are as important for the preservation of economic freedom and our free enterprise system as the Bill of Rights is to the protection of our fundamental personal freedoms ...

Without competition, resources are not allocated efficiently by the market. Where competition is excluded or restricted, producers can charge more for their products and sell fewer of them, thereby making a greater profit but denying the consumer the benefit of having more goods to buy at the lower price, leaving unmet consumer demand.

*Note*

For a full treatment of the economics of competition law, *see* Posner, *Antitrust Law: an Economic perspective* (Chicago University Press, 1976).

Within the EC, competition policy has an important additional role to play in the creation of the common market. Attempts to partition the market are strictly controlled by the competition rules.

Competition laws are aimed at two basic types of restraint:

- *Vertical restraints*, which exist between enterprises at different levels in the supply chain, eg. between manufacturers and distributors; and

- *Horizontal restraints*, which exist at a single level, eg. among a group of competing manufacturers or on the part of a single dominant firm.

Competition laws therefore have something to say about many distribution agreements and licences, as well as controlling the creation and exercise of monopoly power.

## 2.3    An outline of US competition law

There are several federal and state antitrust statutes, enacted since the late nineteenth century. This outline is concerned only with federal law. These laws fall into two general categories:

- Those designed to prevent abuses related to excessive concentration of economic power or monopoly; and
- Those designed to prohibit specific types of unfair, collusive and predatory practices.

The legislation was a reaction to the practice whereby stockholders in a number of corporations would assign their stocks (shares) to a board of trustees in return for dividend-bearing trust certificates. The trustees were able to operate all the corporations as a group, eg. the Standard Oil Trust held all the stock in 14 corporations and limited partnerships, plus stakes in a further 20. Similar trusts were active in the cotton, whisky, lead and sugar industries.

These trusts came to dominate economic life. Eventually the public outcry became so great that so-called 'antitrust' legislation was enacted.

### 2.3.1    Basic antitrust provisions

**Antitrust laws**
Both federal and state laws prohibit antitrust violations. The most important federal antitrust statutes are:

- The *Sherman Act of 1890*, which prohibits:

  every contract, combination in the form of a trust or otherwise or conspiracy in restraint of trade among the several states or with foreign nations: s.1.

  It also makes it a felony to:

  monopolize or attempt to monopolize or combine or conspire with any other persons to monopolize any part of the trade or commerce among the several states or with foreign nations.

- The *Clayton Act of 1914*, s.3 of which makes it unlawful for those engaged in commerce to lease or sell goods in commerce for use, consumption or sale in the USA on the condition that the lessee or purchaser should not use or deal in the goods of a competitor, where that would lessen competitiveness or tend to create a monopoly in any line of commerce. (This was a response to the Supreme Court's decision in the *Standard Oil Co of New Jersey v US* (1911) which severely limited the Sherman Act.)

- The *Federal Trade Commission Act 1972*, which prohibits unfair trade practices and unfair methods of competition.
- The *Robinson-Patman Act 1936*, which amends the Clayton Act and prohibits price discrimination between buyers of the same product.

Nearly every state has antitrust laws that contain provisions quite similar to these key federal laws.

### Enforcement

The federal antitrust laws are enforced by the Antitrust Division of the Department of Justice (Antitrust Division) and by the Federal Trade Commission (FTC). The Antitrust Division brings both criminal prosecutions and civil suits against violators of the antitrust laws, while the FTC brings only civil suits.

Only certain types of serious, hard-core antitrust violations are *prosecuted*. These violations include such practices as:

- Price fixing;
- Bid rigging; and
- Group boycotts.

An individual convicted of a criminal antitrust violation may be fined up to $250,000 and imprisoned for up to three years; a corporation convicted of such a violation may be fined up to $1 million.

Lesser federal antitrust violations result in *civil suits* by the Antitrust Division for injunction, damages and/or costs and attorneys' fees, or by the FTC for injunction. Private parties also can bring suit in federal court to recover damages suffered as a result of antitrust violations and, if successful, will recover three times the damages proven, plus costs and attorneys' fees.

### Agreements in restraint of trade

2.3.2

#### Rule of reason

The prohibition in the Sherman Act appeared to cover any agreement which could result in a restraint of trade, however minor. The Supreme Court took the view in the *Standard Oil* case that this had not been the intention of Congress.

Instead, the Supreme Court decided that the agreement

had to be examined to determine whether it was *unreasonably* restrictive of competition. This gave rise to the so-called Rule of Reason.

### *Per se* violations

The courts found the Rule of Reason very time-consuming to apply in each case. Often it demanded sophisticated economic analysis. They therefore began to develop the idea that some practices could never be reasonable. Thus some practices were considered to have no redeeming features and were therefore *completely prohibited*.

### Where is the boundary?

It is not always easy to tell whether the Rule of Reason should be applied in a particular case or whether an agreement is *per se* prohibited. Economic fashions dictate where the boundary is drawn.

The (free-market) Chicago School (in the ascendancy for most of the recent past) argues that the purpose of antitrust laws is to maximise economic efficiency and that free competition is not necessarily the way to achieve this. This favours a Rule of Reason approach, examining each agreement for its effect.

In *Continental TV v GTE Sylvania* (1977) the Supreme Court first gave credence to Chicago School assumptions. In an earlier case, *US v Schwinn* (1967) it had decided that attempts by a seller to enforce retail restrictions were illegal *per se*. In *Sylvania* it reversed that decision, stating that *per se* rules only apply where the pernicious effects of an agreement or practice on competition and their complete lack of any redeeming features mean that they can be conclusively presumed to be unreasonable.

### Horizontal practices

Several types of horizontal agreements are still considered to be illegal *per se*. These include:

- Price fixing agreements;
- Attempts to divide markets; and
- Group boycotts; and
- Tying arrangements.

However, mere 'conscious parallelism' of prices charged, unless there is a conspiracy, is not prohibited provided that there is no additional exchange of price information.

### Vertical practices

**Distribution agreements and IP licences** Vertical practices include distribution agreements and intellectual property licences. The basis of this law is *Sylvania*, which was concerned specifically with the extent to which a supplier could control the location of its distributors' outlets. The manufacturer terminated the distributor as part of a programme of reducing the number of outlets it had, and the distributor argued that the limitation on the locations from which it could sell Sylvania television sets was a *per se* violation of s.1, Sherman Act 1890.

The Supreme Court held that while the restriction limited *intrabrand* competition by restricting the number of outlets vying for the business of a particular group of customers, manufacturers could achieve efficiencies in the distribution of their products and *interbrand* competition would be enhanced. Vertical restraints should *not* therefore be conclusively presumed to be unreasonable.

**Tying** Tying was considered by the Supreme Court in *Jefferson Parish Hospital District v Hyde* (1984). There one firm of anaesthesiologists had the exclusive right to provide their services in a particular hospital. The Supreme Court accepted that certain tying agreements had to be considered illegal *per se* but not every refusal to sell two products separately could be considered to restrain competition. *Per se* condemnation would only follow if it is probable that a substantial portion of the market would be forced to purchase the tied product. Otherwise, the rule of reason should be applied.

On the facts, the court decided that hospital services and anaesthesiology services did not constitute the 'two distinguishable product markets' required by the Sherman Act for there to be a *per se* violation. On a Rule of Reason analysis the Court held further that the agreement was not unreasonable.

*Note*

For the purposes of the Sherman Act a parent and subsidiary must be considered as a single enterprise. A 'Bath Tub Conspiracy' – an agreement between a parent and subsidiary – would not violate the Act.

### Monopolisation                                           2.3.3

Monopolisation is prohibited by s.2, Sherman Act 1890, which makes it (and attempted monopolisation) a felony.

More than mere possession of monopoly power is necessary for the felony.

In *US v Grinnell Corporation* (1966) the Supreme Court held that if there was also

the wilful acquisition or maintenance of (monopoly) power as distinguished from growth or developments as a consequence of a superior product, business acumen or historic accident ...

the felony would be committed. In other cases the additional element which was required has been defined as 'the purpose or intent to exercise power.'

In the *Aspen Highlands Co v Aspen Highlands Skiing Corp* (1985) the Supreme Court held that s.2 was violated where the owner of three skiing areas in one resort terminated an arrangement whereby a single ski lift ticket covered its three areas and another owned by a third party. This termination had a severe adverse impact on the other third party. The Court found that the reason for the termination was purely anti-competitive and exclusionary.

Predatory pricing is another form of monopolization which the Courts will consider unlawful. So too may be seeking to enforce a patent obtained by fraud: *Walker Process Equipment v Food Machinery Co* (1965).

### Attempted monopolisation

Generally, a plaintiff in an attempted monopolisation case must show not only that the defendant has attempted to monopolise a given market but also that there was a 'dangerous possibility' that it would succeed: *Swift and Co v US* (1905).

### Mergers

Acquiring the stock, share capital or assets of another person where the effect may be substantially to lessen competition or tend to create a monopoly is prohibited by s.7, Sherman Act 1890. The expression 'any asset' can include intellectual property rights.

Pre-notification of certain mergers is required by the Hart-Scott-Rodino Act 1976. The FTC and the Department of Justice have to be told before the merger is effected. The Department of Justice has issued guidelines to its policy on mergers, making clear that the primary thrust of its policy is improving efficiency in American industry.

The degree of market concentration is the key criterion used in consideration of *horizontal* mergers, although there may be special factors (such as the probability that a merger will breathe new life into a failing business). In *vertical* mergers, the Department will be concerned about whether the merger will increase the barriers to others entering the market and whether the merger will facilitate collusion.

**2.3.4**      **Federal Trade Commission**

Section 5, Federal Trade Commission Act 1972 deals with unfair methods of competition and unfair or deceptive acts or practices. The Commission must take action against such practices unless it appears to be in the public interest not to do so.

There is no longer a requirement that the practices in question must infringe the letter or spirit of the Sherman or Clayton Acts: *FTC v Sperry and Hutchinson & Co* (1972). The 1972 Act can therefore be used against incipient restraints.

## Enforcement 2.3.5

### Criminal actions
Criminal violations of ss.1 and 2, Sherman Act 1890 are felonies. Actions are brought in the Federal Courts by the Department of Justice.

*Note* _____

US law still draws a distinction between felonies – more serious offences – and misdemeanours – less serious ones.

Proceedings normally begin with a letter requesting a voluntary supply of information, and if the inquiry is proceeded with formal federal grand jury proceedings will follow. If the grand jury thinks that there is sufficient evidence, it will issue an indictment and the case will go to a trial before judge and jury.

### Civil action by the Department of Justice
The Department may also institute civil proceedings. This will normally happen where it is not clear that there has been a purposeful violation of the law. Typically, civil cases brought by the Department are settled by a consent decree without the need for a trial.

If asked, the Department may comment about the legality under antitrust law of a proposed course of conduct. It does so in a *Business Review Letter*, a document which is open to public inspection.

### FTC enforcement
After the due procedure has been followed, the FTC may issue a *cease and desist order* to those indulging in unfair competition. The FTC has extensive powers of investigation and cases are brought to a hearing before one of its own administrative law judges. An appeal lies to the full five-member Commission and thence to a Circuit Court (a second-instance Federal court).

### Private civil actions
Since the Clayton Act 1914, enforcement of the antitrust laws by private civil action has also been possible. Section 4 provides that a plaintiff may receive triple damages (though subsequent amendments have reduced damages available in certain cases). Section 16 deals with granting injunctions.

The bulk of antitrust actions are private ones, during the Reagan era the Department of Justice's Antitrust Division was reduced in size by one-third. But note that a successful criminal action raises *prima facie* evidence for a subsequent private claim.

## Self-assessment questions

1  What are the two categories of restraints on competition which may be encountered?
2  What types of agreements are commonly caught by competition law?
3  Why is it in the interests of consumers to have competitive markets?
4  What are the two basic US Antitrust statutes?
5  What is the Rule of Reason?
6  What is a *per se* violation?

Chapter 3

# Restrictive agreements and concerted practices

## UK law: restrictive trade practices 3.1

The Restrictive Trade Practices Act 1976 (RPTA) applies to restrictive agreements relating to:

- Goods: s.6(1); or
- Services: s.11; and
- Information agreements relating to goods: s.7 and SI 1969/No 1842.

Any such agreement must be *registered* if:

- Two or more parties to it carry on business in the UK; and
- Two or more of the parties (not necessarily carrying on business in the UK) accept restrictions on certain specified matters, unless it is exempt: s.1.

The intention of this formalistic approach is to secure certainty in commercial arrangements – it can be seen immediately whether an agreement is caught without having to wait for the competition authorities to decide whether it has a deleterious effect on competition – *but* it means that the Act is *easily circumvented*. Agreements can often be drafted so that only one party accepts restrictions, especially since many restrictions are disregarded. And if there is a foreign party that too can serve to remove the agreement from the scope of the legislation – the mere fact that a foreign company has a UK subsidiary does not mean that it is 'doing business' in the UK.

What constitutes an agreement is construed very widely. Agreements may be written or oral; even a 'gentlemen's agreement' which is not intended to be legally binding may be caught. Additionally, the RTPA deems trade association recommendations to be agreements between all members of the association: s.8(1).

### Exemptions 3.1.1

Certain types of agreement which would otherwise be registrable are exempted, but only if they meet detailed requirements. These are listed in Sched. 3 to the Act. They include:

- Agreements authorised by statute;
- Exclusive dealing agreements;

- Trademark agreements;
- Agreements relating to patents and registered designs;
- Know-how agreements;
- Copyright agreements (added by s.30, Competition Act 1980); and
- Agreements with overseas operations.

Agreements which are important to the national economy may be exempted (s.29) as may agreements relating to particular occupations or businesses (Sched. 1).

*Note*

On agreements relating to intellectual property, *see* Chapter 19.

### 3.1.2 Disregarded restrictions

Certain restrictions in an agreement will be disregarded. This means that no account is taken of them when considering the registrability of the agreement. However, other restrictions in the agreement may still mean it has to be registered, though the disregarded restrictions will not be considered when the agreement is reviewed.

**Goods or services**

Restrictions concerned only with the goods or services supplied under the agreement will be disregarded, but not where they are accepted by more than one supplier or by more than one purchaser: ss.9(3) and 18(2), *see Registrar of Restrictive Trade Practices v Schweppes (No 2) (1970)* and *Topliss Showers Ltd v Gessey and Sons Ltd (1982).*

This provision refers to restrictions which affect the goods which the contract provides will be supplied *and no other goods.* An obligation to sell those goods only to specified customers would be within the scope of this provision. A master distribution agreement is covered, even though the goods are supplied under subsequent contracts of sale: *Re Diazo Copying Materials (1984).*

**Compliance with standards**

Agreements to comply with British Standards or standards adopted by another body and approved by the Secretary of State (who has only approved a handful of such agreements) will also be disregarded: ss.9(5) and 18(5).

**Business transfer agreements**

The Restrictive Trade Practices (Sale and Purchase and Share Subscription Agreements) (Goods) Order 1989 (SI 1989 No 1081) and the Restrictive Trade Practices (Services) (Amendment) Order 1989 (SI 1989 No 1082) provide that certain terms in share sale and purchase and subscription agreements will be disregarded when considering whether an agreement is registrable under the Act. The conditions set out in the instruments are:

- More than 50% of the issued share capital of the company or the whole of the vendor's interest in the business is transferred (share sale and purchase agreements only);
- The agreement does not contain price restrictions;
- Such restrictions as are accepted are accepted only by vendors, their associated companies or individuals;
- The restrictions which are to be disregarded only limit the extent to which the persons accepting them may compete with the company or business sold; and
- The restrictions to be disregarded will not last for more than five years from the date on which the agreement becomes operative or for more than two years beyond the expiry of any relevant employment or service contract, whichever is the later.

*Note*
The Orders do not cover asset sale and purchase agreements.

## Other

Restrictions relating to employment (ss.9(6) and 18(6)), certain restrictions on loan, rental, and guarantee agreements (ss.1 and 2, RTPA 1977), and agreements which contain restrictions only affecting certain professional services (ss.11 and 13, Sched. 1 and SI 1976 No 98), will be disregarded. Restrictive covenants in property leases will sometimes be caught.

## Registration     3.1.3

The full details of any registrable agreement (not just the restrictive provisions) must be provided to the Office of Fair Trading (OFT) before the restrictions take effect, and in any case within three months of the making of the agreement: s.24, Schedule 2. Only one party to the agreement has to provide the details. The procedure for registration is set out in SI 1984 No 392.

*Note*
Variations to an existing agreement must be registered in the same way unless they make it less restrictive. This also applies to the ending of a registered agreement.

Two copies of all documents must be supplied, one of them

signed by the person providing them. That person must also certify (on an OFT form) that these particulars are accurate and complete. There is no charge for registration.

Where agreements are in common form it is sufficient to register once and furnish details of the parties to, and minor differences between, subsequent agreements.

A section of the register is confidential and the Secretary of State may direct that some details be put on it to protect the legitimate business interests of any person: s.23. A formal request should be made for confidentiality when sending the agreement to the OFT. Such directions are very rarely given.

Section 26 provides that the OFT's decision to register an agreement can be challenged in the courts.

Failure to register in time makes the restrictions in the agreement *void*: s.35. A person affected by the unlawful operation of a void restriction may sue for damages.

### 3.1.4          Reference to the Restrictive Practices Court

Every agreement which is registered must be referred to the Restrictive Practices Court unless either:

- The Director General of Fair Trading (DGFT) recommends to the Secretary of State that it does not need to be referred (the grounds for doing so are very limited): s.21(2); or
- The DGFT thinks it appropriate not to do so in view of EC provisions which may authorise or exempt the agreement: s.21(1)(a); or
- The agreement has expired or the restrictions in it have been removed or have expired: s.21(1)(b).

In practice, most registered agreements never get to the court because the DGFT or the Secretary of State is able to exercise their discretion. This will often happen after modification of the agreement following discussions between the authorities and the parties to it.

If the agreement does go before the court only the restrictions in it will be examined. The Court is concerned with whether the restrictions are *against the public interest*.

If they are, the agreement is void and the Court can (and usually does) make an order restraining the parties from:

- Giving effect to any condemned restrictions;
- Enforcing or purporting to enforce them; and
- Making any agreement to like effect: s.2.

Breach of such an order amounts to contempt and substantial fines (£185,000 in one 1980 case) can be levied.

### The public interest 3.1.5

Restrictions will be held to be against the public interest unless they get through one of the 'gateways' set out in the Act: ss.10(1) and 19(1). Even if they do, they must also get past the 'tailpiece' which requires that the restriction is reasonable having regard to the balance between the gateway and any detriment caused to the public by the restriction.

### Proceedings 3.1.6

Once proceedings begin they usually go on to a conclusion even if the agreement is subsequently abandoned. The court may make an interim order precluding the operation of restrictions if they can reasonably be assumed not to fit any of the gateways: s.3.

### Reform of the law 3.1.7

In 1989 the government published its proposals to replace the registration system of the RTPA with a prohibition system modelled on Article 85, Treaty of Rome, in the white paper *Opening Markets: New Policy on Restrictive Trade Practices* (Cm 727, 1989). (Legislation is still awaited at the time of writing.)

## Competition Act 1980 3.2

### Introduction 3.2.1

The Competition Act controls *anti-competitive practices*. A person engages in an anti-competitive practice if in the course of a business they pursue a course of conduct and that course of conduct either alone or together with a course of conduct pursued by persons associated with them restricts, distorts or prevents competition or is intended to do so: s.2(1).

*Note*

If such a course of conduct is caught by the RPTA it is not regarded as an anti-competitive practice under the Competition Act: s.2(2)).

### Investigation 3.2.2

The Act empowers the DGFT to investigate possible anti-competitive practices and to report on the matter: s.3. In reporting the DGFT must specify the persons concerned, the goods or services in question, and whether it is considered necessary to refer the matter to the Monopolies and Mergers Commission (MMC): s.5.

### Competition references 3.2.3

References to the MMC are known as competition references. The persons concerned may avoid a competition reference by giving undertakings to the DGFT.

### 3.2.4 MMC Investigation

If a competition reference is made the MMC investigates whether the conduct has taken place, and whether it operates against the public interest. The public interest criteria are the same as those applied in the case of monopolies and mergers.

If the MMC reports adversely, the Secretary of State may ask the DGFT to seek appropriate undertakings from the persons concerned. If they refuse to give undertakings, or fail to comply with them, the Secretary of State may make an order prohibiting them from engaging in the practice: s.9.

## 3.3 Resale Prices Act 1976

### 3.3.1 Introduction

Resale price maintenance (RPM) – the practice whereby a manufacturer fixes the prices at which their goods may be resold – is prohibited. The practice of *recommending* resale prices is not affected.

### 3.3.2 Collective and individual resale price maintenance

Part 1 of the Act prohibits *collective* RPM. This covers agreements or arrangements entered into collectively by suppliers to boycott or discriminate against traders who breach resale price conditions.

Part 2 of the Act prohibits *individual* resale price maintenance. It makes void any term or condition in a contract of sale (or other agreement relating to a sale) between a supplier and a dealer which would establish a minimum price to be charged on the resale of goods.

### 3.3.3 Enforcement

The provisions of Part 1 can be enforced by the DGFT. Any person harmed by the collective action would be able to take action for breach of statutory duty.

### 3.3.4 Exemption

Application may be made to the Restrictive Practices Court for exemption from the provisions of Part 2 covering classes of goods on public interest grounds: s.14. The applicant must establish that maintaining minimum prices is necessary for:

- The maintenance of *quality and variety*;
- The maintenance of *retail outlets*;
- Keeping *prices low*;

- Avoiding *danger* to health arising from misuse by the public; or
- Providing *necessary services*.

There is an overriding requirement that such restrictions must be in the *public interest*. Only two exemptions (for books and medicaments) have been given.

## EEC competition rules     3.4

### The prohibition     3.4.1

Article 85(1) prohibits agreements between undertakings, decisions of associations and concerted practices where:

- There is collusion;
- Competition is, or is intended to be, prevented, restricted or distorted; and
- There is an effect (or a potential effect) on trade between Member States.

Article 85(2) makes such agreements automatically void.

Article 85 does not seek to create perfect competition. It acknowledges that this is unattainable, so mechanisms are put in place to exempt certain agreements from the rules. The aim is what the European Court of Justice (ECJ) has described as 'workable competition': *see Metro v Commission* (1977). This approach is less dogmatic than the American system.

The concept of an *undertaking* is very broad, encompassing almost any economically active unit (whether profit-making or not): *see Van Landewyck v Commission* (FEDETAB) (1980). Article 85 is *effects based*. This means that the law looks for an *effect on competition and on trade* between Member States, whereas the UK law is *form-based* and considers only whether there is a restriction of a particular type in an agreement. (Under proposals made in 1989 the UK will move shortly to an effects-based system (*see* 3.1.7.))

The form and content of a restriction on competition is immaterial to Article 85. While the Article contains an illustrative list of prohibited practices, it is not exhaustive. In *Consten/Grundig v Commission* (1966) the ECJ held that Article 85 prohibited an arrangement that perpetuated national boundaries as barriers to the free circulation of goods.

Nor does Article 85 distinguish between *horizontal* restraints (which are normally much more damaging to competition) and *vertical* restraints, which are usually benign and generally recognised as such in US law (*see* Chapter 2, para. 3.2.2). However, it can be difficult to distinguish agreements on this basis as both types of effects are frequently present.

### 3.4.2        Collusion

*Unilateral* action by an undertaking is outside the scope of Article 85 (though if the undertaking is dominant Article 86 may well prohibit whatever it is doing). However, an agreement of some sort is frequently found to exist.

*Example*

1   In *AEG v Commission* (1983) the court held that a refusal to admit a dealer to a manufacturer's network is not unilateral. It had to be considered as part of a contractual system, involving agreements with the existing dealers.

2   In *Sandoz* OJ (1990) the inclusion of a notice saying 'not to be exported' on invoices for goods was held to be an agreed export ban rather than a unilateral declaration.

### 3.4.3        Effect on trade

The requirement that there is an effect on trade between Member States is a jurisdictional threshold which the authorities must get over. The requirement has been interpreted in such a way as to ensure that it does not constitute a serious obstacle. Even if the arrangements concern only one Member State, an effect on trade may be found.

*Example*

In *Vereeniging van Cementhandeleren v Commission* (1972) an agreement limited to Dutch cement companies was found to have 'inevitable' implications for other markets. Dutch price fixing affected the ability of German or Belgian producers to enter the market.

#### Extraterritorial application

Any agreement having the prohibited effect in the Common Market is caught. It does not matter if the agreement is made wholly outside the Community, by foreign companies. In *Ahlstrom Osakeyhito & Others v Commission* (1988) – the 'Woodpulp Case' – the ECJ upheld the Commission's approach, holding that if a contract made by non-nationals outside the Common Market is implemented within it, the Commission is competent.

### 3.4.4        Prevention, distortion or restriction

The necessary effect (or intended effect) is often perfectly clear from the agreement. Many such agreements (if not all of them) are entered into because they are expected to have these effects.

*Example*

In *Zanussi* (1979) the manufacturer's warranty scheme

prescribed that warranty claims be made in the country of purchase, which would not wash with the Commission.

### Exceptions

Certain situations are outside the scope of Article 85(1), eg. some commercial agency agreements and agreements between companies in the same group. In *Christiani v Neilsen* (1969) the Commission decided that the Dutch subsidiary of a Danish company was incapable of entering into a prohibited agreement with its parent. It was already effectively controlled by the parent and had no economic independence. The ECJ has several times upheld this view where the parties constituted a single economic unit. Further exclusions cover the coal and steel sectors which are subject to special regimes.

*Note*

Transport is something of a special case and outside the scope of this Companion.

The Notice on Minor Agreements (OJ [1986] C 231/2) applies if the parties' market share is so small (less than 5%) and their turnover so low (less than 200 million ECU) that competition is not distorted to any significant extent.

The Notice sets out formal criteria for the application of a *de minimis* rule which has always been used in Article 85 cases. Where one of the parties is part of a larger group the whole of the group's market share and turnover may have to be included.

For some types of agreement or practice the Commission has issued a Notice delineating the scope of the prohibition. Co-operation agreements, sub-contracting agreements and certain joint ventures are currently covered.

### Negative clearance

Negative clearance – a statement that Article 85(1) does not apply – may be applied for: Regulation 17/62, Article 2. The procedure for doing so is described below (*see* 3.4.9).

### Exemption

An agreement which is within the scope of Article 85(1) is prohibited and automatically void (Article 85(2)) unless it is exempted by Article 85(3).

Exemption is granted to agreements or practices which:

- Contribute to an improvement in production or distribution, or to economic progress;
- Give a fair share of the benefits to consumers (including trade customers);

- Impose no restrictions which are not indispensable to realising the benefits; and

- Do not afford the parties the possibility of eliminating competition in respect of a substantial part of the products in question.

*Note*
_____

Only the Commission has the power to declare Article 85(1) inapplicable.
_____

Article 85(3) seeks to balance the costs of the restrictive practice against its benefits. The restrictions must go no further than is necessary to achieve the benefits of collaboration. Unnecessary ancillary restrictions must not be included.

The Commission must first look at the broad economic context of the collaboration. If the market would have realised the claimed benefits itself, the justification for the restriction is undermined. The market must be examined without the restriction in operation so the benefits unavailable without it can be seen. For example, in an exclusive distribution agreement the parties' freedom of action is restricted, but it may mean that a manufacturer is able to enter a new market which, without the help of a distributor, would remain closed to the manufacturer.

The possibility of third party competition must remain. The economic benefits of an agreement are only likely to continue if the parties remain exposed to competition from other undertakings. Crisis cartels will be permitted under Article 85(3) if they permit restructuring (and therefore preserve jobs) which would otherwise be impossible: *see Synthetic Fibre Cartel*.

### 3.4.7        Block exemptions

Council Regulation 17/62, Article 9.1 lays down conditions for automatic exemption under Article 85(3). This enables the Commission to exempt categories of agreements, thereby clearing some of the logjams of notified agreements which have built up. Block exemption regulations express in concrete form for particular categories of agreements the requirements of Article 85(3).

The following main block exemption regulations have been made under this power (*see* further Chapter 7):

- Exclusive distribution agreements: Regulation 1983/83;

- Exclusive purchasing agreements (including special rules for beer and service station agreements): Regulation 1984/83;

- Patent licensing agreements: Regulation 2349/84;
- Motor vehicle distribution and servicing agreements: Regulation 123/85;
- Specialisation agreements: Regulation 417/85;
- Research and development agreements: Regulation 418/85;
- Know-how licensing: Regulation 556/89;
- Franchising: Regulation 4087/88.

An agreement which is not inside one of these regulations may still benefit from individual exemption.

### Notification                                                    3.4.8

Negative clearance can only be given if application has been made for it, and the Commission can only give individual exemption to an agreement which has been notified. In practice the two are normally done together, with exemption being sought as an alternative to negative clearance: Regulation 17/62, Articles 2 and 4.1.

Notification *must* be made on Form A/B. In fact the form itself is very brief; the important information has to be provided in an extensive annex. The questions to be addressed are set out in the explanatory note to the form, which is prescribed by Commission Regulation 2526/85.

Notification does not have to be made by all the parties to an agreement, but the notifier must be a party.

Failure to submit accurate, complete and truthful information (whether intentionally or negligently) is punishable by a fine of up to 5000 ECU: Regulation 17/62, Article 15.1.

Certain agreements do not have to be registered. If needed, retrospective exemption can be given for these agreements. Included are:

- Purely domestic agreements (no affect on trade between member states);
- Certain unilateral restrictions in bilateral agreements;
- Bilateral agreements concerning standards;
- Joint research and development and specialisation agreements where the parties' market share is less than 15% and their turnover less than 200m ECU.

Notification secures immunity from fines from the date of notification (*see* below). There is no fee.

### The Commission's powers                                         3.4.9

#### Own initiative investigations
The Commission may investigate matters under the competition rules of which it learns through the media, ques-

tions in the European Parliament, etc but is under no obligation to do so: *see Automec v Commission* (1992).

It is also empowered to conduct general enquiries into economic sectors where it thinks competition may be restricted: Regulation 17/62, Article 12.

### Fact finding

The Commission has far-reaching powers to investigate a suspected infringement. It may request information and may carry out an investigation: Regulation 17/62, Articles 11 and 14.

### Requests for information

Article 11 empowers the Commission to obtain 'all necessary information'. There is a privilege against self-incrimination.

Requests for information are made in writing to suspected infringers or to third parties who may be able to provide information. Initially, such requests are informal, but supplying incorrect or incomplete information can result in a 5,000 ECU fine: Article 15.1.

If a request is ignored or refused or the reply is incomplete, a formal decision may be made by the Commission ordering the information to be supplied: Article 16.1. Daily default fines of up to 1,000 ECU can be imposed if this is ignored.

### Investigations

Investigations also come in varying degrees of formality, though there is no two-tier system; the Commission may choose to be informal first, or it may go straight in with a formal investigation.

An inspection visit is like a request for information. Officials may:

- Examine business records;
- Take copies;
- Request explanations; and
- Enter property.

Incomplete production of records, etc, carries a penalty of up to 5,000 ECU: Article 14.2, 15.1.

*Note*

Commission inspectors must show their authorisation and prove their identity by means of their staff card.

A firm may refuse to submit to an investigation. If so, this is recorded and the firm may have a copy of the minute. If it voluntarily submits, it accepts all the ensuing obligations.

Investigation may also be ordered by *decision* of the Commission: Article 14(3). This procedure is followed if the:

- Firm refuses to submit to investigation;
- The infringement is serious and the Commission fears that evidence may disappear if the firm is forewarned; or if
- The firm has a bad record for co-operating in the past.

A visit by decision need not be announced. The firm is required to submit to the investigation and fines and periodic penalties may be imposed in default. The decision may be annulled on application to the Court of First instance of the ECJ.

Firms which receive a visit may insist on having a legal adviser present provided this does not unduly delay the inspection.

**Final decision**

The Commission's final decision can be to:

- Grant negative clearance; or
- Grant exemption; or
- Order the termination of an infringement.

Negative clearance or exemption must be preceded by publication of details of the case in the Official Journal, giving interested parties an opportunity to comment. Member states' authorities must also be consulted, through the Advisory Committee on Restrictive Practices and Dominant Positions.

A decision to grant negative clearance states that the Commission finds no infringement on the facts before it. New facts may arise causing it to reconsider whether an agreement or concerted practice violates Article 85(1) and what its saving graces are for the purposes of Article 85(3).

A decision to grant exemption indicates why the agreement violates Article 85(1) and what its saving graces are for the purposes of Article 85(3): Regulation 17(62), Article 8. Exemption lasts for a set time but may be extended. Sometimes modifications are required to the agreement before exemption is given.

Before reaching a decision that an infringement has occurred, the Commission gives the parties a statement of objections with a copy of its file attached. A time limit – usually one or two months – is specified for a written response to the objections: Regulation 99/63 Article 2.

Parties can request an oral procedure before the Hearing Officer, a Commission Official charged with ensuring that due account is taken of all the facts. Following the hearing, if there is one, the Advisory Committee must be consulted.

Where it finds an infringement the Commission will issue

a cease and desist order. If the infringement has already been terminated the decision will state that it was an infringement.

Positive actions may also be required, eg. to restore supplies to a customer from whom they have been withheld.

Fines can also be imposed for infringements of Articles 85(1) or 86, up to 1 million ECU or 10% of the worldwide turnover of the firm concerned in the previous business year – which may include the turnover in all products of the whole group: Regulation 17/62, Article 15.2. Fines of 3 million ECU are regularly imposed, 10 million is not unknown and in *Tetra Pak Rausing SA v Commission* an Article 86 case, the fine was 75 million. The level of the fine depends on:

- The seriousness of the conduct;
- Its duration;
- Whether deliberate or negligent;
- The firm's past record; and
- Whether the Commission has previously targeted for such practices (in which case the offender should have known better).

Interim measures may be taken to preserve the *status quo*; a final decision may take years and immense damage could be done if protective measures were not available.

*Example* _____

In *Peugeot* (1990), the Commission ordered the manufacturer to recommence supplies to the parallel trader whom the manufacturer had ordered its Belgian and Luxembourg dealers to stop supplying.

_____

Provisional decisions, which terminate immunity from fines, amount to a warning that the Commission considers that Article 85(1) has been infringed and exemption is not justified. Since fines can be imposed again, such warnings should not lightly be ignored.

Administrative (or 'comfort') letters inform the parties that the Commission does not intend to take action. They do not have the legal status of decisions but such a letter could be useful evidence in the UK courts; if it says the agreement is outside the scope of Article 85(1) that would rebut a challenge to the validity of the agreement but if it says the agreement may be exempted that merely proves that it infringes Article 85 and the court must regard it as void because only the Commission can grant exemption.

Informal settlements may be reached by negotiation; the firms involved agree to modify the agreement or change their behaviour to the satisfaction of the Commission.

Decisions must be published in the Official Journal, except for procedural decisions publication of which is optional. Press releases are issued publicising decisions, and also informal settlements where a point of general interest is covered.

## Using the competition rules as a weapon            3.5

The Commission also takes action on complaints received from interested parties. When a complaint is received the Commission examines whether a violation is taking place. If it finds no infringement it will inform the complainant who then has an opportunity to make comments, following which the Commission will either continue its investigation or reject the complaint.

A complaint may be made using Form C (available from the Commission or its information offices) but a simple letter is sufficient.

Articles 85 and 86 form part of the law of the UK and can be used in legal actions in the British courts, eg. for a declaration that an agreement is void under Article 85(2) or that a dominant position is being abused. The courts, unlike the Commission, can award damages but they lack the Commission's powers of investigation. Very few such actions have been brought.

## The European Court of Justice            3.6

Competition cases are heard by the Court of First Instance of the ECJ, with an appeal to the full court.

The Court may confirm, reduce, cancel or increase fines or periodic penalties imposed by the Commission. It can also review and, if necessary, annul all formal decisions of the Commission. Appeals can also be brought against the Commission's failure to act.

## Self-assessment questions

1   What agreements must be registered under the Restrictive Practices Act 1976?
2   What type of restrictions may be disregarded in deciding whether the registration is necessary?
3   What sort of agreements are excepted from the need to register?
4   With what is the Restrictive Practices Court concerned?

5   What does the Competition Act control?
6   What is individual resale price maintenance?
7   What does Article 85 of the Treaty of Rome prohibit?
8   What are the criteria in the Minor Agreements Notice?
9   What is the difference between exemption and negative clearance?

# Chapter 4

# Abuse of market power and mergers

## Introduction 4.1

EC and UK competition law contain provisions to deal with the abuse of market power. This abuse may take the form of a:

- *Monopoly*; or of a
- *Dominant position*.

Both systems also set out to control mergers.

## Fair Trading Act 1973 4.2

### Introduction 4.2.1

This applies to monopolies and mergers and in each case provides for reference to be made to the Monopolies and Mergers Commission (MMC).

### Monopolies 4.2.2

Under ss.44–56 *monopoly references* may be made where there is either a scale monopoly or a complex monopoly.

**Scale monopoly**
A scale monopoly is a business or group of inter-related businesses which supplies or buys at least 25% of a product or service in the UK.

**Complex monopoly**
A complex monopoly is a group of firms which supply at least 25% of the market who act in such a way as to prevent, restrict or distort competition. There is no need for there to be collusion for a complex monopoly situation to exist.

> *Note*
>
> There is no obligation on firms to notify the authorities if the 25% threshold is crossed. The Director General of Fair Trading (DGFT) is specifically given the job of monitoring commercial activity and collecting information about monopoly situations and uncompetitive practices.

### Mergers 4.2.3

Sections 63–77 deal with *merger references*. They require all mergers which would lead to one firm supplying 25% of the market, or which would involve assets of more than £30 million, to be considered by the DGFT for referral to the MMC.

In practice, because of the possible disastrous consequences of a reference being made after the merger has taken place, most mergers are brought to the DGFT's attention before being formalised. Often, predatory firms will agree to divest themselves of that part of their target which is likely to give rise to a referral.

*Note*

The Companies Act 1989 has instituted a pre-notification system for mergers. This has the drawback that it involves publicity being given to the intended merger, and there are fees payable.

### 4.2.4    The public interest

In both monopoly references and merger references the MMC must consider the public interest. The Act lays down guidelines but does not indicate what weight is to be given to different factors. Moreover, the list in the Fair Trading Act is not exhaustive. Section 84 states that the MMC must have regard to 'all matters which appear in the particular circumstances to be relevant'. These include the desirability of:

- Maintaining and promoting effective competition;
- Promoting the interest of consumers;
- Reducing costs;
- Developing new products;
- Maintaining and promoting the balanced distribution of industry and employment in the UK; and
- International competitiveness.

### 4.2.5    Powers of the Secretary of State

The Secretary of State has wide powers to act on an MMC report. Under Schedule 8 the Secretary of State can:

- Prohibit or modify a particular practice;
- Transfer or vest property in other bodies; or
- Keep a practice under surveillance (Schedule 8).

The Secretary of State may also ask the DGFT to consult with the parties concerned and obtain undertakings from them: s.88(1).

### 4.2.6    Newspaper mergers

Newspaper mergers raise significant non-economic issues and are therefore subject to a special regime: ss.57–63 (*see* Chapter 4, para. 4.2.6).

## Abuse of dominant position                          4.3

A firm which enjoys a dominant position must not abuse its economic power in any way. Any such abuse is prohibited: Article 86. This controls firms whose economic strength makes them immune from the normal pressures of a competitive market.

Market share is the best indication of dominance, but other factors may be equally, or even more, important. In *United Brands v Commission* (1976) the ECJ said that Article 86:

... relates to a position of economic strength enjoyed by an undertaking which enables it to prevent effective competition being maintained in the relevant market by giving it the power to behave to an appreciable extent independently of its competitors, customers and ultimately ... consumers.

Access to raw materials or capital may enable a firm to act regardless of its competitors, suppliers and purchasers.

*Note*

It is not the existence of a dominant position which is unlawful, but only the abuse of such a position.

The dominant position must be in the Common Market or a substantial part of it. What constitutes a *substantial part* is a question of fact and will vary according to the nature of the product. A distinct geographical market partitioned from the rest of the Common Market will be treated as a distinct market in itself. The product market in which dominance must be judged is an important consideration.

*Example*

In *United Brands v Commission*, where the company supplied bananas, consideration had to be given to whether the market for fresh fruit should be considered. Some fruits are not available all the year round so could not compete effectively with bananas, which are. United Brands argued that other fruits were readily substitutable for bananas, but the Commission and the Court both disagreed. Bananas had certain features (soft texture, etc) which made them particularly suitable for the very young, the elderly and the sick. There was no substitute for them to these classes of consumers, so the market in which dominance had to be tested was that for bananas alone.

A dominant position is abused if advantage is taken of it so as to cause injury to third parties. Examples include:

• Charging unfair prices;
• Price discrimination;

- Refusal to supply; and
- Fidelity rebates.

There is no provision for exemption to be granted under Article 86, but it would not be necessary anyway. The concept of abuse is flexible: if the conditions for exemption existed in that the practice complained of has beneficial effects it would not be considered abusive.

## 4.4    Merger control

In the past, mergers have been controlled under Article 86 (*Continental Can v Commission* (1972) and Article 85 (*BAT and Reynolds v Commission* (1987). Neither has proved particularly well-suited to the task. The Merger Control regulation (4064/89) now requires pre-notification of certain mergers, and aims to achieve predictability through 'one stop shopping'. The criteria are designed to ensure that only mergers with a Community dimension are caught, so the Community regime should not in theory overlap with national ones.

The Regulation controls *concentrations*. This includes the situation where two or more previously independent undertakings merge, and where control of another undertaking is acquired. The second is difficult to apply precisely: control depends on the ability to exercise decisive influence, which could be achieved by acquiring a minority interest.

*Example*

In *Arjimori Prioux/Wiggins Teape* (1990) acquisition of 39% of the shares, where the remaining shares were widely dispersed, gave the buyer control. On the other hand, in *Renault/Volvo* where 25% of the companies' car manufacturing and 45% of their truck manufacturing operations were merged the trucks deal was caught but not the cars one.

The thresholds prescribed by the regulation are:

- The parties' aggregate worldwide turnover exceeds 5,000 million ECU; and
- The aggregate Community-wide turnover of each of at least two of the undertakings concerned exceeds 250 million ECU; unless
- Each of the undertakings concerned achieves more than two-thirds of its aggregate Community-wide turnover within one and the same member state.

Mergers which are caught have to be notified no more than a week after the agreement, announcement of public bid or acquisition of a controlling interest. The procedure for notification is set out in Regulation 2367/90 and form CO is prescribed. The merger may not be put into effect before, or for three weeks after, notification. Failure to observe these procedural requirements may result in fines and periodic penalty payments.

*Note*

A joint venture may be regarded as a 'concentration' to which the regulation applies (as does the Fair Trading Act). The question is whether the joint venture performs, on a lasting basis, all the functions of an autonomous economic entity. If it gives rise to co-ordination of the parties, or between them and the joint venture, Article 85 will still apply. The question is whether the joint venture is collaborative, ie. within Article 85, or concentrative, ie. within the Merger Control Regulation. The Commission produced guidelines to help in telling the difference in 1990.

Whether the merger is permitted depends on its effect on competition in the EC. If it creates or strengthens a dominant position as a result of which effective competition would be significantly impeded in the Common Market or in a substantial part of it, it will not be permitted or conditions may be attached by the Commission. The notion of dominance requires consideration of what the market is.

*Example*

In *Aerospatiale/MBB* (1991) the parties had more than 50% of the European helicopter market, but the entire world market was open to them. They were not dominant at the global level so the merger was allowed.

## Exceptions to the 'one stop' principle          4.4.1

The 'one stop' principle does not apply where:

- There is dominance in a distinct *national market*, national law may be applied if the Commission authorises this: Article 9;

- Article 21(93) enables a Member State to protect interests affected by a merger other than those specifically covered by the Regulation. This permits intervention on grounds of public security, plurality of the media, 'prudential rules', and 'other legitimate interests'.

A merger which does not satisfy the Community dimension criteria may nevertheless be subject to Community control if a member state requests it. The merger must significantly affect competition within that member state's territory.

Perfect one stop shopping has therefore not been achieved and, indeed, is unattainable. There will always be situations where it is not possible to work out if the thresholds have been reached, eg. in a contested take-over where the parties do not have full information. In such cases national and Community requirements will still have to be followed.

Nor does the Regulation exclude Articles 85 and 86 from the field, although by prohibiting overlap between itself and Regulation 17/62 (the instrument which gives the Commission the power to apply Articles 85 and 86) the Merger Regulation does oust a large part of the jurisdiction of those provisions.

## Self-assessment questions

1  What is a complex monopoly?
2  What does the Monopolies and mergers Commission consider in a monopoly or merger reference?
3  What powers does the Secretary of State have following a MMC Report?
4  What does Article 86 control?
5  What threshold does the merger control regulation prescribe?
6  When does the 'one stop' principle in the merger control regulation not apply?

# Chapter 5

# Patents: scope and procedure

## Subject matter                                              5.1

In *Re Asahi's Application* (1991), Lord Oliver of Aylmerton said:

The underlying purpose of the patent system is the encouragement of improvements and innovation. In return for making known his improvement to the public the inventor receives the benefit of a period of monopoly during which he becomes entitled to prevent others from performing his invention except by his licence. The necessarily technical process of applying for a patent, which involves the formulation of precisely expressed claims defining the extent of the monopoly applied for, and the equally technical process of investigating the claims made, inevitably involve a considerable lapse of time between the date when the inventor first makes his application and the date when his invention is exposed to the public and his patent is granted.

A patent is a monopoly right to the exclusive use of an invention. The right lasts for 20 years provided renewal fees are paid on time. It is granted in return for a complete disclosure of the invention, so the learning it embodies is available to anyone who is interested.

Patent law in the UK is contained in the Patents Act 1977 and secondary legislation made under it (most importantly, the Patents Rules 1991 and the Patents (Fees) Rules 1992) Before the 1977 Act came into operation, the law was found in the Patents Act 1949.

The 1977 Act was made necessary, in part at least, by the European Patents Convention of 1973 (EPC) (*see* Chapter 11, para. 11.3.3). Certain provisions of the 1977 Act are expressly framed so as to have the same effects as the corresponding provisions of the EPC, the Community Patent Convention (CPC) (*see* Chapter 11, para, 11.3.2) and s.103(7), Patent Co-operation Treaty (PCT) (*see* Chapter 11, para. 11.3.4).

*Note*

All references in this chapter are to the Patents Act 1977 unless stated otherwise.

## Obtaining UK patents                                        5.2

There are three ways to obtain UK patents:

- Apply under the 1977 Act;
- Apply under the EPC, specifying the UK as a country in which a patent is desired; at the end of the process, if successful, a European Patent (UK) will be granted identical to an ordinary UK patent: s.77;
- Make an international application under the Patent Co-operation Treaty for a UK patent.

The Community Patent Convention is intended to make it possible to obtain a European Patent under the EPC procedure which is valid throughout the European Community. However, not all Member States have been able to ratify the Convention to date, so it will be delayed or may come into operation with less than all the 12 Member States.

### 5.2.1 Priority

The *priority date* of an invention which is the subject of a patent application, and of any matter contained in the application, is a concept of crucial importance. This date is the date on which the application is filed, or an earlier date (within the previous 12 months) on which an application was filed in the UK or abroad which disclosed matter which supports the later application ('the application in suit'): s.5.

## 5.3 Requirements for obtaining protection

Section 1 lays down the conditions for a patent to be granted. To be patentable, an invention must:

- Be *new*;
- Involve an *inventive step*;
- Be capable of *industrial application*; and
- *Not be excluded* by the Act.

### 5.3.1 Novelty

**State of the art**

A patent will only be granted if the invention does not form part of the state of the art at its priority date: s.2. If it has been anticipated in this way, it is not new, and it is remarkably easy to do something which destroys the necessary novelty.

*Example*

1   In *Fomento v Mentmore* (1956) (CA) knowledge by a handful of people who were under no obligation of confidentiality was enough to invalidate a patent for a new method of making ball-point pens. Pens embodying the claimed invention had been given to members of the public.

2   In *Lux Traffic Signals v Faronwise and Pike Signals* (1993) (not

yet reported) use of portable road traffic signals in a trial on a public road, where a bystander who knew about such things could have deduced how the invention worked, destroyed the novelty of the invention.

The *state of the art* comprises all matter which has been made available to the public. This includes a product, process, information about either, or anything else, and it may be disclosed by written or oral description, by use or in any other way: s.2(2).

*Example*

In *Catnic Components v C Evans & Co* (1983) the question was whether the applicant's invention was anticipated by an earlier one. The only people to whom the earlier invention (a new type of lintel) had been shown were under confidentiality obligations, so that did not amount to making it available to the public. The earlier inventor had only had a small section made up to his design, insufficient to use as a lintel. There was therefore no question of disclosure by use either.

### Priority date

The key date for determining novelty is the priority date of the application (*see* 5.2).

Matter contained in an application for a patent which is unpublished at the priority date may also be relevant. If the application is published on or after the priority date of a later invention, it forms part of the state of the art when considering the later invention's novelty, but only where the matter in question was contained in the application as originally filed and as published, and where the priority date is earlier than that of the later invention: s.2(3).

Disclosing a prior invention does not, however, amount to prior publication of a later invention if the former is merely '[a] signpost, however clear, upon the road to the patentee's invention ... The prior inventor must be clearly shown to have planted his flag at the precise destination before the patentee.': *per* Sachs LJ in *General Tire and Rubber Co v Firestone Tyre and Rubber Co* (1971).

Disclosure in circumstances of confidentiality or secret prior use does not amount to making available to the public. Professional advisers – lawyers and patent agents – are bound to treat information given to them by the inventor as confidential. Details can also be shown to interested parties under confidentiality agreements, essential to secure financial support or to interest a manufacturing company in exploiting the invention.

---

*Example*

---

In *Pall Corp v Commercial Hydraulics (Bedford) Ltd* (1988) delivering samples in confidence to people who knew they were secret and experimental did not prejudice the novelty of the invention.

---

**Unauthorised disclosure**

Matter which has been obtained unlawfully or in breach of confidence, or which has been divulged in breach of confidence, is disregarded in considering the novelty of an invention: s.2(4).

Where a patent application is filed, there is a six month period during which no such disclosure will prejudice the application. An invention may also be displayed at an international exhibition during this period of grace.

However, publication of information about the invention anywhere in the world can ruin the inventor's chances of obtaining a patent. Since many inventors' first instincts are to write a paper about their invention for publication in an academic journal, this can be a problem.

---

*Note*

---

It makes little difference if the journal in question is obscure. By s.130(1) a document is taken to be 'published' if it can be inspected as of right at any place in the UK by members of the public. Whether they have to pay to do so is immaterial. So extensive are the holdings of the British Library (including the Science Reference and Information Service, which keeps patent information from around the world) that the scope of his definition is very wide indeed.

---

**5.3.2    Inventive step**

**Non-obviousness**

An invention involves an inventive step if it would not be obvious to someone with good knowledge and experience of the subject compared with what is already known: s.3.

All matter forming part of the state of the art is to be taken into account, but not in this instance matters included in patent applications with earlier priority dates published after the invention's priority date. (Such applications do form part of the state of the art when considering novelty (*see* 5.3.1.))

**Inventive step and novelty**

This requirement is not unrelated to the requirement of novelty. If an invention has already been disclosed it forms part of the prior art and therefore the invention cannot involve an inventive step (except in the special case of an earlier unpublished patent application). But the need for an inventive step goes further; even if the invention is new, it may be obvious (but no-one ever thought of it before).

Consideration of obviousness involves a 'skilled worker' test, similar to that used when considering novelty. In the case of obviousness, statute specifically provides for this test.

The meaning of 'obvious' is not elaborated on in the Act. In *Firestone* the Court thought it unnecessary to go further than the dictionary definition and took it to mean 'very plain'.

Commercial success goes a long way to showing that invention was not obvious. If it was it would have been thought of before if it satisfied such a need. However, the question of obviousness is decided according to technical, not commercial, considerations.

*Example*

In *Technograph Printed Circuits Ltd v Mills & Rockley (Electronics) Ltd* (1972) the invention (a method for making printed circuit boards using silk screening) was not an immediate commercial success because manufacturers could make all the boards they wanted using old manufacturing techniques. The invention was not used for some years, but then it was highly successful. The House of Lords held the invention was non-obvious and valid.

Remember also that commercial success may be attributed to other factors, such as advertising: *Molnlycke AB v Proctor and Gamble Ltd (No 3)* (1990).

A second use of existing technology may satisfy the inventive step requirement (though novelty may be difficult to prove).

*Example*

In *Parks-Cramer Co v G W Thornton & Sons Ltd* (1966) the patentee solved a long-standing problem concerning cleaning the floor between textile machines. The invention consisted basically of an overhead vacuum cleaner. In the High Court the Judge considered this obvious. The Court of Appeal overturned the first instance judgment, giving weight to the many unsuccessful attempts to solve the problem and to the immediate commercial success of the invention.

## Industrial application                                      5.3.3

To be patentable an invention must be capable of being used in some sort of industry: s.4(1). It could be a process or a product.

The expression 'industry' must be understood in its

broadest sense. It includes almost any useful, practical activity but not purely intellectual or aesthetic activities.

Public policy demands that medical practitioners and veterinary surgeons should not be constrained by other peoples' patents when treating patients: *John Wyeth & Brothers' Application*: *Schering AG's Application* (1985). Methods of treatment themselves are therefore not considered capable of industrial application (s:4(2)) but just because a product is invented for use in a method of treatment does not stop it being patented.

## 5.4 'Excluded' inventions

Some things are excluded from patent protection despite being ingenious, beneficial and unusual: s.1(2). The Act declares that they are not inventions. The exclusion applies to these matters 'as such', so an invention which *incorporates* excluded matter may still be patented.

An idea is not patentable if it is:

- Merely a discovery, or a scientific theory or mathematical method (which already exist and are just waiting to be discovered);
- A literary, dramatic, musical or artistic work or an aesthetic creation (which are properly protected by copyright or design law);
- A scheme or method for performing a mental act, playing a game or doing business, or a computer program (again, these are proper to the copyright system); or
- The presentation of information.

Animal and plant varieties and immoral inventions, though they may be inventions, may not be patented: s.1(3).

### 5.4.1 Computer programs

Copyright is almost universally regarded as the most appropriate means for protecting computer programs. They were not patentable under the 1949 Act because they were not a 'manner of manufacture' (the predecessor of the industrial application requirement of the 1977 Act) but they could form part of a machine or industrial process.

Following the leading US case of *Diamond v Diehr* (Supreme Court 1981), if the operation of a programmed computer gives rise to a *technical effect* an application for a patent may succeed. The courts must consider whether the end result is an excluded item: if, for example, it is a manner of doing business, no patent will be granted.

The method of storage of a program should now be considered irrelevant to the question of patentability, though in earlier cases punched cards were considered a method of manufacture (*Gevers' Application* (1970)) and programs permanently embedded in a computer's circuits were held to be patentable (*Borroughs Corporation (Perkin's) Application* (1974)).

The words 'as such' in s:1(2) have given rise to two different approaches.

- The application can be considered without the excluded matter. If the application is for a computer with a program running on it, the court must consider whether the machine *itself* adds anything to the state of the art. If the invention's novelty and inventiveness resides entirely in the program, no patent will be granted: *Re Merrill Lynch's Application* (1989).

- Where the subject matter of the invention is the *technical effect* of the computer program, that technical effect should be patentable since the patent is granted for the technical effect (which must therefore be novel and non-obvious), and it is of no significance that the effect is found in the program. In this approach the method by which the invention is implemented is immaterial: *Vicom Systems Inc's application* (1987).

The different approaches of the Patent Office and the EPO were dealt with in *Genentech Inc's Patent* (1989). The application in suit was for the technical application of a discovery which concerned nucleotide sequences of DNA. The Court of Appeal held that the practical application of a discovery could be patented even though it was obvious once the discovery had been made.

The Court of Appeal went on to apply this ruling to computer programs in *Re Merrill Lynch's Application* and in *Re Gale's Application* (1990). There must be some technical effect resulting from the use of the program which is novel and non-obvious.

### Animal and plant varieties                5.4.2

If the invention is a new animal or plant variety, it cannot be patented. Microbiological processes (which have always been employed in brewing and baking) are, however, patentable (*see American Cyanamid Co (Dann's) Patent* (1971)) as are their products. The EPO has granted a patent for a genetically-engineered mouse (*Onco-Mouse/Harvard* (1990)) and the EC Commission has produced a draft directive which will ensure the patentability of biotechnological inventions (OJ [1989] C10/3).

*Note*

1   Microbiology is the science of microscopic organisms – bacteria, viruses, fungi etc. Biotechnology is concerned with modern forms of industrial production using living organisms, especially micro-organisms.

2   Plant varieties, though not patentable, may be protected under a special (and similar) regime: Plant Varieties and Seeds Act 1964.

### 5.4.3     Public policy grounds

Inventions may not be patented if their publication or exploitation would generally be expected to encourage offensive, immoral or anti-social behaviour: s.1(3).

This means more than mere illegality: s.1(4). It has formerly been used to prevent contraceptives being protected (*Riddlesborger's Application* (1936)) but more recently inventions in this field have been held to be patentable (*Schering AG's Application* (1971)).

## 5.5     Procedure for obtaining protection

### 5.5.1     Application

An application has to be made on an official form, and must (of course) be accompanied by the appropriate fee: s.14(1).

The fees charged at the early stages are modest, currently only £15; the Patent Office does not expect to break even on a patent until it has been in force for some years. Renewal fees (payable annually) are progressive, on the basis that the longer a patent is considered worth protecting the more valuable the proprietor must think it is.

The application has to contain three matters (apart from the fee):

● A request for a patent (though completing the form takes care of this one);

● The applicant must be identified; and

● There has to be a specification, comprising a description of the invention, a claim or claims, and an abstract: s.14(2).

The specification must disclose the invention clearly and completely enough to enable it to be performed by someone skilled in the art, ie. a notional, unimaginative skilled technician in the field rather than the leading expert: s.14(3). The claim or claims must:

● Define the matter for which the application seeks protection;

- Be clear and concise;
- Be supported by the description, ie. cover only things included in the description; and
- Relate to one invention or to a group of inventions which form a single inventive concept.

When these items (not necessarily including the claims or abstract, which may be filed up to a year later) have all been presented, the Office will give the application a filing date.

After filing, there is a period of grace of 12 months in which the applicant can decide what to do next. The invention's commercial value can be assessed, finance can be obtained, industrial partners sought. Foreign protection can be applied for. If at the end of this time nothing further is done, the application dies. An application may also be withdrawn at any time before it is granted.

### Search and publication                                              5.5.2

During this 12 months, the applicant must pay a search fee for a preliminary examination (s.17) and file claims (if they were not filed in the first place).

The preliminary search report which the examiner will issue will list any documents the examiner considers to be relevant to the question of novelty. The applicant, after considering the results of the search, may file amendments to the description and claims.

However, these are not acted on immediately; rather the patent goes forward to publication in exactly the form in which it was filed. The only addition will be any new claims filed since then but prior to the completion or preparation of the application for publication.

At this stage copies of the application are available to anybody who wishes to inspect or purchase them. The Patent Office file is also open to public inspection.

The application as published will also include an abstract, a summary of the invention covering the main technical features. This too has to be supplied by the applicant. Like the claims and search fee, the abstract has to be filed within 12 months of the application date if it is not filed at the same time as the rest of the application.

### Substantive examination and grant                                    5.5.3

The final stage before a patent can be granted (covered by s.18) is known as the substantive examination. At this stage, the applicant has to pay a further fee (called the Examination Fee) and if this is not done within six months after publication the application will die.

A Patent Office Examiner will examine the specification, ie. the description of the invention and the claims, to see whether it meets all the requirements of the Act.

In particular, the Examiner will look to see whether the documents which were reported at search stage, or any others which have come to light since then, indicate that the claimed invention is either not new or is obvious.

A report is then sent to the applicant, who may then amend the application to overcome any adverse findings by the examiner or present arguments in reply.

This procedure may be repeated as many times as necessary until the examiner is satisfied that the specification meets all the requirements.

Once the examiner is so satisfied, the patent is granted and the specification is published.

**Timetable**

The search report is normally sent out within three months after a search request is made. Publication takes place just over 18 months from the filing date (or priority date) and the first full examination report is issued about 18 months after that.

The patent may be granted at any time after the first examination report once the application is in order.

There is a maximum permitted time of four and a half years from the filing date (or priority date) for the application to meet all the requirements.

It is possible for an application to be published earlier on request: s.16. The applicant can also shorten the period between publication and full examination and grant if they can make out a case for accelerated processing.

### 5.5.4    Amendment of application

Applicants may amend their applications before grant: s.19. The specification may also be amended after grant, with the Comptroller's permission: s.27.

Amendments may not be made to granted patents under s.27 where there are proceedings pending (in the Court or before the Comptroller) in which the validity of the patent may be put in issue. Instead, with the leave of the Court or the Comptroller, the proprietor may make amendments subject to such conditions concerning advertising the proposed amendments and costs or expenses as the Court or the Comptroller thinks fit. Such amendments may be formally opposed by third parties. The Comptroller must be given notice of any such proceedings brought in the Court.

No amendment to an application or a patent may include new matter: s.76(2).

## Duration 5.6

The basic term of protection under a UK patent, and under a European Patent (UK), is 20 years.

Under the 1949 Act it was only 16 years, and patents in existence when the 1977 Act came into operation received an extra period of protection, ie. possible protection up to 1997. To make things a little fairer, this additional windfall period was made subject to licences of right – that is, anyone wishing to work the invention in that time would be able to get a licence on request provided that he paid the licence fee demanded by the patentee.

Some products, particularly pharmaceuticals, take a long time to get to market. Extensive tests and trials are required, so that by the time the patentee begins selling products covered by the patent there is often little protection left. Under the Copyright, Designs and Patents Act 1988 pharmaceutical patentees are given the possibility of extending the term of protection of their pre-1977 patents by being relieved of the licensing of right requirements referred to in the preceding paragraph. This concession was later also extended to pesticides.

The European Community has also recognised the need for additional protection for proprietors of pharmaceutical inventions and a regulation has been adopted providing for the grant of supplementary protection certificates (Council Regulation 1768/92, OJ 1992 L 182/1). *See* also the Patents (Supplementary Protection Certificates for Medicinal Products) Regulations 1992 (SI 1992 No 3091) and the associated Rules (SI 1992 No 3162). These will have the effect of giving an extra period of protection for pharmaceutical products, lasting up to five years. The actual period of supplementary protection will equal the period between the application date and the date of the first authorisation to place the product on the market, less five years, but subject to the five year maximum.

## Self-assessment questions

1 What are the three routes to a UK patent?
2 What is the priority date of:
    (a) an invention;
    (b) matter contained in a patent application?

3 What are the four requirements for the grant of a patent under the 1977 Act?

4 What is the 'state of the art'?

5 When does an invention involve an inventive step?

6 In what circumstances will a computer program be patentable?

7 How are new plant varieties protected?

8 What are the three components of a patent application?

9 What must the specification achieve?

10 What is the final stage of the application procedure before grant?

11 How can an application be amended before grant, and when can a specification be changed after grant?

12 How long does a patent last?

# Chapter 6

# Registered designs: scope and procedure

## Subject matter                                                      6.1

Designs can be protected by registration under the Registered Designs Act 1949, as amended by the Copyright, Designs and Patents Act 1988. Protection can be given in this way not only to the:

- Shape; or
- Configuration;

of an article but also to any

- Surface pattern; or
- Ornament on it;

applied to it by any industrial process – printing, embossing, moulding, etc.

Registration gives the owner the *exclusive right* to the design in the UK and the Isle of Man.

Protection lasts initially for a period of five years, after which it is renewable for further five year terms up to a maximum of 25 years from the filing date.

*Note*

References in this chapter are to the Registered Designs Act 1949 unless stated otherwise.

## Requirements                                                        6.2

### Eye appeal                                                         6.2.1

To be registrable, the features mentioned above (*see* 6.1) must appeal to and be judged by the eye. Aesthetic merit is therefore required.

### Novelty                                                            6.2.2

To qualify, a design must be new at the date on which the application for registration is filed: s.1(2). To be considered new it must not have been previously registered or made available or disclosed to the public in any way whatsoever in the UK: s.1(4).

Its *shape, configuration, pattern* or *ornament* must make a materially different *appeal to the eye* when compared with an earlier design: s.1(3). Any differences of a kind commonly used in the trade as a variation will be disregarded for this purpose, and in making the comparison individual features are not compared – both articles must be viewed as a whole.

**Permitted disclosure**

It is possible to disclose the design without losing its novelty (and therefore making it unregistrable). This is extremely useful for designers who are not sure whether articles made to their design will sell; it allows them to test the market before incurring the cost of applying for registration. This exception, however, is very limited. It applies only to display at an exhibition certified by the Department of Trade and Industry, and even then an application for registration must be filed not more than six months after the opening of the exhibition.

Otherwise, any disclosure will have to be under circumstances of confidentiality.

### 6.2.3   Application to an article of manufacture

Designs must be applied to a specific type of article, which must be an article of manufacture: s.44. A design for a part of an article may be registered if that part is made and sold separately.

Sometimes, designs may be applied to two or more articles which form a set. To qualify as a set, the articles must be sold, or intended for use, together and must share a common identity of design. That means that they may be slightly varied versions of the same basic design and similar in appearance, but not merely decorated in the same style.

*Example*

1   The settee and arm chair of a three piece suite may constitute a set since the settee maybe considered a widened version of the chair design, but pieces of a chess set which are specifically designed to be distinguishable from each other will not make up a set. They will have to be registered individually.

2   Similarly the design for a letter of the alphabet in a particular typeface may be registered, but the complete font of characters will not be a set because the essence of them is that each is different.

3   A tea set where all the pieces are decorated with the same pattern or slight variations of it may be registered as a set only if protection is claimed for the pattern or ornament and not for the shape or configuration.

Where a design which is applied to a set is registered, the

proprietor gets the same protection as if the design for each article had been registered individually.

### Excluded designs 6.2.4

The designs of certain types of articles are specifically excluded from registration. They may be protected under other provisions of the Copyright, Designs and Patents Act 1988, in particular by unregistered design right or copyright.

Where the shape of an article is dictated by the *function* which it has to perform, as would be the case with a stackable crate for example, the design of the article will be specifically excluded from registration. Design right is the appropriate way of protecting such items.

Works of sculpture (unless they are going to be used for mass production), wall plaques, medals and medallions, and printed matter primarily of a literary or artistic character, are also excluded from registration. These are all matters which are proper to copyright.

## Obtaining protection 6.3

### Applicants 6.3.1

Applications for registration may only be made by the owners of designs. Applicants may be of any nationality, not necessarily resident in the UK, but they must have an address for service in the UK.

An application to register a design is made on Form 2A with the appropriate filing fee, accompanied by clear representations or specimens of the design. For most designs a statement of novelty must also be included, although this requirement does not apply when the design is for wallpaper, lace or textile articles.

On receipt by the Registry, an application will be given a filing date and a number. The applicant or agent will then be sent an official receipt. The Registry will then check that all the documents have been prepared correctly and make a search.

### Examination 6.3.2

Pre-existing designs, including those registered in the Design Registry itself, will be searched, along with other designs published in periodicals, catalogues and other sources, to establish that the design is new.

There is no way, however, that this search can be exhaustive, so the mere fact that a design is accepted for registration cannot be a guarantee of its validity.

*Note*

This process does not apply to checked and striped patterns which are applied to textile articles, nor does it apply to lace designs. These are registered without a search.

If the search indicates that the design is not new, the Registry will notify its objections to the applicant. The relevant pre-existing designs will be cited.

### 6.3.3    Registration

Where no prior designs are cited against an application, there may still be amendments to be made to the documents to bring them into line with standard requirements. But once all the documents are in order the application can go forward for the grant of a certificate of registration. The process normally takes about four months.

A period of 12 months from the application date is allowed for the application to be put in order for registration. This period may be extended by up to three one month terms using designs form 8 and paying additional fees. If an application is not in order after 15 months, it will be deemed to be abandoned and cannot then be registered.

*Note*

It is impossible to start again from scratch because the necessary novelty will have disappeared.

At any time after the application has been filed the applicant may manufacture and sell articles made to the design. Corresponding protection abroad may be obtained using international conventions, which will give priority based on the UK filing date.

### 6.3.4    Objections

If the Registry objects to registration of a design, the applicant has two months to argue against the objection either by making observations in writing or by applying for a hearing.

A hearing will decide a case on its merits and may overturn the initial objections. It may be that certain modifications still have to be made to the documents before registration can take place. If an application is refused, an appeal may be made to the Registered Designs Appeal Tribunal (part of the High Court).

### 6.3.5    Representations of the design

#### The application
The representations which must be filed as part of the applica-

tion are included to present an accurate and complete picture of the design to be registered. They must also identify those features of the design which are novel and for which protection is sought. The representations therefore consist of a series of views of the article and a statement of novelty.

Four identical copies of the representations must be filed, except where the application is for a design of a set of articles in which case five identical copies are required. One copy will be incorporated into the certificate of registration, the second and third copies are held by the Registry for public inspection, and the remaining copy or copies will be kept in the Registry's search files.

Representations must contain a sufficient number of different views of the articles to leave no doubt about the precise features of shape, configuration, pattern and/or ornament for which protection is sought. For a set, there must be views of all the different articles which make it up.

Perspective views are generally much more revealing than straightforward elevational views. No descriptive matter may be included in the views, nor must their be any indication of the size of the article.

If the article's design includes words, letters or numerals the representations or specimens should carry a disclaimer of any right to their exclusive use.

Where piece goods or articles in sheet form have a repeated surface pattern, the representation or specimen must show the complete pattern plus a sufficient proportion of the repeat.

### Statement of novelty
Each set of representations must include on the top sheet a statement which clearly identifies the novel features of the design. The novel features must be expressed in terms of shape, configuration, pattern, and/or ornament.

*Example*

The features of the design for which novelty is claimed are the shape and configuration of the article as shown in the representations.

As shape, configuration, pattern and ornament are the only features which can be protected by design registration, the statement of novelty must therefore not include any description of the use of the article or its features, or of its advantages or method of construction.

Often, only a particular part of an article will be capable

of being protected. If the proprietor only wishes to protect part of a design, the parts in which novelty are claimed must be clearly and unambiguously identified. This could be done by colouring them or by encircling them in red ink.

**Statement of article**

The application must specify the precise type of article to which the design is applied. For wall coverings and lace, use of these words alone is sufficient, but when a design is to be applied either to other textile articles or any other article a suitable and concise description must be provided. The statement of article of a set of articles should make plain how many different articles make up the set.

**Association with earlier design**

The proprietor of a design, or of an application for a design, may apply to register revised versions of the same design. A proprietor may also obtain further registrations if the design is to be applied to different types of article from those named in the original application.

In these cases, the later registration must be associated with the original. This formal requirement ensures that the period of protection of the later registration expires at the same time as the protection of the earlier.

### 6.3.6    Renewals

Applications for renewals must be made using Form 9A during the last three months of the current period of protection. If a registration lapses by more than six months it cannot be renewed and will give the proprietor no further protection.

Where protection has lapsed because renewal fees have not been paid, application may be made using Form 29 to restore protection. This must be made within one year from the date the protection lapsed, and the Registrar must be satisfied that the proprietor took reasonable care to see that the registration period was extended at the proper time.

*Note* ⎯⎯⎯⎯⎯⎯⎯⎯⎯⎯⎯⎯⎯⎯⎯⎯⎯⎯

This does not apply to designs registered on applications filed before 1 August 1989. This provision was inserted by the Copyright, Designs and Patents Act 1988.

A design which has been registered in association with an earlier design may only be extended if the registration of the earlier design has not lapsed or expired.

The Registry is required to issue a reminder when extension is overdue, but responsibility to apply in time rests entirely with the proprietor or the proprietor's agent.

### The Register 6.3.7

Registered designs are open to public inspection. Details of the registration are recorded in the Register of Designs and published in the Official Journal (Patents). The representations of registered designs, the application documents and the entry on the Register may be inspected from the date on which the certificate of registration is issued. Designs registered for wallpaper or lace are, however, not available for public inspection until two years after the date of registration, and no public inspection of textile articles is permitted for three years.

Particulars of registrations, but not representations of the designs themselves, are recorded in the Register of Designs. This is open to public inspection on payment of a fee. The Registry will undertake searches to determine if a particular design is identical to or closely resembles an existing registered design which is still protected. The public is not permitted to search through the representations of registered designs.

### Changes in proprietorship

Changes in the proprietorship of a design must be notified to the Registrar so that the Register can be amended. A certified copy of the assignment, stamped with the appropriate duty, should be filed with the relevant form (Form 12A).

If such a document is not entered in the Register it will not be admitted as evidence of title in any court, unless the court directs otherwise.

### Marking 6.3.8

There is no legal requirement that articles made to a design should be marked. Proprietors should, however, be aware that, in proceedings for infringement, damages will not be awarded against a defendant who proves that at the time of the infringement there were no reasonable grounds to suppose that the design was registered.

Once a valid certificate of registration has been issued, all articles made to that design may be marked to indicate that registration has taken place. For such a mark to establish that a design has been registered it must include the registration number.

*Note* _____

It is an offence to mark articles to indicate their design is registered when it is not, or when registration has lapsed or expired.

## Self-assessment questions

1 What features of a design may be protected by registration?

2 How long may protection last?

3 What requirements must these meet before they can be registered?

4 In what circumstances may a design be shown at an exhibition?

5 When may a design for a set of articles be registered?

6 What designs are excluded from protection?

7 What documents must be filed to apply for registration?

8 When is a statement of novelty required?

9 What is the purpose of a statement of article?

10 If an article made to a registered design is marked to show it is registered, what is it essential to include in the mark?

Chapter 7

# Trademarks: scope and procedure

## Introduction                                          7.1

### What is a trademark?                                 7.1.1

Traditionally, a trademark is a badge applied to goods to tell people who made them. Section 68(1), Trade Marks Act 1938 defines a mark as including a 'device, name, signature, word, letter, numeral or any combination thereof'. If it is used in a way which indicates a *trade connection* between the goods to which it is applied and its proprietor or registered user (licensee) it is referred to as a 'trademark'.

*Example*

1  In *Aristoc v Rysta* (1945) the House of Lords held that use of a mark on stockings to indicate that the proprietor had repaired them did not indicate a connection with the goods 'in the course of trade'.

2  In *Smith, Kline and French v Sterling Winthrop* (1976) the House of Lords allowed the registration of particular combinations of colours for capsules containing pharmaceuticals. The combinations constituted marks, and they had come to indicate a trade connection between the goods and the applicant.

3  In *Coca Cola TM* (1986) the House of Lords upheld the refusal to register a distinctive bottle shape, on the grounds that the bottle was a container, not a mark.

*Note*

The Trade Marks Bill will permit containers to be registered if they are capable of distinguishing the applicant's goods.

### The Trade Marks Bill                                 7.1.2

The 1938 Act will shortly be replaced by new legislation, required by the First EC Directive on the harmonisation of trademark law (*see* Chapter 12, para. 12.2.2): the effects of the Trade Marks Bill are noted where appropriate.

Under the Bill, any sign capable of being represented graphically, and which is capable of distinguishing the proprietor's goods or services, is a trademark. In addition to the matters mentioned in s.68(1), it includes:

● The *shape* of goods and their *packaging*;

and could also embrace:

● Music and (conceivably) smells.

*Note*

1   All statutory references in this chapter are to the Trade Marks Act 1938 (as amended by the Trade Marks (Amendment) Act 1984) unless otherwise stated.

2   American usage runs the words 'trade' and 'mark' together, in the same way as English usage ran the words 'copy' and 'right' together years ago. Anticipating that the American usage will spread to this country in due course, we have adopted the word 'trademark' in this Companion.

## 7.2     The modern role of trademarks

Trademark law still stresses that marks are indications of origin, though for decades the actual source of goods has mattered less and less to consumers. For example, people continue to buy 'Smarties' in blissful ignorance of Nestles' takeover of Rowntree MacIntosh. Indeed, it is the strength of brands like that which gives some companies their value, and the identity of the brand owner is often irrelevant (*see McDowell's Application* (1926)).

A trademark embodies the *goodwill* or *reputation* of the business which makes the goods. In an increasingly impersonal market place, it gives the customer a sign to which to return for goods of the same quality and characteristics. You may buy a chocolate bar from any convenient shop but you rely not on the shop's reputation, about which you know nothing, nor even on the identity of the manufacturer of the bar, which you may well not know either, you go for the brand name and the distinctive wrapper.

A particularly succinct explanation of the function and purpose of a trademark is found in an anonymous note in the *Yale Law Journal* for 1925 (p.115 at 116):

... a trade-mark is merely the visible manifestation of the more important business goodwill, which is 'property' to be protected against invasion.

'Goodwill' has been defined as consisting of a number of elements, one of which is 'the attractive force which brings in custom': *Inland Revenue v Muller's Margarine* (1901).

### 7.2.1    Registered or unregistered trademarks

The owner of an *unregistered* trademark cannot sue for infringement (s.2) but it is protected by the action for passing off (*see* 7.3). *Registration* brings significant benefits.

A registered trademark is protected under the 1938 Act and the proprietor can sue someone who infringes the rights given by registration for infringement. Broadly speaking, this is much less expensive than suing for passing off.

### Service marks 7.2.2

Similar badges can be used by service industries to distinguish what they provide from what other people in the same business provide. Marks applied to services in this way are known as service marks, although this is a distinction which UK law will drop in the near future. They became registrable in the UK after the Trade Marks (Amendment) Act 1984.

> *Note*
>
> Unless the context requires otherwise, the expression 'trademarks' in this chapter covers trademarks and service marks. The new legislation will remove this distinction.

### Brand valuation 7.2.3

Brand valuation – placing a value on a company's trademarks and putting them in the balance sheet as assets – is a relatively new science. It became particularly important during the late 1980s when there was a great deal of merger and takeover activity and companies were keen to boost their asset values. That led to a new awareness of the value of intellectual property rights in general and trademarks in particular which seems likely to last for a long time.

## Passing off 7.3

Passing off is concerned with the protection of traders and prevention of commercial dishonesty (*see* Chapter 14). 'Trading must not only be honest but must not even unintentionally be unfair' *per* Lord Morris in *Parker-Knoll Ltd v Knoll International Ltd* (1962).

Unfair trading as a wrong actionable at the suit of other traders who thereby suffer loss of business or goodwill may take a variety of forms, to some of which separate labels have become attached in English law. Conspiracy to injure a person in his trade or business is one, slander of goods another, but most protean is that which is generally and nowadays, perhaps misleadingly, described as 'passing off': *per* Lord Diplock in *Erven Warnink BV v J Townend & Sons (Hull) Ltd* (1980) – the 'Advocaat case'.

Action may be taken by one trader against another. No rights of action are given to those upon whom deception is practised.

## 7.4        Registering a trademark

Most countries of the world have systems for registering trademarks. Registration of a mark confers a statutory monopoly enabling the owner to sue for infringement if somebody else uses the same mark or one nearly resembling it on the same goods or for the same services as those specified in the registration. This is much simpler than suing for passing off, where you have to begin by showing that you have a reputation in the mark.

*Note* _____

Many trademark systems, particularly those in continental Europe, are deposit systems rather than true registration systems. Registration follows immediately upon filing, unlike the UK (and other common law countries) where extensive searches for prior rights are carried out. In a deposit system, owners of prior rights have to take legal action to remove later conflicting rights.

### 7.4.1        Classification of trademarks

The goods and services for which marks can be registered are broken down by international agreement (the Nice Agreement) into 42 different classes, and a mark has to be registered for particular goods or services or classes of goods or services.

If the goods or services on which you use the mark fall into more than one class (for example, beer (class 32) and spirits (class 33)), to get complete protection you have to apply separately in each of those classes.

*Note* _____

Multi-class applications will be permitted under the new legislation.

### 7.4.2        The applicant

Any person who claims to be the owner of a trademark or service mark which they use or propose to use in the UK may apply for registration. There is no requirement that the applicant is a British subject but an address for service in the UK is required.

Application is made on form TM3, which is used for both trademarks and service marks. A fee (currently £185) must be paid on application and three additional representations of the mark on form TM4 must accompany each application.

### 7.4.3        Priority

Applicants may claim priority from an earlier registration

in another country. Section 39A (which implements Article 4 of the Paris Convention – *see* Chapter 11, para. 11.2) gives applicants the right of priority if their application to register is made in the UK within six months of their application in another convention country. Where this right is exercised and the mark is consequently registered in the UK, it is given the date of the foreign, not the British, application. Damages for infringement may however only be claimed from the date of the British application.

If priority is claimed under s.39A the convention country must be named and the date of the basic foreign application must be stated.

An applicant who wishes to claim priority must furnish a certificate by the registering authority of the foreign country (and a translation, if necessary) or must otherwise verify the foreign application to the satisfaction of the Registrar in the UK. This must be done before acceptance of the mark for registration.

### What marks are registrable                                              7.4.4

Not all trademarks and service marks are registrable. It would not be right to grant a monopoly over a mark which consists of (or which might be confused with) words or symbols which other traders or providers of services should be free to use (*see* below). If a mark contains matter which may not be registered, a disclaimer may allow the applicant to register the mark and therefore secure protection over its other elements.

Some marks are inherently distinctive and are therefore readily registrable. Extensive use of a word or symbol as a trademark or service mark can also result in them becoming distinctive of one person's goods or services, enabling them to be registered. Some marks are, however, totally unregistrable, notwithstanding long use and recognition as trademarks or service marks, because this will never displace their ordinary signification.

*Note*

If a mark comprises a shape (including a container shape) which results from the nature of the goods themselves, or is functional, or which gives substantial value to the goods, it will not be registrable under the new legislation.

## Requirements for obtaining protection                     7.5

### Proprietorship                                                            7.5.1

A person who claims to be the proprietor of a trademark or

service mark used or proposed to be used by them may apply to register it: s.17(1). An applicant to register a service mark may show intent to use by showing that they are about to set up a company to use it or that they are applying to register a user at the same time: *see Genette TM* (1969) (CA); *Rawhide TM* (1962); and *Hollie Hobbie TM* (1984) (HL).

### 7.5.2 Distinctiveness

A mark may not consist of matter which traders may legitimately wish to use for their own goods or services. Ordinary vocabulary must remain free to use. Registration is therefore permitted only where the mark applied for is distinctive.

Depending on how distinctive a trademark is, it may be registered in Part A or Part B of the Register. The difference is material if the proprietor seeks to enforce their rights: *see* Chapter 13, para. 13.2.2.

**Part A**

Part A is for marks which are *inherently distinctive*: s.9.

Names of individuals, companies or firms are not considered inherently distinctive unless they are represented in a *highly stylised form*. Consequently, they will not usually be accepted for registration in Part A. As to what constitutes an invented word, *see Eastman Photographic's Application* (1898).

The same goes for:

- Surnames, unless they are very rare (a matter assessed by referring to the telephone directory, and in the case of a foreign name a telephone directory for the appropriate country);
- Nearly all geographical names;
- Words that are descriptive of the character or quality of the goods or services; and
- Any other matter which should be free for all to use in the normal conduct of their trading or business activities. This last category includes letters of the alphabet, laudatory words and devices representing a feature of the relevant goods or services.

*Example*

1 In *Crosfields' Application* (1909) the Court of Appeal dealt with applications to register certain word marks with a descriptive content, including 'Perfection' and 'Orlwoola'. Word marks in general had only recently become registrable under the 1905 Act, previously, only specified types of words had been protectable. The Court held that the word 'Perfection' had to remain part of 'the great common of the English

language' (*per* Cozens-Hardy MR) and could not be 'enclosed' by the applicant. The Court also refused 'Orlwoola', for textile fabrics. Recognising it as a 'grotesque mis-spelling', the Court held that the word had to be either descriptive of wool textiles or deceptive if applied to non-wool textiles.

2 In *Electrix Ltd's Application* (1959) the House of Lords held that the word 'Electrics' (for vacuum cleaners) would be inherently unregistrable and the same went for the mis-spelt version.

In *Smith, Kline and French v Sterling Winthrop* (1976) the House of Lords allowed registration of distinctive colour combinations for capsules for drugs.

### Part B

The standards of distinctiveness for registration in Part B are less rigorous: s.10. Geographical names may be registered if it is unlikely that others will wish to use the name for the same goods or services (*see York TM* (1984)).

Surnames which are more common (but still rare) and words which, according to the dictionary, are descriptive of the nature of the relevant goods or services but not necessarily the most apt word to describe their nature, may also be registrable in Part B. So may words which resemble words which are descriptive or non-distinctive, provided they are sufficiently different from them not to hinder the use of the descriptive or non-distinctive word by others. Letters of the alphabet, devices, and so on represented in a novel manner may be registered in Part B.

Where a mark has already been used, it may have acquired distinctiveness and become registrable even though it does not strictly fit the above criteria. The amount of use required depends on the inherent qualities of the mark, the more descriptive or non-distinctive it is, the stronger the acquired distinctiveness must be.

*Note*

The Bill will create a unitary register. The criteria for registration will be very similar to those for Part B

### Disclaimers

7.5.3

It is possible to include descriptive or other non-distinctive matter in a trademark or service mark, provided that it also contains elements which are distinctive: s.14. The mark as a whole will be registrable (in one or other part of the register) depending on the registrability of whatever distinctive elements it contains, but in most cases it will be necessary to disclaim exclusive rights in the descriptive or non-distinctive matter.

No disclaimer is necessary for words which are obviously descriptive or laudatory, such as the name or ordinary description of the services, or a word such as 'super' – it is unthinkable that any one trader or business could claim exclusive rights in them.

Where a disclaimer has been entered, the right to sue for infringement arises only where the distinctive matter is infringed.

### 7.5.4 Deceptive material

Marks may not be registered if they are likely to lead the public to believe that the goods for which they are registered are of a different type or nature from what they are in fact: s.11.

The goods or services for which the mark is to be registered in such cases must be limited to those which the mark does actually indicate.

### 7.5.5 Conflict with other marks

Marks may not be registered if they are identical with, or if they nearly resemble, marks already on the register for the same goods (or goods of the same description) or services (or services of the same description), or goods associated with a service or vice versa: s.12 (1).

*Note*

The comparison which is carried out here is not restricted to goods or services within the same class as that for which registration is sought.

Goods of the *same description* can be difficult to recognise.

*Example*

In *Jellineck's Application* (1946) Romer J found that shoes and shoe polish were not goods of the same description. He took into account:

● The nature and composition of the goods;

● The respective natures of the goods; and

● The trade channels through which the goods would be bought and sold.

This test is employed by the Registry in all cases where the question arises.

Where an application has been made to register a conflicting mark, priority will be given for the earliest application unless the later application is able to establish use from a date earlier than the date of the earlier application.

Where both applicants have used their marks before filing their applications (referred to as 'honest concurrent user'), the application with the earliest use will be given priority unless both have been in use for a considerable period of time (normally seven years). In that case, both applications may be registered so long as the marks are not identical or virtually identical or, alternatively, so long as the goods or services are not the same: s.12(2).

*Note*
_____

The Bill provides that a mark will not be registrable if it is identical or similar to an earlier mark registered for identical or similar goods. Whether goods are similar depends on whether the use of the mark on them would confuse the consumer.

## Protected matter                                      7.5.6

There are certain matters the inclusion of which, in a trademark or service mark, will make it totally unacceptable for registration.

The first of these categories is matter protected by the Geneva Convention, including the Red Cross symbol and the Red Crescent symbol and other related designs and wording. The second is the Royal Arms (or Arms so nearly resembling them as to be calculated to deceive) where the use is in a manner to lead people to believe that the person is authorised to use them.

The third category, for historical reasons, is the word 'ANZAC' (Australian and New Zealand Army Corps). Use of this word in connection with any trade, business, calling or profession is prohibited unless authority has been given.

Other matter appearing in marks may cause an application to be refused. The Registrar must give particular consideration to, *inter alia*:

- Representations of the royal crests or armorial bearings, or of insignia so nearly resembling any of them as to be likely to be mistaken for them;
- Representations of the Royal crown, or of the Royal or national flags;
- Representations of the Queen or any member of the Royal family;
- Words, letters or devices the use of which is likely to lead people to believe that the applicant has, or has had, Royal patronage or authorisation;

- Any word or words the false use of which would amount to the offence of falsely representing a design as registered or claiming patent rights or that a patent has been applied for;
- Any word or words suggestive of copyright or similar protection, or suggesting that trademark infringement is a criminal offence;
- Any representation of the name, initials, armorial bearings, insignia, orders of chivalry, decorations or flags of any international organisation, state, city, borough, town, place, society, body corporate, institution or person unless the consent of the appropriate body or person to that use has been given;
- The name or representation of any person living or recently dead unless the appropriate consent has been given;
- Varietal names, or words confusingly similar to them, of a type of seed, grain, plant, flower, fruit, vegetable or of vegetative stock where an application is for a mark to be used on such goods.

*Note*
The Bill contains a similar, though not identical, provision.

## 7.6    The specification

### 7.6.1    Purpose

The purpose of the specification is to *define the extent of the monopoly* conferred by registration. The specification must be an unambiguous list of all the goods or services covered by the registration. It must not be a description of the goods or services.

All goods or services of interest to the applicant *must* be covered. The scope of the specification may not be extended after application; if it is necessary to add further matter a new application will be needed.

However, the Registrar may *refuse* to register a mark if it is thought that:

- It is not going to be used on all the goods or services included in the specification; or
- Its registration may be opposed by someone with an interest in the same mark (or a similar one) for goods within the wording of the specification; and
- Even if registration is achieved, the mark may subsequently become vulnerable to attack for non-use.

## Drafting the specification

All goods or services in each application must belong to one class only. The applicant must have a genuine intention to use the mark for all the goods or services claimed in the specification.

The first step in acting for an applicant for a trademark is to obtain a list of goods or services for which protection is required. Isolate the important headings and make a single list. Include any likely or proposed developments. Then:

- Compare the list with class headings and divide accordingly;
- Order goods or services within each class to conform with the class definition;
- Amalgamate into general terms where appropriate, remove tautology and repetition;
- Punctuate properly.

The following may not form part of any specification:

- Laudatory words incapable of interpretation;
- Words appearing as marks in the Register – no evidence may be adduced that the word has become generic;
- Words such as 'including' and 'especially' which do not serve to define the rights claimed;
- Words such as 'and similar goods', 'and the like', 'etc' which leave the ambit of the specification open and may extend to cover goods from other classes;
- Words of vague meaning which are collective nouns or comprise a number of different goods/types of goods.

The following words should be used rather than the alternatives shown:

- System – use 'apparatus';
- Equipment – use 'machine'/'apparatus';
- Media – be specific;
- Accessories – use 'parts and fittings';
- Peripheral(s) (computer-related usage) – specify, eg. printer;
- Machinery – use 'machine';
- Devices – use 'apparatus'/'instrument'/'appliances';
- Kits – specify parts to be included and add 'all for inclusion in kits'.

The governing principle is that the specification should be comprehensible to someone having no knowledge of the background or circumstances of the application.

### 7.6.3    Words with special meanings

- 'Stationery' – includes everything normally sold at stationers (staplers and staples, letter knives etc);
- 'Parts and fittings' – always expressed as 'for the aforesaid goods' and used instead of words such as 'accessories'. Not to be used with materials which cannot have parts and fittings or goods which are parts and fittings themselves;
- 'Principally': *see Vacu-u-Flex* (1966) where although 56% of the tubing was metal it was not 'principally' of metal and the mark held invalid through non-use;
- 'Wholly' or 'substantially wholly' may be used to avoid deceptiveness objections where goods are classified by material.

### 7.6.4    Qualifications and exclusions

*Qualifications* are used to exclude goods or services which are not proper to the class. Use the words 'other than' followed by the objectionable goods/services, immediately after the goods concerned.

*Exclusions* are used to remove from the specification items otherwise falling within the class. They are usually used to overcome official objections.

*Example*

'Wines and spirits, all included in class 33, excluding gin.'

### 7.6.5    Punctuation

Use semi-colons to separate different groups of goods or services. Use brackets for qualifications if it assists clarity.

## 7.7    The Registry's approach

The 1938 Act (as amended) and the Trade Marks Rules 1986 define the Registrar's powers affecting classification of goods and services:

... any question arising as to the class within which any goods fall shall be determined by the Registrar whose decision shall be final. (s.3)

... each application shall be for registration in respect of services in only one class of Schedule 4 to (the) Rules. (Rule 21(3))

### 7.7.1    Criteria used

In examining specifications in the light of these provisions, five questions are considered:

- Is the specification too wide to be credible?
- Are the goods/services restricted to one class only?

- Are the terms clear?
- Is the list of goods and services tautologous?
- Is the punctuation clear?

1   *Credibility.* Most claims for 'all goods in Class ...' or 'all services in Class ...' are queried except for Classes 14, 23 and 33, which are relatively narrow. Claims for half the services named in one of the service classes are also generally queried. Account, however, is taken of the name and nature of business of the applicant to decide whether to query wide claims. Objections will be taken if the wide claim appears unreasonable and cannot be justified by the applicant.

2   *One class only.* Rule 21 requires applications to be made in one class only. It is now unusual for specifications to include goods which clearly fall into more than one class but it happens frequently with services. Any type of goods or services belongs in one class only.

Where a term could cover goods or services falling into more than one class it must be qualified in some way.

*Note* _____

1   To restrict it to the appropriate class simply add the Class number at the end of all specifications, ie. '...; all within class X'.

2   Multi-class applications are permitted under the Bill.

3   *Clarity.* Most defective cases occur in applications for service marks.

4   *Tautology.* The Registry prefers superfluous items to be deleted from specifications. This makes the specification easier to read and understand. The Registrar does not insist on the total elimination of tautologous items if the applicant has good reasons for having them. This would apply, for example, where an item was new to the market or represents a new venture for the applicant.

5   *Punctuation.* Where there is a simple list of goods or services it does not matter whether commas or semi-colons are used between the items. Conventions have developed, however, where qualifications, limitations and exclusions are concerned, and these are set out in the Registry's Work Manual, which is widely used by practitioners.

## Objections          7.7.2

The application will be examined at the Trade Marks Registry and if it fails to meet any of the criteria described above the Examiner may raise objections to it. If this happens, the applicant may put forward arguments in support of the mark, either by a considered reply in writing or at an oral hearing before a senior officer of the Registry.

Before that happens, the Registrar has discretion to allow the applicant to try to resolve the objection by informal correspondence. If this does not make progress the applicant will be obliged to rely on the statutory right to make a considered reply in writing or apply for a hearing.

At this stage, any significant use of the mark prior to the date of application may help establish distinctiveness, so evidence of this use may be submitted for consideration. Otherwise, in some cases an objection may be overcome by a slight amendment of a mark or of the specification of the goods or services in the application.

If the objections are maintained, the applicant can appeal to the High Court or to the Secretary of State. To do so they will need a written statement of the grounds for refusal which can be obtained by filing form TM5 and paying the appropriate fee.

*Note*

The Community Trade Mark system (*see* Chapter 12, para. 12.2.1), in common with continental European systems, will not have a pre-grant search. Conflicts with earlier marks – 'relative grounds for refusal' – will be resolved by the owners of the rights taking opposition proceedings. In the expectation that in time the UK will have to follow this model, the Bill provides for a change to the search requirements to be made by statutory instrument. This can only be done at least 10 years after the Community system becomes operational.

## 7.8      Advertisement and opposition

Once an application has passed the examination test and has been accepted it must be advertised: s.18(1). This is done in the *Trade Marks Journal*, a weekly publication. Advertising enables anybody who has cause to do so to oppose the registration of the mark. Such oppositions must be lodged within one month after the date of the advertisement: s.18(2). Trademark practitioners must keep an eye on advertised applications in case something of interest to a client appears.

Any person who wishes to oppose the registration of a mark must give notice by filing form TM7 and paying the fee. The time for doing this may be extended by the Registrar on application by the person opposing the registration. The notice of opposition must state the grounds for it and the opponent's address for service in Great Britain or Northern Ireland. A duplicate must also be provided for transmission to the applicant by the Registrar.

Formal oppositions should not be lodged until after notice has been given by letter to the applicant. This is to give the applicant an opportunity to withdraw the application before any expense is incurred because of the opposition.

*Note*
_____

If no such notice is given this will be taken into account by the Registry when it comes to consider any application an opponent may make for an order for costs in the event that the opposition is uncontested.
_____

Once an opposition procedure has been started, the applicant may file a counter statement, then the opponent and the applicant will file evidence and the opponent may file evidence in reply. These matters are regulated by Rules 48–57, Trademarks and Service Marks Rules 1986.

When the process of submitting evidence has been completed the Registrar will fix a time for a hearing. Each party which attends must file Form TM9 and pay the hearing fee.

## Registration                                                    7.9

Once an application has been advertised, and either no opposition has been entered within the time allowed or any opposition which has been entered has proved unsuccessful, and when all the conditions precedent to registration have been complied with, the mark will be entered on the Register: s.19(1).

The applicant must file Form TM10A before this can happen. No fee is payable at this stage. (The application fee includes the registration fee whether or not the mark actually gets as far as being registered.)

A certificate of registration is issued to the applicant without request. The effective date of registration will be either the date of receipt of the application or, if a priority date is claimed, the priority date.

## Duration and removal                                            7.10

The initial term of a registration is seven years. The registration is then renewable for periods of 14 years each. This is done by filing Form TM11 and paying the prescribed fee.

*Note*
_____

Under the Bill, these periods will both become 10 years.
_____

7.10.1     **Use**

A registered mark may be removed from the Register under s.26 for non-use where:

● The mark was registered without any *bona fide* intention to use it, and there has been no such use; or

● There was no *bona fide* use of the mark for five years.

In each case the non-use may relate to all or only some of the goods or services for which the mark is registered. If it has been used on some but not all those goods or services it may be part-cancelled.

The period during which non-use must have accrued ends a month before the application for removal or part-cancellation. This avoids the proprietor starting using it to avoid such consequences. An interested party – someone, perhaps, who wants to register or use a similar mark – may open negotiations to secure the proprietor's agreement to a cancellation knowing that there is this period of grace before proceedings have to be started.

The Act provides that application is to be made to the High Court or, at the option of the applicant and subject to s.54, to the Register. Note that once application has been made to the Registrar it is virtually impossible to 'transfer' the matter to the Court.

*Note* _____

Since proceedings before the Registrar are much slower than those before the Court, though also cheaper, you should give careful consideration to which route to take.

The applicant has to be a 'person aggrieved', eg. an applicant for registration of a mark against which the other mark has been cited.

Use of the mark on goods of the same description (*see* above) will save the mark, so if a mark registered for clothing is used on footwear it will not be vulnerable to cancellation (*see* also *Lyons' Application* (1959) (CA)). Use of the mark on services associated with the goods for which it is registered, or vice versa, can also save it: s.26(1)(ii).

Where a mark is in use only in a limited geographical area, and a second proprietor has been allowed to register an identical or nearly identical mark under the honest concurrent user provisions (s.12(2)), the second proprietor may apply to have the first proprietor's rights limited to that area.

7.10.2     **Words becoming descriptive**

Section 15 covers the situation where a word or words

contained in a trademark is used as the name or description of an article or substance. 'Gramophone', 'Linoleum' and 'Shredded Wheat' all started off as trademarks. The section states the general rule as being that this does not invalidate the registration.

However, this does not apply if there is a well-established use of the word or words by a trader in the goods which it describes, and those goods are not connected in the course of trade with the proprietor of the mark, or goods were formerly manufactured under a patent which was in force on 23 December 1919 where the word or words are the only practicable name for the article or substance.

In those cases, the mark will be completely invalid if it consists only of the descriptive word or words. If it contains other matter, it may be allowed to stay on the Register but the Registrar may require a disclaimer of the descriptive elements. In other words, a word which is used to describe an article will not be protected, but if it is incorporated in a logo, at least the appearance of the logo may be protectable.

### General power to rectify                                    7.10.3

Section 32(1) allows anyone aggrieved by:

- The non-insertion in, or omission from, the Register of any matter; or by
- Any entry made without sufficient cause; or
- Wrongly remaining on the Register; or by
- Any error or defect in any entry on the Register;

to apply to have it rectified. They may apply to the Court or (at their option) to the Registrar.

> *Note*
>
> While it is generally cheaper to go to the Registrar than the High Court, the process is very much slower. Having once applied to the Registrar it is exceedingly difficult to switch proceedings to the Court. If speed is required, application must in practice be to the Court.

### Defensive trademarks                                        7.10.4

Owners of trademarks which are very well known may wish not only to ensure that they have a monopoly to use them on the goods for which they are registered, but also to register them for other goods to stop anybody else using them. Such a registration is known as a defensive registration.

Under s.27(1) the additional goods concerned must be such that it would be reasonable to expect the public to assume, seeing the mark used on those goods, that it indicated the owner of the registered trademark was using the mark on and trading in those goods.

*Example*

In *Ferodo's Application* (1945), the applicant sought registration in class 5 for pharmaceutical products and in class 34 for tobacco, smokers' articles and matches. The mark, an invented word, was already registered in several classes, but used principally only for brake and clutch linings. The applicant argued that it served many customers, had a high turnover and advertised extensively, and that the mark was therefore sufficiently notorious for the requirements of s.27.

The judge took the view that he would have to be satisfied that the word had become so well known that a consumer seeing Ferodo aspirins would assume they came from the brake lining manufacturers. The more special the character of the goods for which the mark was registered, and the more limited their market, the less likely it was that a consumer would draw this conclusion.

On the other hand, the judge also considered that if a mark is well known in its application to a particular product, that could indicate that its use on another product would be unlikely to cause a consumer to infer a connection in the course of trade. As a topical example, he suggested that no-one would be likely to think Spitfire toothpaste had anything to do with the aircraft manufacturer.

As for Ferodo, the judge felt that the narrow fields of the mark made it difficult to argue that its use on other goods would lead to an inference of common origin. The appeal against the refusal to register was dismissed. However, the judge also added some useful observations:

● That the mark had not already been used on the goods concerned;

● How important brand names are in the marketing of such goods; and

● For trade witnesses to be called to say what effect seeing the other goods bearing the mark would have on them.

An important limitation to the use of defensive trademarks is that it only applies to marks which are *invented words*.

Form TM 32 is used to apply to register a defensive mark.

There is no such thing as a defensive service mark.

*Note*

Defensive registration will be replaced in the new legislation

by a general right for the owner of a well-known trademark
(defined in the Paris Convention) to restrain the use of a similar
or identical mark. The Registrar will also be required to refuse
to register marks similar or identical to earlier well-known
ones, even though they are not registered.

## Certification trademarks 7.11

Certification trademarks are used to indicate that goods
possess certain defined characteristics. These may relate to
the goods' origin, materials, method of manufacture, quality or accuracy, or other features.

Registration of a certification trademark gives the owner
exclusive rights in it. Others may be authorised to use it
according to the regulations applicable to its use, a draft of
which has to be filed with the application. Commonly,
certification trademarks are owned by trade associations,
an example is the wool mark.

These regulations are designed to ensure that the goods
to which the mark is applied possess the relevant characteristics. The owner of a certification trademark may not trade
in the goods concerned.

The requirements for acceptance of a certification trademark are much the same as those for registration of an
ordinary trademark in Part B.

Consideration of applications for registration of certification trademarks is shared between the Registrar and the
Consumer Affairs Division of the Department of Trade and
Industry. The Registrar is concerned with distinctiveness,
the latter with matters of public interest and the approval of
regulations governing the use of the mark.

Approval is dependent on the benefit to the public accruing from registration, the applicant's competence to certify the
goods and to operate the scheme, and the availability of the
mark for use by anyone whose products meet the requirements. A copy of the regulations must be deposited at the
Trademark Registry and is available for public inspection.

Any alteration to the deposited regulations requires the
specific approval of the Consumer Affairs Division. The
same applies to any transfer of ownership of a registered
certification trademark.

The form to use to apply for registration of a certification
mark is TM6.

*Note* _____

The new legislation will also permit collective marks to be

registered. Such marks indicate a connection in the course of trade with the association, eg. a mark used to denote membership.

## Self-assessment questions

1 What matters may constitute a trademark? What is the significance of a connection in the course of trade?

2 How is a trademark which has not been registered protected?

3 What is a service mark?

4 How many classes of goods and services are there?

5 What are the tests of distinctiveness for Part A and B?

6 When may a mark be considered deceptive?

7 In what circumstances will a mark conflict with an earlier one?

8 What are 'goods of the same description'?

9 What purpose does the specification serve?

10 How long does protection last?

Chapter 8

# Copyright: scope of protection

## Nature of copyright

8.1

Copyright, unlike the rights examined in Chapters 5–7, arises *automatically* when the requirements of the law are met. Under s.1(1), Copyright, Designs and Patents Act 1988, copyright protects:

- *Original* literary, dramatic, musical and artistic works;
- Sound recordings, films, broadcasts and cable programmes (derivative works which are protected by 'neighbouring rights' and which normally belong to entrepreneurs);
- The typographical arrangement of published editions – the appearance of the printed page. This is another type of 'neighbouring right'.

*Note*

All statutory references in this chapter are to Part 1 of the Copyright, Designs and Patents Act 1988.

### Original literary, dramatic and musical works

8.1.1

Section 3 protects original literary, dramatic and musical works.

Literary and dramatic works include not only books, pamphlets, plays and articles but virtually anything else which is written, spoken or sung: *University of London Press v London Tutorial Press* (1916). However, a single word is not substantial enough to constitute an original literary work: *Exxon Corp v Exxon Insurance Brokers* (1982) (CA).

Computer programs and preparatory design material for them are types of literary works (*see* Chapter 22, para. 22.2), and so are tables and compilations such as railway timetables, football fixture lists (*Ladbroke (Football) v Wm Hill* (1964)) and trade directories.

A computer database is a form of compilation and may therefore be protected as a literary work, although the scope of protection is narrow because the originality in a compilation lies in the selection and arrangement of the material which it includes (and which may or may not be protected in its own right).

*Note*

Databases are the subject of a draft EC directive (*see* Chapter 12, para. 12.4.6).

Dramatic works include works of dance or mime. Musical works do not include any accompanying words or action. Operas therefore combine musical, dramatic and literary works.

There is no requirement that the work is published. Even private correspondence is protected. However, it must be recorded in writing or otherwise for copyright to come into existence (s.3(2)) although the author's consent is not required for this purpose. If someone other than the author makes the recording they may own rights in the recording independent of the author's rights in the work.

### 8.1.2          Original artistic works

Section 4 protects original artistic works.

Artistic works include graphic works (paintings, drawings, diagrams, maps, charts and plans; engravings, etchings, lithographs, woodcuts and similar works) photographs, sculptures and collages.

*Note*

Protection applies irrespective of artistic quality, which sounds strange but is designed to avoid judges having to act as arbiters of artistic value.

The Act does not elaborate on the meanings of the various categories of graphic works, but the Court of Appeal has held that make-up, however distinctive, is not a painting: *see Merchandising Corp of America v Harpbond* (1983) – the 'Adam Ant' case.

Design drawings for typefaces and industrial designs are included although what constitutes an infringement of them is limited (*see* Chapter 13, para. 13.2.4).

Works of architecture – either buildings or models of buildings – are also artistic works. Architects' drawings are within the definition of graphic works.

Also included are works of artistic craftsmanship, a category of doubtful scope but which clearly includes matters such as pottery and wood carvings.

*Example*

1   In *Hensher v Restawile* (1976) the House of Lords failed to settle on a definition of a work of artistic craftsmanship while agreeing that the prototype furniture in suit was definitely not included.

2   In *Merlet v Mothercare* (1986) (CA) a waterproof cape created by the plaintiff purely to protect a baby from the elements was not artistic (though it involved craftsmanship). The plaintiff had not set out to create a work of art.

### Sound recordings and films                                         8.1.3

Sections 5 and 6 protect sound recordings and films.

Any recording of sounds from which the sounds may be reproduced is capable of protection. The medium on which the recording is made or the methods by which the sounds may be reproduced is immaterial.

Copyright in a sound recording exists completely independently of copyright in the matter recorded. Thus, the recording of a piece of music will embody rights belonging to the composer and rights belonging to the record company, and if the piece of music is vocal the author of the lyrics will have a separate right in it too.

A recording in any medium from which a moving image may be produced by any means is a film. Video tapes are therefore included, as may be computer programs.

### Broadcasts and cable programs                                      8.1.4

Broadcasts are only protected if made within the UK and if members of the public can lawfully receive them, and they have been transmitted for presentation to the public. The public which can receive the broadcast may be in any country of the world.

The reference to 'lawful reception' by the public embraces two concepts. First, the broadcast must be properly licensed (so satellite transmissions of pornographic material from the Continent which are not licensed in the UK will not be protected). Secondly, if a broadcast is transmitted in encrypted form, members of the public would only be able to receive it lawfully if they had the requisite de-coding equipment. However, this does not stop it qualifying for copyright protection provided the decoders have been made available by or with the authorisation of the broadcaster.

*Note*

The Act does not distinguish between terrestrial and satellite broadcasts for these purposes.

A cable programme will also be protected by copyright. However, note that many cable programme services simply re-transmit the broadcasts of others, an activity which does not attract copyright protection.

## 8.2          Conditions for protection

### 8.2.1          Originality

The requirement that a literary, dramatic, musical or artistic work must be original does not go so far as to require novelty. It simply means that the work must be the author's original work, not copied either from someone else's or from an earlier work: *Interlego v Tyco Industries* (1988) (PC).

The requisite originality is therefore *originality of expression*, not of thought, and that must originate from the author: *see* the *University of London Press* case. A translation may be an original literary work independently of the work from which it was translated: *Byrne v Statist* (1914).

### 8.2.2          Sound recordings, films and broadcasts

Sound recordings and films do not have to be original but insofar as they are copies of previous sound recordings or films they get no new copyright. The release on video of a classic film, or the re-release in CD form of an old recording, will not start protection running again.

A broadcast is not eligible for protection if it infringes copyright in another broadcast or a cable programme. Nor is a cable programme eligible for protection if it infringes copyright in another cable programme or in a broadcast.

Also excluded are those cable operations which, in broad terms, do not serve the public. This excludes closed-circuit television transmissions from protection.

### 8.2.3          Independent creation

If two people independently produce identical works, each work will be protected by copyright.

### 8.2.4          Fixation

Copyright does not subsist in a literary, dramatic or musical work until it is recorded in some medium, in writing or otherwise: s.3(2). The recording may be made by the author or by anyone else, not necessarily with the author's consent, eg. a reporter may have copyright in the verbatim report they write of a speech, independent of the rights of the person who made the speech: *Walter v Lane* (1900).

A record of spoken words, made for reporting or broadcasting purposes, may be freely used subject to conditions set out in s.58.

## 8.3          Duration

The length of copyright protection varies from one category

of work to another.

Copyright in literary, dramatic, musical and artistic works expires at the end of 50 years after the year in which the author died: s.12(1). The fact that copyrights always expire at 12 midnight on 31 December makes it unnecessary to know exactly when the author died (unless it was at a New Year's Eve party). There are, however, some exceptions to this rule.

### Exceptions

1 *Commercial exploitation.* Where an artistic work has been commercially exploited with the permission of the copyright owner the term of protection is reduced to 25 years after the first marketing. This will happen if articles which are copies of the work have been marketed.

2 *Typeface design.* Typeface design (though a type of artistic work in the UK) is outside the system created by the international copyright conventions, being the subject of a convention all of its own (the Vienna Agreement). The maximum term for protection for a typeface in the UK is 25 years after the year in which articles specially designed or adapted for producing material in that typeface were first marketed.

3 *Anonymous works.* These receive protection for 50 years from the end of the year when they were first made available to the public with the authority of the copyright owner. Pseudonymous works are protected in the same way. If during that period of protection it becomes possible to identify the author, the ordinary rules will apply: s.12(2).

4 *Co-authors.* Where two or more authors create the same work together, and their contributions are not capable of being distinguished, protection will run for 50 years from the end of the year in which the last of the authors dies: s.12(4).

5 *Crown copyright.* Crown copyright in a literary, dramatic or musical work lasts for 125 years from the end of the year in which the work was made. If it was published commercially within 75 years after being made, copyright will run for 50 years from the year of publication: s.163(3).

6 *Acts of Parliament/Measures of the General Synod.* Crown copyright also protects Acts of Parliament and measures of the General Synod of the Church of England, and expires at the end of 50 years from the year of Royal Assent: s.164. Prior to Royal Assent, copyright in a parliamentary Bill belongs to Parliament. Parliament also owns copyright in the literary, dramatic, musical or artistic works, which expires after 50 years from the year in which the work was made: s.165.

Copyright in sound recordings and films lasts for 50 years

from the end of the year in which the work was made. If the work is released to the public before the end of that period the period of protection is 50 years from the end of the year of release. The expression 'release' includes broadcasting and inclusion in a cable programme, and public performance of a film: s.13.

Copyright in a broadcast or cable programme expires at the end of 50 years from the end of the year in which it was made: s.14.

Copyright in a typographical arrangement (a different matter from typeface design) expires at the end of the 25th year after the year in which the edition incorporating the arrangement was first published: s.15.

For the first time in a modern copyright statute anywhere in the world, the 1988 Act makes special provision for computer generated literary, dramatic, musical and artistic works. These are works where there is no identifiable human author. Where this is the case, copyright expires at the end of 50 years after the year in which the work was made and belongs to whoever made the arrangements for it to be created (often a company).

The EC directive on the harmonisation of the term of protection of copyright and neighbouring rights (OJ [1993] L 290/0) will increase the term of copyright protection to life of the author plus 70 years. It will come into operation by 1 July 1995 and will extend the life of copyright in works still protected at that time. The 1988 Act will have to be amended.

## 8.4        Moral rights

Since 1988, copyright law has also protected two important moral rights of authors. These are:

- *Paternity* right, which covers the author's right to be identified as the author of a work;
- *Integrity* right, which protects the author against unjustified modifications to the work.

These rights are covered in Chapter 13.

## Self-assessment questions

1 What categories of original works are protected by copyright?

2 What is meant by 'neighbouring rights'?

3 How are computer programs protected?

4 Are unpublished works protected?

5 How may the words of a song be protected?

6 What is a work of artistic craftsmanship?

7 What constitutes a sound recording for copyright purposes?

8 What conditions must be satisfied for a broadcast to be protected?

9 What does the requirement of fixation mean?

10 What is the term of protection for:

   (a) original copyright works;

   (b) neighbouring rights?

# Chapter 9

# Unregistered design right: scope of protection

## Introduction

9.1

Part III of the Copyright, Designs and Patents Act 1988 introduced an important *new* form of intellectual property – unregistered design right – to oust copyright as the basic vehicle for the protection of functional designs. This new right has much in common with copyright but offers much less protection.

Section 51 imposes severe restrictions on the copyright protection of industrial designs (*see* Chapter 13, para. 13.2.4). Designs will be protected not by copyright but by the new design right. If they have the requisite eye-appeal they may also qualify for protection under the Registered Designs Act 1949, as amended.

*Note*

All references to legislation in this chapter are to the Copyright, Designs and Patents Act 1988 unless otherwise stated.

## Subject matter

9.2

Design right subsists in original designs. There is no need for there to be a design drawing or other document although the design does have to be fixed in some form. This could be data stored in a computer.

Section 213(2) defines 'design' to mean the design of any aspect of the shape or configuration of the whole or part of an article. This means the *overall appearance or form* of an article, or any part of it. (Registered designs, by contrast, are largely concerned with particular features of a design.)

Design right only subsists if the design is of an *article*; the designer must have intended it to apply to articles. The Act does not contain a definition of 'article'.

### Functional and aesthetic designs

9.2.1

Design right is primarily intended to cover designs which are functional rather than aesthetically pleasing. Artistic designs are not disqualified from design right protection but will enjoy 25 years' protection if they are registered under the Registered Designs Act 1949 as amended. Thus, there is a strong incentive *not* to rely on design right if registration is available.

The point that design right applies irrespective of how functional a design might be is reinforced by the fact that the definition of a design specifically includes the internal as well as the external shape or configuration of an article. The design, when applied to an article, need not even be visible to the naked eye.

## 9.3      Exceptions to design right

Design right does not subsist in certain situations. Some of these designs are also excluded from the definition of 'design' in the Registered Designs Act 1949, as amended, so cannot be registered either.

### 9.3.1      Method or principle of construction

The definition of design excludes the underlying principles or ideas behind the design. If these are to be protected at all, they are properly matters for the patent system.

### 9.3.2      Mandatory design features

The 'must fit' and 'must match' exceptions are intended to prevent design right conferring a monopoly and thereby to preserve competition. They permit copying where design constraints compel it.

**Must fit**

Design right does not subsist in those parts of the design of an article which are used to fit or connect an article to another so that either article may perform its intended function. This exception is particularly intended to withdraw protection from spare parts which must fit in to existing equipment.

*Example*

A car exhaust pipe has to fit to the exhaust manifold and must conform to the configuration of the underside of the car, in particular, passing close to the mounting points. Those features of the design are mandatory – there is no design discretion – so protection does not cover them.

Notice that it is not the design for the spare part itself which is excluded from protection, but only the design for those features of shape or configuration of the article which enable it to fit. A competitor who wishes to produce an article will still be prevented from copying the free-standing parts of the design but will be able to copy the connecting features. These may be applied to the second design to produce a competing article which will fit and function.

**Must match**
The 'must match' exception excludes from protection features which are dependent upon the appearance of another article of which the article is intended by the designer to form an integral part.

It is intended to apply where there is a need for articles which are part of a single object to match the appearance of the rest of that object as a whole – it does not, for example, apply to pieces from a set of cutlery. In fact, it was created to deal with the problem of car body panels, and it may have no application outside that area.

The exception is intended to cover the situation where a part is needed to restore the aesthetic appearance of an article. In such a case certain features of the design may be covered by the 'must fit' exception. The other features of the design are not free-standing since the designer has to reproduce the shape of the item being replaced if their article is going to serve as a viable replacement. So, wherever, aesthetically, there is no design freedom, design right will not arise.

### Surface decoration                                        9.3.2

Surface decoration is excluded from the scope of design right, again because the right is concerned with the overall form of an article. However, it may be registered (registration being concerned with features of an article) and may also be protected by copyright.

## Requirements for protection                                9.4

### Originality                                                9.4.1

Design right only subsists in original designs. The basic test of originality is that the design must be independent in the sense that it is not a copy – although it need not necessarily be novel.

> *Note* _____
>
> In *Interlego v Tyco Industries* (1988) the Privy Council held that a design was not original where the only original input of the designer was to make modifications to the design drawings which were undetectable in the article made to the design. Among other changes, the radii on the corners of the bricks were altered. This was not enough to make the 'new' design original.

Section 3(4) therefore adds a further limitation – it requires that a design is not commonplace. Thus, designs are excluded which, while they are not copies, are no more than an expression of what is widely known in the particular design field. For example, a design for a door will have to depart significantly from convention if it is not to be excluded under this heading.

### 9.4.2    Qualification

#### Qualifying persons

A design may qualify for design right protection by reference to the designer, to the commissioner or employer of the designer, or to first marketing. If the designer is a 'qualifying person' the design will be protected. If the designer is (as is likely to be the case) employed, or has been commissioned to make the design, the question is whether the employer or commissioner qualifies.

A citizen, subject or habitual resident of the UK or another EC Member State, is a qualifying person. So too are citizens or subjects or habitual residents of certain other specified qualifying countries (which do not include important trading partners such as the USA and Japan).

A body corporate qualifies if it is organised under the laws of the UK or another qualifying country and has a real business presence – more than just a mailbox – there.

#### First marketing

If the design is not protected under the 'qualifying person' rules, it may be protected if it was first marketed in the UK or elsewhere in the EC.

#### Foreign designers

The benefits of the legislation will be extended to foreign designers on a reciprocal basis. Countries will only be designated under the legislation if they give UK designers the same rights as UK law will give their designers. The UK legislation is, however, unique, and this provision will rarely if ever apply.

### 9.4.3    Fixation

There is no design right in a design until it has been fixed in a material form. This could happen either by the design being recorded in a design document, or in electronic media, or in an article being made to the design.

*Note* _____

A design document is defined as any record of a design whether in the form of a drawing, a written description, a photograph, data stored in the computer, or otherwise.

### 9.4.4    First marketing

If the design qualifies for protection by reference to its first marketing then design right will only arise when it is first marketed.

## Existing designs 9.5

Design right will not subsist in designs which were fixed in a material form before the commencement of Part III of the Act, 1 August 1989. They will remain protected by copyright under the then existing law (the Copyright Act 1956) subject to the transitional provisions set out in paragraphs 19 and 20 of Schedule 1 to the Act.

These provide that:

- Protection is limited to a maximum of 10 years from commencement (1 August 1989), unless under the old copyright law it expires earlier;
- Licences of right are available for the whole of this period;
- The 'spare parts exception' expounded by the House of Lords is *BL v Armstrong* (1986) applies. This holds that copyright will not protect the design of a spare part. The reason for the decision is the same as that underlying the 'must fit' exception.

## Duration 9.6

Protection begins when the design is first recorded in a material form or when articles made to the design are first made available for sale.

It will generally expire 10 years after the end of the year in which articles to the design are made available for sale or hire, but to avoid perpetual protection for unmarketed designs, s.216(1)(a) provides for an overall period of 15 years from the end of the calendar year in which the design is first recorded.

## Self-assessment questions

1 What designs are protected by design right?
2 What is the key difference between copyright protection for a design and design right?
3 What level of aesthetic appeal is required for design right to apply?
4 What are the exceptions to design right?
5 What tests of originality are imposed?
6 How may a design qualify for protection?
7 When does design right arise?

8 What is a design document?
9 How are designs existing on 1 August 1989 treated?
10 How long does design right last?

# Chapter 10

# Confidential information

## Introduction 10.1

Confidential information is not, strictly speaking, a type of intellectual property. However, the law on confidentiality can protect the same material as some intellectual property rights, especially patents, and it has to be understood as part of any intellectual property course. This chapter sets out the basics of this area of law.

*Note*

Where novelty is a prerequisite for IP protection, as with patents and registered designs, confidentiality agreements are a very important way of protecting inventions or designs before applications are filed. An invention can be disclosed to a prospective financial backer under a confidentiality agreement without compromising its novelty.

There is no statute law on the subject, so there are few hard and fast rules. It is entirely a matter for agreement – express or implied – between the parties.

The courts recognise that information can be protected if it is of the *right sort*. They seek to balance the rights of the proprietor of confidential information against the rights of those who have an interest in using it.

The result is that the use of confidential information may generally be restrained to a reasonable degree and for a reasonable time.

## Subject matter 10.2

The law of confidentiality can cover a wide variety of different types of information, or know-how, including technical information and business intelligence ( of 'trade secrets') such as customer lists. The scope of the right to protect confidential information depends more on the effort involved in duplication than on the nature of the material. The mere fact that the information is simple is no bar to its being protected – all that is needed is that its availability is limited.

The information must be specific and well-defined. Information which is publicly available cannot be protected, though a particular selection of publicly available information may be. The names of a business's customers are not in themselves confidential, but its customer list – a compilation of the names of the people it does business with – may be.

Once information becomes public, no end of confidentiality agreements can restore its confidential status. Any disclosure is fatal to its confidentiality, unless that disclosure is made in circumstances of confidentiality.

The law of confidence protects information against disclosure only. It cannot give protection against reverse engineering or analysis, which may reveal the information to the third party which carries it out. For example, a computer manufacturer may seek to keep secret the information needed to write programs to work on its products, but if an enterprising programmer can work out the information for themselves the manufacturer cannot use the law of confidentiality to stop them using it.

*Note*
_____

This example is subject to agreements to the contrary, and you should also note that copyright will provide protection where confidentiality does not.
_____

### 10.2.1        Disclosures

Confidential information is commonly disclosed to third parties and employees. The nature of the relationship with each requires study.

In both cases, there will usually be a specific agreement to keep the information disclosed confidential, and it should (for ease of proof) be in writing.

Confidentiality may also be implied in certain circumstances. They must be such that a reasonable person would have realised that the information was not being given away. Employees have a general duty to keep their employer's proprietary information confidential.

Specific information may be disclosed for a particular purpose. For example, consultants (non-employees) or freelance experts may need access to confidential information, and will have to be bound by express agreement. Subcontractors will need technical know-how. A competitive tendering process will require the disclosure of trade secrets, probably by both sides. Financial backers and business partners are likely to want to know a company's deepest secrets. Computer bureaux process confidential information for their clients.

### 10.2.2        Written agreements

There is no such thing as a standard confidentiality agreement. Although there are precedents, each agreement should be negotiated afresh and take account of the particular features of the situation. The following are matters which must always be covered.

### Prohibition

The agreement must prohibit *disclosure and publication* of the information, and must include disclosure through the recipient's carelessness. The reason for the disclosure makes no difference to the fact that confidentiality is destroyed by it.

The recipient should be prevented from *using* the information for its own benefit.

> *Example*
>
> In *Terrapin Ltd v Builders Supply Co (Hayes) Ltd* (1967), the owner of confidential information was able to impose restrictions so that the recipient would not use it as a springboard, to compete on equal terms without having to do all the work involved in collecting the information.

The use which the recipient may make of the information must be defined, usually narrowly. The definition of the use may be expressed positively or negatively.

### Duration

The duration of a confidentiality obligation is a matter for the parties, though they are limited to what the law would consider reasonable in the individual case.

### Disclosure by the recipient

The proprietor of the information should usually ensure that the recipient undertakes to impose a similar obligation on its employees, and/or to disclose it only to those employees who need to know it.

### Return of documents

The agreement will usually provide for the return of all documents at the end of the transaction for which they are used, eg. tender documents will have to be sent back by all tenderers.

### Release

10.2.3

The obligation of confidentiality is terminated when the information comes into the public domain otherwise than through the fault of the recipient. The recipient may also be released where:

- It becomes aparent, when the information is disclosed to the recipient, that they already knew it;
- A third party discloses it; or

- The recipient subsequently generates the information independently.

Establishing when one of these situations exists is potentially very difficult.

## 10.3　Implied confidence

### 10.3.1　Professional advisers

Professional advisers are under an implied duty to respect the confidentiality of information given to them by their clients. Information revealed in business meetings is also subject to an implied obligation, provided that a reasonable person would realise that it was not just being given away.

*Note*

Where a confidential disclosure occurs, it is possible (and often sensible) to record the fact and the terms in writing afterwards.

### 10.3.2　Employees

Employees will commonly have confidential information in their possession (often in their heads). The employment relationship implies a duty to keep such information confidential, and employment contracts often also contain express provisions. The employer will have to consider how to protect this information without interfering with the employee's freedom to pursue their career.

**Current employees**

Current employees are under a duty not to disclose confidential information acquired during or as a result of their employment. There is an implied duty of fidelity even if one is not expressly imposed in the contract of employment.

The employer has no right to control an employee's 'skill and dexterity, manual or mental ability' or 'information which is part of the workman himself.' Such information belongs to the employee.

*Example*

A trainee solicitor may have specialised knowledge which could be protected as confidential information, but if it was not information belonging to the employer, the employer would not be able to control its use.

**Former employees**

To the employer, the departing employee is (as one book on the subject puts it) 'confidential information personified.' Great care should be taken of the departing employee who is likely to be in possession of information which the employer considers confidential and which it does not want to see disclosed. In addition to obvious precautions – requiring a terminated employee to leave the premises immediately under escort – the contract can restrict the use of confidential information known to the ex-employee.

An ex-employee has every right to compete with the former employer (subject to express covenants in the contract of employment, of course). However, this does *not* extend to a right to carry away trade secrets. The fact that there is no express agreement restricting the right of an employee to use the employer's confidential information after the employment relationship is terminated does not imply that the information can be freely used.

The scope of the obligation of confidentiality was considered by the Court of Appeal in *Faccenda Chicken v Fowler* (1986). The Court held that a current employee has greater obligations than a former employee, there is some information which cannot be controlled after the employee leaves.

All the circumstances of the case must be considered, including:

- The nature of the employee's employment (the higher the status, and the more frequent the access to confidential information, the greater the control which may be exercised);
- The nature of the information;
- Whether the employee was expressly notified that the information was confidential; and
- Whether the information could easily be isolated from other information.

In *Fowler*, information concerning sales routes was not limited to high-level employees. Pricing information could have been confidential, but was not sufficiently isolated from other information. Finally, management had not instructed employees about the confidential nature of the information. The ex-employee could not therefore be restrained from using it.

During the period of notice, outgoing employees can in an appropriate case be ordered to deliver up all confidential information in their possession; on the other hand, an employer has been refused an injunction against a departing employee who wished to set up a competing business (though without soliciting existing customers).

**Restrictive covenants**                                        10.3.3

Restrictive covenants in employment contracts can include an explicit prohibition on using trade secrets, although such an obligation is implicit in the employment relationship anyway.

A covenant could also prevent an employee from joining a specified competitor for a period of say a year or restrain the employee from competing in a specified geographical area. Such restrictions must be reasonable in all the circumstances.

## Self-assessment questions

1   What is the basis of an obligation of confidentiality?
2   When may a confidentiality obligation be implied?
3   Where is it common to find an express provision protecting confidential information?
4   What does the law require of information before it will treat it as confidential?
5   What does the law give protection against?
6   How long may a confidentiality requirement last?
7   When will the recipient of information be released from a confidentiality obligation?
8   What four circumstances will usually be considered by a court in a confidential information case?

# Chapter 11

# International aspects

## Introduction

Intellectual property laws are national in their extent but the subject matter of the rights they give is international. A network of international treaties and conventions governs the protection of matter covered by other countries' IP laws and ensures that UK rights owners get protection, or applications can be made to secure it, elsewhere in the world, and that rights owners overseas may get protection here.

## The Paris Convention

The Paris Convention for the Protection of Industrial Property (1883), known as 'the International Convention', is the fundamental instrument in international IP law.

The Convention defines industrial property as:

- Patents;
- Utility models;
- Industrial designs;
- Trademarks;
- Service marks;
- Trade names;
- Indications of source and appellations of origin; and
- The repression of unfair competition.

The Convention does not cover copyright.

### National treatment

The Convention establishes the principle of national treatment – that nationals of all member countries should be treated alike under the laws of each member state – as far as protecting industrial property is concerned. National treatment is afforded on the basis of domicile, place of business or nationality of the proprietor.

Countries without patent systems, including the Communist bloc, were able to adhere to the Paris Convention because their laws treated their own nationals and foreign applicants in the same way.

### Priority

The Convention established a priority system. This means that an application in one member state for a patent or for the registration of a utility model, an industrial design or a trademark gives the applicant a period during which to pursue applications in other member states.

*Note*

Utility models are functional articles such as components for cars which are protected by registration in some countries, most importantly Germany. They are similar to patents, but a much lower standard of novelty is required. 'Petty patents' are similar.

The priority period for *patents* and *utility models* is 12 months, during which time nothing done by the applicant will have the effect of destroying the novelty of the application, nor may other applicants file applications which will take priority over that of the first applicant.

The priority period for *industrial designs* and *trademarks* is six months.

If the original application is withdrawn or abandoned, or refused, without being published, the priority date may be accorded to a new application filed within the appropriate time limit.

## 11.2.3     Compulsory working

The Paris Convention system tries to deal with the problem that national patent laws tend to encourage national exploitation of the rights they grant. Governments – especially of developing countries – do not happily give protection to multinational companies just so they can sell products made elsewhere to that country. They want to see local manufacturing, not just imports.

These 'compulsory working' provisions are permitted by the Convention to a limited extent; compulsory licences may be granted if a patent is not worked for three years after grant, and if that fails to achieve the desired result the patent can be revoked.

Developing countries offer patent protection to attract foreign technology, but then commonly seek to ensure that it is exploited locally so there is direct benefit to the economy. The demands of the developing world for an international system more favourable to their needs has resulted in some pressure on the Paris system.

In the late 1970s the UNCTAD Code of Conduct on Transfer of Technology gave practical expression to the search for a new international economic order. Drafts were prepared but differences between the Group of 77 developing countries, the industrial nations and the Communist bloc prevented any agreement being reached. Similarly, a revision conference on the Paris Convention had to be adjourned due to the Group of 77 demands for the power to impose *exclusive* compulsory licences if a patent was not worked in the national territory.

These developments led to pressure particularly from the USA for the subject of intellectual property rights to be included in the Uruguay Round of GATT Talks. Trade Related Aspects of Intellectual Property (TRIPS) have formed a major part of the current Round, which will result in much wider acceptance of the principles of IP protection.

## Patents                                                           11.3

### International applications                                        11.3.1

A patent has to be applied for in each country in which the inventor needs protection, otherwise they will have no control over people exploiting the invention in that country. Since UK patent gives the inventor the right to stop people importing the invention (if it is a product), a UK patent alone may sometimes suffice.

However, the rules on free movement of goods within the EC mean that it is inadvisable to rely on a patent in one member state only. In any case, it is rare to find an invention which has no export potential.

There are two ways in which a UK application can be used as the basis for obtaining protection in other countries:

- *European Patent Convention.* Most western European countries (including the UK) are parties to the European Patent Convention (EPC). The applicant files a single application under the EPC and will (if successful) be granted a patent in each of the countries designated in the application. So a UK patent can be obtained by filing a European Application designating the UK; and this process can also secure protection in up to 13 other European countries.

- *Patent Co-operation Treaty.* The Patent Co-operation Treaty (PCT), to which 42 countries including the UK are signatories, simplifies filing on a worldwide scale. So a UK patent could be obtained by filing an international application under the PCT.

In countries which are members of neither the EPC or the PCT systems, separate national applications will have to be made.

### Defence considerations                                           11.3.2

Seeking protection abroad may raise one problem under UK law. If the Patent Office considers that an application contains information the publication of which might be prejudicial to the defence of the realm or the safety of the public, it may prohibit or restrict its publication or communication. The demands of national security may therefore make an invention completely unpatentable outside the UK.

A UK resident who wishes to apply abroad for a patent must first obtain permission from the Patent Office. This requirement does not apply if they have already applied for a patent for the same invention in the UK, but in this case no application abroad may be made until at least six weeks after the UK filing. This period gives time for consideration of the defence implications of the invention.

### 11.3.3    European Patent Convention

Making a single European Patent application may be much cheaper than making separate national patent applications in each country in which protection is required.

The applicant has to designate the countries in which the patent is wanted and pay a fee for each. The application may be filed at the Patent Office in London (or any other national patent office in a EPC country) or at the two branches of the European Patent Office, at Munich or The Hague.

> *Note*
>
> As the Patents Act 1977 is based closely on the European Patent Convention, the procedure for the grant of a patent is very similar.

The result of a successful European Patent application is the grant of a bundle of separate national patents, one for each designated country. These national patents will then be subject to the patent legislation of the country in which they are granted.

### 11.3.4    The Patent Co-operation Treaty

The Paris Convention system is concerned with *access* to the patent systems of member states but does little about standardising or simplifying the process of obtaining a patent. The Patent Co-operation Treaty (signed in 1970, operational in 1978 and administered by the World Intellectual Property Organisation (WIPO) in Geneva) complements the Paris Convention by proceeding from the assumption that there is a need at the international level for *examination* before the grant of a patent, since unexamined patents (the validity of which will be doubtful) are a nuisance. However, pre-grant examinations are not cheap, and to have to repeat them many times in different national offices would be extortionately expensive.

Efficiency could be increased and costs reduced by internationalising the system. The PCT is designed to achieve this.

**International application**

The PCT permits a single international application, in one language and in accordance with one set of rules concerning formal requirements and content, to be filed at a single Receiving Office. For UK residents this will generally be the Patent Office in London.

The applicant designates in the international application those countries in which a patent is wanted. The single application is sent to an international searching authority (of which the EPO at The Hague is one) where a search is carried out. The PCT also provides for a single preliminary examination.

As soon as possible after 18 months from the priority date, the application and search report are published by WIPO. Copies of the search report will be sent to the applicant and (with the application) to each of the patent offices of the designated countries.

Each designated country then processes the application as a national one. However, the national fees charged by that office will have to be paid, and in many cases national rules will require a translation to be supplied.

It is also possible to apply for a European patent using the PCT route. If the European patent has been designated that part of the application will be processed according to the EPC's rules.

The PCT offers a much simpler way of filing the applications but it is not necessarily cheaper. Its main effect from the cost point of view is that it *defers* the payment of the fees charged by the national offices, and the decisions on validity taken by those offices can be delayed for 20 months (25 where there is an international preliminary examination). It says nothing about the grounds for validity of the patent application, which are left to national laws. The preliminary examination (which the applicant does not have to have) leads to a report couched in very general terms since validity is not a PCT issue, but it provides a basis on which national offices which lack examination facilities can decide whether to grant a patent or not.

# Trademarks                                                11.4

### The Paris Convention                                    11.4.1

Trademarks enjoy a six month priority period under the Paris Convention. During that time an application filed in one country may be given the filing date of an earlier application in another Convention country. International applications may also be made, using the Madrid system (*see* below).

A copy of the foreign application must be filed to support the priority claim. If this is not already in English, it has to be translated.

The priority application in the UK may not claim protection over anything omitted in the specification of the original foreign application. Due to different meanings of words between British and American English, and different drafting conventions and legal requirements, it can prove difficult to secure a registration of identical extent.

### 11.4.2    The Madrid Agreement

The Madrid Agreement is a special arrangement under the Paris Convention. It enables an applicant who has a registered trademark in the Member State of the Madrid Union in which it has a real and effective industrial or commercial establishment to make an international application. This takes the form of a deposit with WIPO.

*Note*

The meaning of 'real and effective industrial or commercial establishment' is not entirely clear. It means more than just a mailing address but does not require the bulk of the company's activities to be there. The main problem is that most companies operate in other countries through subsidiaries, so the only way a UK company could take advantage of the Madrid system would be to register the trademarks in the name, say, of its French subsidiary.

Registration follows in those member states which have been designated in the international application. Member states may raise objections under their national laws and refuse registration within 12 months of the international deposit.

The UK has always had problems with this system and accordingly is not a member. It would give presumptive access to foreign applicants, whereas UK trademark proprietors using the system would still have to go through the process of securing a UK registration.

The financial arrangements under the Madrid system are also inappropriate for a national system which carries out an extensive pre-grant search (as opposed to continental systems, which are generally deposit systems granting protection immediately on application and relying on third party actions to keep the register clean).

Finally, the possibility of 'central attack' – whereby if the basic or home registration is invalidated within five years all the international registrations based on it fall too – makes the system unattractive to UK users.

To overcome some of these objections, making the system more attractive for the UK, and also to adapt the Madrid system to the introduction of the Community Trade Mark system, a Protocol has been drawn up to the original agreement. The UK has signed the Protocol, which will:

- Permit international applications to be based on national applications (not registrations);

- Give the possibility of charging the national fee for registering a mark for an application which comes under the international system; and

- Change the consequence of a central attack so that the international registration is converted into a series of national applications.

The Trade Marks Bill currently before Parliament will enable the UK to ratify the Protocol.

# Designs 11.5

## The Paris Convention 11.5.1

The Paris Convention requires that industrial designs be protected in all countries of the Union which it creates. It is not specific about the scope of the protection to be given.

Article 4 provides that where designs are protected by registration (as under the Registered Designs Act 1949), an application in one Convention country confers six months' priority during which applications can be made in other Convention countries. The design's novelty is not forfeited because of the earlier application or any subsequent publication.

The Paris Convention enables proprietors to claim priority of registration date from the earliest application made to protect the same design in a signatory country. Subsequent applications claiming that priority must be made not more than six months after the filing date of the earliest application.

An application which claims priority cannot be invalidated if, after the date of the earliest application but prior to the UK application, the design is published or industrially applied in the UK, or if a competitor has produced a similar product.

A priority claim must be supported by filing convention

documents. These include details of the original filing, including representations authenticated officially by the design registration authority in the country where it was filed. If English is not the language in which the documents are written, a certified translation must also be supplied.

The representations filed in the UK must be supported by the representations of the convention documents. Any unsupported views included in the UK application will either have to be withdrawn at the request of the Designs Registry, or the priority claim dropped.

## 11.5.2      Other international arrangements

There is no all embracing international registration system for designs. In general, separate applications for registration must be made in each and every country in which protection is sought. The criteria for protection (if it is available at all) and its duration are extremely variable.

There are several countries (for the most part members of the Commonwealth) which have enacted local legislation under which the UK registration of a design is accepted as being equivalent to an independent registration in the country concerned. Sometimes local formalities may be required.

### The Hague Agreement

The Hague Agreement is a special arrangement under the umbrella of the Paris Convention. It establishes a system similar to that set up for trademarks by the Madrid Agreement, allowing a single international application which will automatically result in registration in the designated countries of the Union created by the Agreement. It differs from Madrid in that there is no danger of central attack.

The Hague Agreement provides for a single deposit of a design with the World Intellectual Property Organisation. There is no examination. This gives protection throughout the countries party to the Agreement unless within a certain period they refuse to give the design protection because it does not conform with the requirements of their laws. The scope and effect of the registration are matters for national laws, the Agreement is solely concerned with applications.

The Hague system has attracted few members. Of the EC Member States, Spain is bound by the 1934 London text of the Hague Agreement, Benelux and Italy by the 1960 revision and France and Germany by both. However, in effect, the only European country actually using the Hague system is Switzerland. The absence from membership of the UK, the USA and Japan makes the Agreement virtually irrelevant.

## Copyright and neighbouring rights                    11.6

In the copyright field there have been international arrangements since 1886, when the Berne Convention was signed. This was supplemented in 1952 by the Universal Copyright Convention, which sought to achieve similar ends but without making the same demands on aspiring members. There are also conventions on neighbouring rights, treated under UK law as a species of copyright.

### The Berne Convention                                11.6.1

Berne established a multinational system of equality, ensuring that either the personal connection of the author with a member state or the first publication in a member state of a copyright work would secure its protection throughout the countries of the Union it created.

Berne has been amended several times. In 1908, for example, formalities and registration requirements were prohibited. Britain was obliged to accept the majority consensus on automatic protection and to remove the requirement which existed until then for registration with the Stationers' Company before infringement actions could be taken. (Similar considerations meant the USA was unable until recently to adhere to Berne, one of the main reasons for the creation of the Universal Copyright Convention.)

That revision also established the term of copyright protection at the minimum period of 50 years after the death of the author, which also required a change in British copyright law.

Berne therefore has a modest harmonising effect on the laws of members of its Union. The most recent development has been the introduction of moral rights, long known to continental (civil law) copyright systems but not previously acknowledged to the same extent in Anglo-American copyright law (*see* Chapter 13, para. 13.2.5).

### The Universal Copyright Convention                  11.6.2

The UCC also imposes the basic obligation of national treatment, but on less stringent terms. The term of protection (minimum of life of the author plus 25 years), subject matter and the extent of protection are more liberally treated. It also permits a requirement that copyright be claimed by including a notice of the existence of copyright and the date of creation. There is no recognition of the author's moral rights under the UCC.

The UCC enabled the USA, the Soviet Union and other countries to join the international copyright system. The

USA has now 'graduated' to Berne, justifying the existence of the 'junior' convention.

### 11.6.3 The Rome Convention

Neighbouring rights are outside the international copyright system (although rights in films are generally assimilated to copyright rather than being regarded as neighbouring rights).

The Rome Convention of 1961 was very much a British initiative, reflecting the fact that neighbouring rights had long been protected in this country. It required members:

- To give performers the power to prevent fixation or broadcast of their live (but not recorded) performances;
- To give phonogram producers (record companies) the power to prevent reproduction of their sound recordings (protected in the UK since the Copyright Act 1911); and
- To give broadcasting organisations the power to control rebroadcasts and public performances (where an entry fee is charged) of their broadcasts (but not their diffusion by wire).

### 11.6.4 The Phonograms Convention

The provisions of the Rome Convention are supplemented by the Phonograms Convention, which deals with mutual protection against unauthorised commercial copying of sound recordings.

### 11.6.5 Qualification for copyright protection in the UK

Protection is only given to a work if it meets requirements concerning the author, the country where the work was first published, or (in the case of a broadcast or cable programme) the country in or from which it was made or sent: s.153, Copyright, Designs and Patents Act 1988.

The Act defines at some length what constitutes a qualifying person, which includes British citizens and subjects, persons domiciled or resident in the UK and bodies incorporated under UK law: s.154(1).

If a work is first published in the UK, or a broadcast or cable programme is first made or sent from the UK, it will qualify for protection irrespective of the nationality of its author. 'Publication' means issuing copies to the public; what is referred to as 'merely colourable' publication does not count.

Protection also covers works made by authors who are nationals of or residents in countries which are party to one of the international conventions (the Berne Convention, Universal Copyright Convention, or the Rome Convention) and which are designated by Order: s.154(4). Works first published in those countries will also enjoy protection. Nationals of non-Convention (and non-EC) countries receive protection on a reciprocal basis.

*Note*

For copyright purposes, 'first publication' includes not only the actual first publication but also any publication taking place within 30 days after that: s.155(3).

## Self-assessment questions

1 What does the Paris Convention cover?

2 Explain the principle of national treatment.

3 How does the priority system work?

4 What two systems exist for a UK applicant to secure foreign patents?

5 What are the main drawbacks to the Madrid Agreement?

6 Which body handles international applications for trademarks and designs?

7 What is the minimum term of copyright protection under the Berne Convention?

8 What are the main differences between Berne and the UCC?

9 What does the Rome Convention cover?

10 How may a copyright work qualify for protection in the UK?

# Chapter 12

# EC proposals

## Introduction

12.1

The internationalisation of intellectual property law has served to highlight the need for rights enforceable throughout the EC, or for a degree of harmonisation of Member States' laws. This chapter describes the EC's initiatives in the IP field.

## Trademarks

12.2

The EC's approach to trademarks is twofold:

- With the *Community Trade Mark Regulation*, it proposes to create a new type of trademark, valid throughout the area of the Community – based on registration, a Community Trade Mark will have identical effect in every Member State;

- By means of a harmonising *directive*, it will bring together the national trademark laws of the Member States.

### Community trademark

12.2.1

The Regulation will create a unitary trademark, equally valid throughout the Community. Once a Community Trade Mark is registered, any national registrations of the same mark will be suspended.

**The Community trademark system**
The system will operate on the basis of a minimal pre-grant search of existing marks. This is common in the national systems of continental Member States not the UK. It will, however, bring the benefit of being able to adhere to the Madrid Convention (*see* Chapter 11, para. 11.4.2), so that an international application may be made on the basis of a single filing in the Community (or the UK) Trade Mark Office.

The Community trademark system will be self-contained, with a Community Trade Mark Office (to be situated in Alicante, Spain) running it and Boards of Appeal deciding on appeals from its decisions. Ultimately, the European Court of Justice will exercise appellate jurisdiction.

**Community trademark rights**
Once granted, a Community Trade Mark will be an item of property just like a national trademark. It will be transferable, and the owner will be able to grant rights over it to other people by licensing or mortgaging it. One important

restriction will be imposed on the freedom of the owner to dispose of the mark; assignments will have to be for the whole Community. However, the rights in different Member States may be *licensed* individually.

Use of the mark on the same or similar goods or services will be an infringement of the rights of the registered proprietor of the mark.

Registration will last for 10 years, and will be renewable for as long as the mark remains in use. Non-use for five years will make the registration vulnerable to revocation. Revocation will also be possible if the mark falls into generic use through the acts or omissions of the proprietor, or if its use becomes liable to mislead the public.

### 12.2.2    The First Trade Marks Directive

The conditions which the Directive will impose on obtaining and using a trademark are very similar to those laid down in the Regulation. The difference is that the Directive will impose those conditions in *national* trademark law.

*Note*

The Trade Marks Bill will implement the Directive in the UK. Most other Member States have already implemented it.

The Directive does not set out to achieve total harmonisation of trademark law throughout the Community. It only touches on those areas where differences in national laws have an *affect on trade* within the Community. It aims to apply the rules developed by the Court of Justice on the 'specific subject-matter' of trademarks providing that the rights given by registration are exhausted once that essential purpose has been realised (*see* Chapter 20, para. 20).

It will also prohibit the partitioning of markets by registering different marks for the same goods in different Member States. So the whole Community eats Snickers bars rather than having Marathon bars in the UK; but how would the English consumer react to being offered mineral water under the established French brand, 'Pschitt'?

## 12.3    Patents

European patent law consists of two conventions: the Community Patent Convention (CPC) and the European Patent Convention (EPC). The two are closely related.

### 12.3.1    The EPC

The EPC (which includes non-EC members) is basically a

centralised filing system, with a certain amount of harmonisation built in. It offers a simplified route to obtaining a bundle of national patents based on a single application to the European Patent Office in Munich.

Both form and substance of the application are examined in Munich, and if the application is acceptable, patents are granted in the countries specified by the applicant. All issues of infringement, and most questions of validity, are dealt with at the national leve (*see* Chapter 11, para. 11.3.3).

## The Community Patent Convention                    12.3.2

The EPC system is seen as a stepping stone on the way to a true Community patent. The aim of the CPC is to produce such a creature, with applications and questions of validity being handled by the EPO and national courts dealing with infringements. The problem has been getting the entire EC to ratify it.

Like a Community trademark, a Community patent can only be assigned, revoked (except in exceptional circumstances) or allowed to lapse throughout the Community. Licences can, however, be restricted territorially. The exhaustion principle will apply; once a product has been placed on the market in the Community by or with the consent of the patentee, the patent cannot be relied upon again to control the resale or importation of that product from another Member State.

A common appeal court, known as COPAC, will hear all appeals relating to infringements of Community patents and their validity, whether the appeal lies from a decision of the EPO or of a national court. This should ensure a degree of uniformity in the way the law is implemented.

The CPC seems unlikely to come onto operation without at least some compromise. Some sort of 'two speed' approach may well be adopted among the EC countries according to whether they are for or against the CPC as presently formulated.

## Other patent initiatives                    12.3.3

In addition, there are two further Community instruments dealing with aspects of patent law.

### Biotechnological inventions
A draft directive (OJ 1989 C 10/3) will ensure that Member States' patent laws do not exclude matter from patentability simply because it relates to living matter. As such it addresses some extremely topical issues.

It provides that a process that requires human intervention consisting of more than merely selecting an available biological function under natural conditions must at least potentially be patentable. National laws will also have to provide that merely because something existed in mixed form in nature, this does not prevent it being patentable.

*Note*

Plant varieties will not be capable of being protected under the Directive. They will be protected instead under a proposed Community system of protection for plant varieties (*see* Chapter 22, para. 22.1.1).

Where the patented process concerns the production of living matter (or matter containing genetic information, such as a strand of DNA) it can be difficult to determine when an infringement takes place. Do the progeny of the living organism infringe the patent? And if bacteria are produced by replication of a cell into which the DNA material produced by the patented process has been inserted, do they infringe the patent? The draft Directive prescribes that these will be regarded as direct products of the patented process and will therefore be infringements of the patent.

The draft also makes provision concerning the deposit of micro-organisms and other biological material.

### Pharmaceutical patents

The regulation on the extension of the term of protection for pharmaceutical patents provides for supplementary protection certificates for medicinal products (*see* Chapter 5, para. 5.6).

## 12.4        Copyright

The Commission's 1988 Green Paper, *Copyright and the Challenge of Technology* laid out an ambitious harmonisation programme. To the *continental countries* it was too economically oriented, and the balance of the proposals has since shifted a little.

*Note*

There are two different schools of copyright thought in the EC: the common law countries (the UK and Ireland) have laws derived from the first English Copyright Act, the Statute of Anne (1709), which was enacted to protect English publishers. The continental countries have laws based on the French Revolutionary decrees on *droit d'auteur*, which start from the proposition that the protection of a person's creative output is a fundamental human right. This approach was subsequently exported by Napoleon throughout the continent, while the common law model became established throughout the British Empire.

The Commission has not taken upon itself the wholesale harmonisation of copyright law. The Green Paper focused on those areas where divergences in national laws affect 'the functioning of the common market by distorting the competitive conditions under which enterprises operate in different parts of the Community'. Or, in other words, it identified areas where co-ordinating actions at the Community level is preferable to independent action by the Member States.

## The Software Directive                                    12.4.1

The first instrument of copyright harmonisation to be adopted was the Directive on the legal protection of computer programs (Directive 91/250/EEC, OJ 1991 L 122/42). This turned out to be the most controversial measure the EC has ever passed. (*See* Chapter 22 for copyright in computer programs generally.)

It was not clear whether computer programs enjoyed protection in all Member States prior to the Directive. Given the size of the industry and the ease with which its products can be copied the Commission felt that a harmonising directive was needed, ensuring protection.

### Basic principles

Under the Directive, computer programs have to be protected by the laws of Member States as literary works. The UK had already adopted this approach, but other Member States had developed specific rules governing software. The Directive also covers preparatory design material.

*Originality* is required for a literary work to enjoy protection, and this requirement has been interpreted differently in different Member States. The Directive applies one simple test – a program is original if it is the *author's own creation* – and no additional criteria will be allowed.

The purchaser, or as the Directive says the 'lawful acquirer', of a program enjoys the right to perform certain permitted acts. They may do what is necessary to use the program – error correction, making back up copies – and may also observe, study, and test the functioning of the program, to determine the ideas and principles underlying it, while performing any of the acts which they are entitled to perform.

### Interoperability

The Directive also had to deal with the problem of interoperability. Computer programs need to interoperate with hardware, and with other programs. The Directive allows programmers first to find out what is going on at that important interface, then to design a match for it. (For example, this text was generated in one program on a PC, translated for an Apple Mac by a second program, edited in a third program and the pages set in a fourth. Although the electronic operations were automatic a good deal of matching took place.)

The Directive permits users to decompile or reverse engineer programs, but only provided this is necessary to achieve interoperability between the original program and an independently created one. It therefore strikes a nice balance between the interests of the user and of the rightholder, between access and incentive.

The term of protection must be the life of the author plus 50 years. As we shall see, this is to be extended under another directive, dealing with the term of copyright protection.

The necessary amendments to the CDPA were made by statutory instrument, the Copyright (Computer Programs) Regulations 1992 (SI 1992 No 3233).

### 12.4.2    Adherence to international conventions

The Council has also adopted a resolution on adherence by the Member States to the Berne and Rome Conventions, the two primary treaties on international copyright and neighbouring rights. It notes that Member States undertake by 1 January 1995 to sign up to the latest version of the Berne Convention (1971) and to the Rome Convention, and make the necessary amendments to national laws. It also stresses that non–EC countries should be encouraged to sign the conventions too.

### 12.4.3    Rental and lending rights, and neighbouring rights

The Commission's second Directive in the copyright field deals with the right to control the rental and lending of copyright works, and with the protection of performers, phonogram producers and broadcasting organisations – neighbouring rights owners.

**Rental right**
The Directive enables copyright owners to control both rental and lending of all classes of works except works of architecture and industrial design. The distinction between rental and lending is that rental means making copyright works (or copies of them) available for profit, while lending means public institutions such as libraries making them available for non-profit making purposes.

The owner of these additional rights is intended to be the first owner of copyright in the relevant works. The treatment accorded to films may cause some interesting problems; in continental jurisdictions, both director and producer are likely to be given rental and lending rights. In the UK the producer is clearly the author for copyright purposes.

The acts to be restricted under the Directive are only those which are limited in time. Sales of copyright works will not generally be caught; but sales with an option to repurchase will be.

The copyright owner will be able to authorise others to rent copies of the work to third parties. It is immaterial whether the persons renting out the works have legitimately purchased copies of it or are licensees of the relevant copyright authorised to do other restricted acts. Thus, no distinction is drawn between the purchaser of a computer program and the holder of a licence to reproduce that program.

The new rights are not exhausted by *exercise* of the distribution right. (If they were, they would count for little.) The fact that right-owners have put copies on the market, and had one bite at the cherry, does not deprive them of the right to remuneration when those copies are hired out, or lent.

The lending right will allow Member States to operate public lending rights schemes, giving 'equitable remuneration' to authors and other copyright owners from central government funds or requiring the libraries to do so according to the use made of the authors' works.

*Note*

At present only four Member States protect a lending right (and there is doubt whether the UK's public lending right gives equitable remuneration).

### Neighbouring rights

The rights of performing artists, producers of phonograms and videograms and broadcasting organisations are dealt with in the second part of the same Directive. Member States must protect certain neighbouring rights, in particular the right to authorise the fixation (recording) of performances, reproduction right, and distribution right.

Performing artists are to have the right to authorise or prohibit the fixation of their performances. Similarly, broadcasting organisations are to have the right to authorise or prohibit the fixation of their broadcasts.

The right to authorise or prohibit the direct or indirect reproduction of certain works is also covered by the Directive. For performing artists, this applies to fixation of their performances; for phonogram producers, it applies to phonograms; for film producers, it applies to first fixation of their films etc; and for broadcasting organisations it applies to the fixation of their broadcasts.

The same people are also given the exclusive right to make the same works available, for an unlimited period of time, to the public by sale or otherwise. However, the doctrine of exhaustion applies to distribution right. If the subject matter of the distribution right has been put into circulation within the Community by the owner of the distribution right or with the owner's consent, its importation into another Member State cannot be prohibited.

Fixation right, reproduction right and distribution right may be limited by Member States. The limitations permitted by the Directive will cover:

- Private use;
- The use of short excerpts for reporting current events;
- 'Ephemeral fixation' by a broadcasting organisation using its own facilities and for its own broadcasts; and
- Use solely for teaching or academic research.

Member States may also limit these rights in the same way as they limit the protection of copyright in literary and artistic works. Compulsory licences may, however, only be provided for if they are compatible with the Rome Convention.

To protect its position on private use, the Commission specifically says in the Directive that Member States' power to limit fixation, reproduction and distribution rights is without prejudice to any existing or future legislation on remuneration for reproduction or use.

### Duration

The Directive then turns to the question of the duration of rights. As for authors' rights, it simply places a floor under the term of protection permitted by national laws. This floor is set at the minimum provided by the Berne Convention: life of the author plus 50 years. Similarly with neighbouring rights, Article 10 adopts the minimum term of protection from the Rome Convention: 50 years (but *see* 12.4.4).

All the various rights given under the Directive will apply to all copyright works, performances, phonograms, broadcasts and first fixations of cinematographic works and moving images referred to in the Directive which enjoyed protection under national legislation on 1 January 1993. That is also the date on which Member States will be required to bring into force the necessary legislation to comply with the Directive.

## The term of protection

Minimum periods of protection are laid down in international conventions, but contracting states are free to apply longer periods, and some Member States do this. Consequently, the duration of protection varies within the Community from country to country and from one type of work to another. Such disparities can create obstacles to free movement of cultural goods and services and lead to distortions of competition. A work within the public domain in one country may be protected in another.

*Note*

Chapter 20 contains further detail about the case law on the free movement of goods and intellectual property.

Accordingly, the Commission has adopted a directive which will harmonise the term of copyright protection at 70 years after the death of the author. Member States must implement the Directive by 1 July 1995. Works still in copyright on that date will gain an extra period of protection. The term for neighbouring rights is set at 50 years.

## Satellite and cable

The draft EC directive on satellite broadcasting and cable retransmission is designed to produce uniform rules governing:

- What acts require authorisation from copyright owners;
- Minimum standards of protection for copyright works used in satellite broadcasts; and
- The acquisition of the necessary consents for cable retransmission.

*Note*

This proposal is dealt with in detail in Chapter 22.

## Databases

### Introduction
Closely related to protecting software is protecting what it mainly processes – compilations of information within computerised databases. An EC-wide information services market is high on the Commission's agenda, and the legal protection of databases is closely tied up with it.

The Berne Convention requires collections to be protected. This is taken to cover databases.

The Commission's proposals for databases envisages harmonisation of the copyright rules which apply to them, and a *sui generis* type of intellectual property protection, lasting 10 years (which the European Parliament has since increased to 15).

Similar *sui generis* laws, designed to protect catalogues and like works, are already in operation in the Scandinavian countries. The new proposal also adopts some principles of unfair competition laws which are found in other Member States.

### The scope of protection

Databases must be protected as collections within that Article's meaning: a compilation (which is presumably the same thing as a collection, or is at least included in the expression) is protected in the UK as a type of literary work.

The *sui generis* right is completely outside the Berne system. The new right will not apply to non-electronic collections, nor will the Directive have any effect on copyright in them. If Member States protect such works, they may continue to do so.

Databases are defined to include collections of any type of material in the literary, artistic and musical fields. The definition includes text, images, sounds, numbers, data, facts and pieces of information. There are no minimum numbers of items which, taken together, constitute a database: each case will have to be decided on its own merits.

### Originality

The key matter requiring harmonisation is the standard of originality demanded for a database to be protected. The draft's definition of originality is the same as that in the Software Directive: originality must be shown to reside in the selection or arrangement of the material.

The originality of the contents themselves is immaterial, and individually they may enjoy no protection at all. Equally, some of them may be protected and some not. They will get no additional protection from the Directive in their own right.

Copyright will protect the original element of a database which lies in its selection and arrangement (the works which comprise the database may qualify for protection themselves). Therefore, the rights are of limited use, as the selection or arrangement will only be copied if a large amount of the data is copied.

### Term

The term of copyright protection for a database will be the same as that given to literary works by copyright law. However, the Directive will not permit the owner of the rights in the database to keep extending protection by adding little bits of information to it (which is likely to be a daily occurrence). A significant change in the selection or arrangement of the material in the database will be necessary for the period of protection to start again.

**Unfair extraction**

The new *sui generis* right will exist quite independently of copyright, so there will be cumulation of the two forms of protection for databases, since the two rights are directed to different matters. Copyright in a database will only be infringed if the *selection or arrangement* of the data is copied: the new right will cover the *contents* of the database even though the extraction does not infringe copyright in the database itself.

---

*Example*

A legal database contains copyright and non-copyright case reports. The selection and arrangement of that material is protected as a collection or compilation by copyright law. But copyright gives no remedy if an unauthorised person gains access and extracts a non-copyright judgment. The new right would cover this situation.

---

There will not, however, be any cumulation of the new right with copyright in the contents of the database. The right of unfair extraction cannot apply to the individual works themselves.

The new right, to do a different job from that done by copyright, will apply only one test to determine whether a user is permitted to extract data from a database: is it *fair*?

The new right will be subject to a *licensing of right* provision. This applies where the database is made publicly available and the works contained in it cannot be created independently, collected or obtained from any other source. Then the right to extract the material for commercial purposes must under the Directive be available on fair and non-discriminatory terms.

**Other areas**                                                    12.4.7

Further initiatives are promised on a range of copyright issues:

● Moral rights;
● Reprography;
● Resale rights;
● Home copying.

**Moral rights**

There are differences between Member States in the extent

to which and the period for which authors' *moral rights* are protected. The use of moral rights, in particular the integrity right, to stop the colourisation of black and white films and to dictate where breaks should take place in films which are broadcast on television has lead the Commission to believe that moral right entitlements can generate restrictions on the public. Indeed, this is their entire purpose.

### Reprography

The Commission undertook a similar study in 1990 of the problems raised by *reprography* and of possible solutions to those problems. If Community action is thought necessary, we might expect a compulsory licensing system, possiblyallied to a hardware levy (the Commission actually uses the word 'tax', which might create problems of *vires*).

### Resale rights

The Commission also proposes to examine the *resale rights* which are optional features of national laws under Article 14 of the Berne Convention. These include the *droit de suite* enjoyed by artists under some copyright laws (particularly France): the artist (or their heirs) may claim a proportion of the proceeds of sale of works, previously sold by the artist. So, the starving artist who swops a painting for a meal early in their career may benefit when they become famous later.

### Home copying

The Green Paper addressed differences in the treatment of home copying and the difficulties involved in remunerating authors and rights owners. The advent of digital audio tape (DAT) was particularly on peoples' minds. The Green Paper favoured technical solutions to the DAT problem (*see* example below).

The Commission intends to lay a proposal before the Council for a directive on *home copying*. The Commission is also favourably disposed to the general use of the serial copy management system (SCMS) for DAT recording equipment. This allows copies to be made while at the same time limiting how many generations of copies can be produced; it reflects the rights of authors and of consumers and maintains a balance between them. The Commission also promises consideration of the possibility of extending such a system to other forms of digital reproduction.

## 12.5     Designs

### 12.5.1     Introduction

Within the 12 countries making up the EC, the problem of

disparate intellectual property rights is worst in the field of
designs. Even the idea of having a system for registering
designs is not universal, although it is only Greece which does
not provide a system for this. And among the 11 Member
States which do have registered design systems, what can be
registered in one country may not be registrable in the another.

### An EC designs system                                    12.5.2

The Commission's 1991 Green Paper on Industrial Designs
proposed a two-stage approach, as with trademark law.
The first stage is a limited harmonisation of Member States'
laws, the second is the establishment of a system under
which a single instrument – a Community design – will give
protection in all 12 Member States. A third stage, the granting of a limited period of unregistered protection, meets
some special needs.

A revised version of the proposed Directive has now
been published: OJ 1993

### The Directive

Any harmonisation which the Commission may contem-
plate has to be limited. If it sought to approximate laws
which really had no effect on trade between Member States
its *vires* would be called into question.

### Definition

The first requirement of a design law is to define what it is
talking about. The definition of a design is common to both
the Directive and the Regulation. It includes features of the
appearance of a product 'capable of being perceived by the
human senses as regards form and/or colour ...'. The product may be two dimensional or three-dimensional. Functional designs will not be excluded from protection, although
the Commission originally proposed that they should be.

There is another exception for features of the design
which have to be the way they are to enable the article in
question to inter-operate with something else. This is based
on the 'must fit' exception found in UK design law, although many people think this is properly a matter for
competition law rather than for intellectual property law.

'Must match' designs are accommodated by a 'repair
clause' which limits their protection to three years.

To be protected, designs must have a distinctive character. There are two tests by which this will be determined:

- Whether the design is known 'in the circles specialised in the
  sector concerned operating within the Community'; and
- Whether it distinguishes itself from any design known

to those circles through 'the overall impression it displays in the eyes of the relevant public ...'

Novelty tests are usual in design protection legislation, and the effect of the Directive and the Regulation will be to bring together the tests employed in different jurisdictions to determine the registrability of designs within the scope of the definition. The same test will apply to Community designs.

The problem of disclosure resulting in the loss of the necessary novelty and making the design unregistrable is dealt with. Both the Directive and the Regulation give designs a one-period of grace, providing that nothing done within that year will affect the novelty of the design if an application for registration is then filed.

### Unregistered protection

In the Community design system (but not under the Directive), designers will enjoy even more flexibility in the early part of the design's life. Designs which meet the criteria for registration will also enjoy a short period of unregistered protection. This will cover the period of grace and is likely to afford some designers all the protection they need. At present the regulation contemplates this unregistered protection lasting for three years. The one drawback of it will be that it will give protection only against copying, not the monopoly protection afforded by registration. (For a discussion of the distinction, *see* Chapter 13, para. 13.1.)

### Pre-grant examination

The value of registered protection depends to a large extent on how carefully the application is examined before registration is granted. The Directive does not prescribe an examination procedure, so it will be up to the proprietors of earlier rights to keep national registers clean. It does, however, set out the grounds on which registration can be refused, but the extent to which Member States will endeavour to keep undeserving designs off the register is a matter for them.

### Community and national design laws

Provisions in national legislation governing unregistered designs will not be affected by the Directive. Nor will national laws concerning trademarks, patent and utility model rights, civil liability and unfair competition. Moreover, designs protected under the Directive may also be protected under the law of copyright of a Member State, at least for the time being. The Directive says that copyright protection should be irrespective of the number of products to which the design is applied and irrespective of whether the design can be dissociated from the products to which it is applied.

The extent and the conditions under which such protection is conferred (including the level or originality) are for the Member States to decide themselves. However, Member States must ensure that their copyright laws give the same protection to designs from other Member States as they do to those produced by their own citizens; in other words, copyright protection must be afforded on a 'national treatment' rather than a reciprocal basis. Designers from other Member States must be protected in the same way as subjects of the UK: protection cannot be based on the extent to which French law protects UK designs.

**The Regulation**
The regulation goes on in some detail to set out the procedures for applying for registration and how the Community Design Office (which will also be in Alicante) will deal with objections and oppositions. It establishes a litigation system based on Community design courts designated by the Member States and deals also with the establishment of the Community Design Office.

## Other IP rights                                          12.6

In the interests of comprehensiveness, other intellectual property rights and Community initiatives require a brief mention.

### Topography right                                        12.6.1

In response to the US Semiconductor Chip Protection Act of 1984 the Council adopted a Directive which required Member States to give a minimum of protection to integrated circuits. As a harmonising measure it was almost totally ineffective because it offered so many options to the Member States. However, it did enable the Commission to obtain reciprocal protection under the US legislation for all 12 countries. As a swift response to a particular situation it has a great deal to commend it.

### Plant varieties                                         12.6.2

Plant varieties enjoy their own system for protection, similar in many ways to patents (*see* Chapter 22, para. 22.1.1 for a description of the UK law). The EC plans to introduce a single system for protecting rights in plant varieties throughout the Community.

## Self-assessment questions

1 What will be the effect of the Community Trade Mark Registration?

2 What is the relationship between the EPC and the CPC?

3 What is COPAC?

4 What criterion of originality does the software directive employ?

5 How does the software directive deal with interoperability?

6 Explain what the rental and lending rights directive seeks to achieve.

7 What will be the duration of copyright under the duration directive?

8 What new right is created to protect database operators?

9 What period of protection will be given to designs under the Directive and Regulation?

10 What will be the criterion for protection of a design?

# Chapter 13

# Intellectual property protection

## Monopoly protection and protection against copying

Intellectual property rights confer limited monopolies on their owners. In fact, it is usual to distinguish between true monopoly protection and protection against copying only.

*Registered rights* – patents, registered designs, and trademarks – confer monopoly protection, whereas *unregistered rights* give the lesser type of protection and are only infringed where there is *actual* copying.

Infringements are also (mostly in the case of unregistered rights) divided into two categories:

- Primary infringements (though the term is not used in the legislation); and
- Secondary infringements.

*Primary infringements* are absolute, in the sense that no knowledge on the part of the infringer is necessary for the plaintiff's action to succeed (but *see* 13.1.3). *Secondary infringements*, which are mainly certain types of dealings in infringing articles, are only committed if the defendant has a degree of knowledge about the infringing nature of the articles.

## Monopoly protection

Monopoly protection enables the rights owner to prevent anyone using their intellectual property whether or not that person knew of the existence of the rights owner's intellectual property.

It is no defence to a *patent* infringement claim to argue that the invention was made with no knowledge of the plaintiff's invention; the details of the invention are available for all the world to see.

Similarly, *registered designs* are notified to the world, and the owner of a registered design has a complete monopoly on its use.

*Trademarks* also confer on their owner a monopoly. However, in this case they are registered only for specified goods, and there may be nothing to stop another person using the same mark on *unrelated* goods and even registering it if the goods or services for which it is registered are sufficiently different.

**13.1.2     Protection against copying**

*Copyright* and *unregistered design right*, on the other hand, protect only against copying. There is no register of copyright in this country (there is in the USA, and registration is a prerequisite for enforcing the owner's rights) so no question of constructive knowledge of the existence of the work.

If another person, without ever having seen the rights owner's work, produces something identical (or similar), no infringement is committed; indeed, two identical copyright works or designs may exist simultaneously, provided the necessary degree of originality is present.

**13.1.3     Innocent infringement**

The question of innocence on the part of the infringer is separate from that of whether the right in question is a monopoly one or not. Damages will not usually be awarded if the infringer can show that they were ignorant of the existence of the owner's intellectual property, whether it is a patent, design (registered or unregistered) or copyright. There is no innocent infringement defence in trademarks law. (*See* also Chapter 21, para. 21.3.5.)

# 13.2     Primary infringement

**13.2.1     Patents**

A patent, once granted, gives its owner the exclusive right to work the invention it protects. Although the information about how to work the invention is made public in the specification of the patent, and is available for others to draw upon, no-one may do precisely what is set out in the patent without the permission of the owner.

This applies equally to both deliberate and innocent infringements, although the remedies available against an innocent infringer will not be the same as those which can be obtained against an infringer who knew full well that the patent existed.

No infringement action can be started before the patent is granted. Infringements taking place after publication of the application may be the subject of a claim for damages (s.69) but the action cannot be started before the patent is granted.

**Infringement: definition**
By s.60, an infringement is any of the following, done without the permission of the patent owner:

● Making, disposing of, offering to dispose of, using or importing a patented product, or keeping it, whether for disposal or otherwise;

- Using a patented process or offering it for use in the UK in the knowledge (or where it would be obvious to a reasonable man) that such use would be without the consent of the proprietor and would be an infringement of the patent;

- Disposing or offering to dispose of, using or importing or keeping, whether for disposal or otherwise, any product obtained directly from a patented process;

- Supplying or offering to supply in the UK a person (other than a licensee or other person entitled to work the invention) with any of the means, relating to an essential element of the invention, for putting the invention into effect.

  This form of contributory infringement requires some element of guilty knowledge on the part of the infringer. The infringer must know, or it must be obvious to a reasonable man in the circumstances, that those means are suitable for putting and are intended to put the invention into effect in the UK.

Whether an alleged infringement is actionable or not depends on consideration of:

- The statutory defences provided in s.60(3) (*see* Chapter 21, para. 21.3.5); and

- The interpretation of the specification of the patent in suit.

### Interpretation of patent specifications

The construction of a patent specification is a matter which has caused some controversy in the past. To amount to an infringement, the act complained of must be within the scope of the specification and the claims (which in turn must be supported by the specification) in the patent application, as amended before grant if this has been necessary to satisfy the examiner.

A literal interpretation is not appropriate for a patent specification, which is a document written for scientists or engineers skilled in the art to which it relates. In *Rodi & Weinberger AG v Henry Showell Ltd* (1969) Lord Reid disapproved a literal approach:

... claims are not addressed to conveyancers: they are addressed to practical men skilled in the prior art, and I do not think that they ought to be construed with that meticulousness which was once thought appropriate for conveyancing documents.

### The 'pith and marrow' approach

Where the issue of infringement is not clear cut, the question may be to consider whether the differences between the defendant's variant and the patented invention are material. Do they differ in essential or inessential respects? This involves the so-called 'pith and marrow' approach, where those components essential to the invention are separated from those which are not. Even though there might be variations in the inessential elements, if the infringer has taken all the essential ones there can be no doubt that the infringement has taken place.

**The purposive approach**
In certain circumstances a purposive approach may be appropriate. This looks at whether the skilled reader would think that the patentee had intended something to be essential.

*Example*

In *Catnic Components v Hill & Smith Ltd* (1982) the House of Lords held that the verticality of the plaintiff's lintel was inessential as the invention worked just as well with a slight incline (as in the defendants' product). The defendants had argued that the verticality was essential and therefore there was no infringement of the pith and marrow of the patent.

Lord Diplock said that 'the kind of meticulous verbal analysis in which lawyers are too often tempted by their training to indulge' was inappropriate in construing a patent specification. The real issue was whether practical persons, skilled in the art, would understand that the patentee intended strict compliance with a particular word or phrase to be an essential requirement of the invention. His Lordship then set down a test for determining whether variants infringe:

- Does the variant have, in fact, a *material effect* on the way the invention works? If yes, it falls outside the claim.

- If no, *would it have been obvious* to the informed reader at the date of publication of the patent specification that the variant had no material effect? If no, the variant falls outside the claim.

- If yes, is it apparent to any reader skilled in the art that *strict compliance* with the primary meaning of the claim was intended? If no the variant is outside the claim, but if yes it is an infringement.

Note also *Improver Corp v Remington Consumer Products Ltd* (1990) where this three part test was applied by the Patents Court.

*Example*

*Improver* concerned a depilatory device. The patent described the use of a 'helical spring' which, when rotated, would catch the offending hairs and pluck them from the skin. The alleged infringing device used a rubber rod with slits in it, which operated in the same way. The variant would have been obvious to the informed reader at the time of the publication, and the Court held that the reader would have understood that strict compliance with the primary meaning of the claim was intended.

## Trademarks 13.2.2

### Content of right

Registration in Part A or Part B of the register gives the proprietor a monopoly in the use of the registered mark on the goods or services for which it is registered.

The right given by registration is infringed if anyone other than the proprietor of the mark or a registered user uses a mark identical with or nearly resembling the registered mark in the course of trade in relation to any goods for which it is registered. A registered service mark is infringed in the same way.

The use made of the mark must be in a manner likely to be taken either:

- As being used as a trademark; or
- As importing a reference to some person having the right to use the trademark or to goods with which such a person is connected in the course of trade.

'Use as a trademark' has to be construed by referring to s.68, TMA (the interpretation section) which contains a definition of 'trademark'. It means:

a mark used or proposed to be used in relation to goods for the purpose of indicating, or so as to indicate, a connection in the course of trade between the goods and some person having the right ... to use the mark ...

### Non-infringing acts

Certain uses do not infringe the rights of the trademark owner. Under s.4(3) these are:

- Use on the proprietor's (or those of a good's registered user) unless the proprietor of the goods (or their registered user) has removed or obliterated it;
- Use with the consent (express or implied) of the proprietor (or registered user); and
- Use on parts or accessories goods on which the trademark has been lawfully used, if the use of the mark is reasonably necessary to indicate that the goods are parts or accessories for those goods. The use must not indicate a connection in the course of trade which does not exist between the goods and any person.

**Part B marks**

An infringement of a Part B trademark will not entitle the plaintiff to an injunction or other relief if the defendant establishes that the use of which the plaintiff complains is not likely to deceive or cause confusion or to be taken as indicating a connection in the course of trade between the goods and a person entitled to use the mark. This does not apply to a s.6 infringement.

**Section 6 infringements**

Under s.6, it is an infringement to breach restrictions contained in a written agreement made by a purchaser or owner of goods with the proprietor or registered user of a trademark by which that person agrees not to do certain acts.

The acts in question are to:

- Apply the trademark to altered goods;
- Alter or partially remove or obliterate a mark already applied to goods;
- Apply another trademark to the goods; and
- Add other written matter to the trademark which is likely to injure the reputation of the trademark.

### 13.2.3    Registered designs

The registered proprietor of a design enjoys the exclusive right to make or import articles for which the design has been registered and to which the design (or one not substantially different from it) has been applied, for sale or hire or for use for the purposes of a trade or business.

They also enjoy the exclusive right to sell such articles, hire them, or offer or expose them for sale or hire. This monopoly right is infringed by anyone who does any of those things without the licence of the proprietor.

The right is also infringed by anyone who (again without the licence of the proprietor) makes anything for enabling such an article to be made where the proprietor enjoys exclusive rights in relation to it. Anything done with a kit is an infringement if it would infringe if done in relation to the assembled article. Making anything for enabling a kit to be assembled or made is also an infringement if the assembled article would be one in which the registered proprietor enjoyed exclusive rights.

The reproduction of functional or 'must match' features, which are left out of account when the design's registrability is assessed, does not amount to an infringement. Proceedings may not be taken in respect of an infringement which pre-dates the issue of the registration certificate.

## Copyright: economic rights                              13.2.4

Since the introduction in the 1988 Act of protection for moral rights, we must distinguish between the two sets of rights protected by copyright. The traditional rights protected by copyright are referred to as economic rights, to distinguish them from moral rights.

The owner of copyright in a work has the exclusive right to do a number of restricted acts: s.16. The right extends to authorising others to do the acts. These are:

- Copying the work;
- Issuing copies of the work to the public;
- Performing, showing or playing the work in public;
- Broadcasting the work or including it in a cable programme service;
- Adapting the work, or doing any of the above acts to an adaptation of the work.

### Copying

Some of these restricted acts may not be applicable to certain categories of copyright work. However, copying a work is covered by the copyright in works of every description: s.17.

For literary, dramatic, musical or artistic works, copying means reproducing the work in a material form. It may be handwritten, typed, printed, photocopied, or recorded, or stored in any medium by electronic means: s.17(2).

Copying an artistic work also includes making a copy in three dimensions of a two dimensional work, or vice versa (s.17(3)), but if the original is a design document (which depends on the intention of the author when the artistic work was created), copyright is only infringed if the three-dimensional object is itself an artistic work. Thus, it infringes copyright in a preliminary drawing for a sculptor to make the sculpture; but if the drawing is of an exhaust pipe there will be no infringement by making the article.

Making a photograph of the whole or any substantial part of an image forming part of a film, broadcast or cable programme amounts to copying it: s.17(4).

The typographical arrangement of a published edition is copied if a facsimile copy is made of it: s.17(5).

Copies which are transient or incidental to some other use of a work are still copies: s.17(6).

### Publishing

Copyright in every description of work also covers issuing copies of a work to the public: s.18(1). This refers to putting into circulation copies not previously put into circulation (in the UK or elsewhere). It does not refer to any subsequent distribution, sale, hiring, loan or importation into the UK of those copies.

This does not, however, apply where the work is a computer program. In that case, it refers to putting into circulation copies of the program which have not previously been put into circulation in the EC by or with the consent of the copyright owner. It does not include any subsequent distribution, sale, hiring or loan of those copies or their subsequent importation into the UK. It does, however, include the rental of copies to the public: s.18(3), inserted by Copyright (Computer Programs) Regulations 1992.

Renting copies of sound recordings and films is a form of issuing copies to the public. In these cases the principle of exhaustion does not apply (if it did the right would be pointless), and the right to control rental continues for the full period of copyright: s.18(2). (*See* also the EC directive on rental and lending of copyright works, Chapter 12, para. 12.4.3.)

## Performing
Copyright in any work except a typographical arrangement is infringed by unauthorised performing, showing or playing a work in public. Public performances exclude performances in domestic situations, but include virtually everything else: s.19.

*Example*

In *Turner v Performing Right Society* (1943) the Court of Appeal held that performances of sound recordings at a place of work for the employees of the defendants was a public performance.

Pubs and shops, even record shops, require licenses (obtained from the Performing Rights Society).

## Broadcasting
Similarly, the restricted act of broadcasting a work or including it in a cable programme applies to every description of work except a typographical arrangement: s.20.

## Adapting
Copyright in a literary, dramatic or musical work covers making an adaptation of that work: s.21. This can include converting a non-dramatic work, eg. a novel, into a dramatic work, eg. a play, or *vice versa*; translating a work; or turning it into a strip cartoon. An arrangement or transcription of a musical work would be considered an adaptation.

If the work in question is a computer program, making

an adaptation means making an arrangement or altered version of the program or a translation of it.

## Infringing

Copyright in a work is infringed if anyone does, or authorises another person to do, any of the acts listed in 13.2.4 to the work without the authorisation of the copyright owner: s.16(2).

*Example*

1   In *Moorhouse v University of New South Wales* (1976), High Court, Australia, it was held that the University had authorised copying and was therefore liable to the owner of copyright in a work photocopied on a self-service machine made available by the University. The notices which the University claimed dissuaded users from infringing copyright merely drew attention to the existence of the exemption for fair dealing for research or private study and then failed to mention the overriding requirement that such copying be fair dealing. The fact that a copy of the relevant statute was also made available was of no assistance, since it would have been unintelligible to a lay person.

2   In *CBS Songs v Amstrad Consumer Electronics* (1988), the House of Lords held that Amstrad did not 'authorise' the commission of an infringement merely by selling twin-deck tape recorders.

An infringing act does not have to be done to the whole copyright work, it is sufficient that it affects a substantial part of it. What constitutes a substantial part is measured quantitatively and qualitatively (s.16(3)), although the two tests do not necessarily carry the same weight. As Lord Reid put it in the *Ladbroke (Football) v Wm Hill* (1964): 'The question whether [the defendant] has copied a substantial part depends much more on the quality than the quantity of what he has taken.'

There is no copyright in the ideas underlying the work, so the taking has to be of the author's expression. The boundary is, however, becoming difficult to define: *see Plix Products v Frank M Winstone* (1986), Supreme Court, New Zealand, and *Independent Television Publications v Time Out* (1984).

A large part of a work will be a substantial part, but so will a small part if its content is important.

*Example*

1   In *Ravenscroft v Herbert* (1980) the defendant, in writing a work of fiction, drew too heavily on material in the plaintiff's historical account of the Hofburg spear (said to have been driven into Christ's body at the Crucifixion).

2  In *Elanco Products v Mandops* (1980) the defendants adopted with little alteration the plaintiffs' instructions for the use of their weed killer, and this was held to infringe.

Infringement only takes place where there is *actual* copying. This will have to be proved by the plaintiff.

*Example*

In *Francis, Day & Hunter v Bron* (1963) the defendant composer admitted that he may have heard the plaintiffs' music but that he was not conscious of having done so and it had not been in his mind when he wrote the allegedly infringing piece. Diplock, LJ held that 'the copyright work must be the source from which the infringing work was derived', so there was no infringement.

### 13.2.5    Moral rights

The Copyright, Designs and Patents Act 1988 introduces two important new rights for authors, and a third right for the commissioners of certain works. The two new authors' rights are:

● The right of paternity; and

● The right of integrity.

They were introduced because the Paris text of the Berne Convention (which the Government wished to ratify) requires them.

**Paternity right**
Paternity right is the right to be *identified* as the author of your own work. The right arises each time the work is commercially exploited or on the happening of other similar events set out in s.77. The author may insist on being identified by a certain name but not on the form of the identification.

Contrary (it is widely thought) to the spirit of the Berne Convention, the law requires that the author assert the right before it is exercisable. Assertion must be in writing and will bind anyone to whose attention it comes.

There are *exceptions* to paternity right, which correspond to the permitted acts under economic copyright law. Computer programs, typeface designs and computer-generated works give rise to no paternity right. Nor does the right apply where the copyright vests in the author's employer under the Act.

**Integrity right**
Integrity right is the right to object to *derogatory treatment* of your work: s.80(1). It belongs to authors of copyright works and to directors of films (producers being entitled to the economic rights).

'Treatment' means:

- Any addition to, deletion from or alteration or adaptation of the work except a translation (no matter, it seems, how bad) of a literary or dramatic work: s.80(2); or
- A transcription of a musical work.

Such treatment is derogatory if it:

- Amounts to distortion or mutilation of the work; or
- Is otherwise prejudicial to the honour or reputation of the author or (in the case of a film) director.

There is no need to assert the integrity right.

### False attribution

The Act maintained the right against false attribution which existed in the 1956 Act. This permits you to take action to stop a work being attributed to you if it is not in fact yours.

### Privacy in photographs and films

Where a photograph or film has been commissioned, the copyright will vest in the photographer or producer of the film. The commissioner is given a new moral right, permitting that person to control (or effectively to veto) the exploitation of the work.

### Consent and waiver

Berne requires that the rights be inalienable and that they endure as long as the economic rights. However, the Act permits the author to whom the rights belong to consent to particular acts which they would otherwise be able to prevent, and to waive the moral rights.

A waiver must be in writing and may relate to a specific work, to a class of works or to the author's works in general. It may be conditional or unconditional and may be expressly capable of being revoked: s.87(2). The possibility of the law of contract or estoppel enforcing an informal consent or waiver is preserved.

The rights may not be assigned. After the author's death the rights become exercisable by their personal representatives.

An author whose moral rights are infringed may sue for breach of statutory duty.

### Design right                                                    13.2.6

The Act sets out a number of restricted acts which if done without the authorisation of the design right owner are primary infringements. Authorising another person to do the act without the consent of the design right owner is also an infringement of design right.

### Commercial reproduction

The owner of design right has the exclusive right to reproduce the design for commercial purposes by making articles to the design. They also have the exclusive right (again, for commercial purposes) to reproduce the design by making design documents recording the design to enable such articles to be made.

Reproduction is for commercial purposes if it is done with a view to the article in question being sold or hired in the course of a business.

Infringement therefore only takes place where the reproduction is done for the purpose of selling or hiring things as part of a commercial enterprise whose business lies in those areas. The Act does not say that the business has to be one in the ordinary course of which such things are sold or hired.

Reproduction other than for commercial purposes (which could include use in a commercial business but not for sale in the course of trade or business) is not an infringement. The owner of a launderette is therefore able to make a part for their washing machines without infringing the design right, notwithstanding the commercial use to which the part will be put.

Reproducing a design by making articles to the design means copying the design so as to produce articles exactly or substantially to that design. Making a design document for the purpose of making articles to the design also amounts to reproduction.

This may also, on the face of it, infringe copyright in the design document, but s.236 says that where there is double protection, copyright is unenforceable.

The expression 'design document' is defined as any record of a design, whether in the form of a drawing, a written description, a photograph, data stored in a computer or otherwise. Making a straightforward copy of a design document may be an infringement of copyright.

### Independent creation

Reproduction does not include reproduction by independent creation. Reproduction only amounts to an infringement if it is by copying and the copy is either exactly or substantially the same as the original.

### Indirect reproduction

Reproduction may be direct or indirect. Indirect reproduction may involve many stages and it does not matter whether the intervening acts are themselves infringements.

It is not an infringement of design right to make a copy of a design document except where this is for the purpose of making an article to the design. However, making a further copy from a non-infringing copy, where the further copy is made for the purpose of making without authorisation an article to the design, would be an infringement notwithstanding the one or more non-infringing, intervening stages.

### Infringing article
If making an article to the design to which it is made infringed design right in the design, then it is an infringing article. In the case of an imported article (or an article proposed to be imported), it is an infringing article if it would have infringed design right in the design to which it is made had it been made in the UK.

## Secondary infringement 13.3

### Patents 13.3.1
Many of the dealings in infringing items which are secondary infringements of other IP rights are primary infringements of patents. Under s.60(2), Patents Act 1977 it is an infringement of a patent to supply or offer to supply in the UK the means for putting the invention into effect if the person supplying knows, or it is obvious to a reasonable person in the circumstances, that those means are suitable for putting and are intended to put the invention into effect in the UK. Although not strictly speaking a form of secondary infringement, it is similar to secondary infringements of other IP rights.

Where the product in question is a 'staple commercial product' this does not apply, unless the supply or offer to supply is made to induce the other party to commit a primary infringement of the patent.

*Note*

The term 'staple commercial product' is not defined in the legislation. Pearson and Miller, in *Commercial Exploitation of Intellectual Property* suggest that the expression includes 'things like petrol, cement, drawing pins, nuts and bolts'.

### Registered designs 13.3.2
There are no acts of secondary infringement set out in the RDA.

### 13.3.3     Copyright

Certain dealings in copyright works are restricted and to do them without the authority of the copyright owner is a secondary infringement. A certain level of knowledge on the part of the infringer is required.

Secondary infringements include:

- Importing an article which the person knows or has reason to believe is an infringing copy of a work, otherwise than for private and domestic use: s.22, CDPA 1988;

- Possessing, trading in, exhibiting in public in the course of a business, or distributing an article which the person knows or has reason to believe is an infringing copy: s.23;

- Making, importing, possessing or trading in an article specifically designed for making copies of the work, knowing or having reason to believe that the article would be used for that purpose: s.24(1);

- Transmitting the work via a telecommunications system, knowing or having reason to believe that infringing copies of the work will be made when the transmission is received: s.24(2);

- Giving permission for a place of public entertainment to be used for the performance of a literary, dramatic or musical work which amounts to an infringement, unless the person giving the permission had reasonable grounds for believing the performance would not be an infringement: s.25;

- Supplying a copy of a sound recording or film which is used to infringe copyright if the person who supplied it knew or had reason to believe that it, or a copy made from it, would be used for that purpose: s.26(3);

- Supplying apparatus which is used for infringing the copyright in a work by playing a sound recording, showing a film or receiving images or sound by electronic means, if the person supplying it knew or had reason to believe that the apparatus would be used for this purpose or did not believe on reasonable grounds that it would not be so used: s.26(2).

If copies of a copyright work are issued to the public incorporating an electronic copy prevention device, copyright in the work will be infringed by anyone who makes or trades in or advertises a device *specifically* designed to circumvent that protection. It will also be infringed by anyone who publishes information intended to help other people to circumvent the protection: s.29(6).

The same applies to dealing in equipment designed to enable people to pick up transmissions without permission: s.29(7).

### Design right

13.3.4

Certain commercial dealings in infringing articles are secondary infringements of design right. This means that they are generally only actionable if the infringer had knowledge that they did infringe.

By s.228, CDPA, it is a secondary infringement of design right to:

- Import an infringing article into the UK;
- Possess an infringing article for commercial purposes; or
- Sell, let for hire, or offer or expose for sale or hire, an infringing article in the course of a business.

The use of the expression 'commercial purposes' significantly narrows the scope of the restricted acts. For a secondary infringement to take place, it must be shown that the alleged infringer knew or had reason to believe that the articles were infringing articles and the onus is on the owner of the design right to prove that the requisite knowledge existed.

The secondary infringer must, as with copyright, know or have reason to believe that the article is an infringing one. The test is objective; if the person dealing in the article was in possession of knowledge which would have led a reasonable person to believe that the article was an infringing article, the dealer will be liable even though he did not appreciate the significance of the knowledge and therefore did not realise that the article was an infringing one.

An article is an infringing article if making it to the design infringed the design right in the design: s.229(2). It is also an infringing article if it has been, or is proposed to be, imported into the UK and making it to that design in the UK would have been an infringement of design right, or a breach of an exclusive licence relating to the design: s.229(3).

There is a presumption that, where design right subsists or has formerly subsisted in a design, the article was made at a time when design right subsisted: s.229(4).

An article which because of an enforceable Community right may be imported into the UK will never be considered an infringing article: s.229(5).

## Self-assessment questions

1 What type of rights give monopoly protection?
2 What is the difference between a primary and a secondary infringement?
3 What is the importance of innocent infringement?

4 Explain the problems involved in construing patent specifications.
5 What use of a trademark infringes the proprietors rights?
6 What acts are restricted by copyright?
7 What are the two moral rights introduced by the 1988 Act?
8 What acts are restricted by design right?
9 What amounts to secondary infringement of a patent?
10 What acts are secondary infringements of copyright?

# Chapter 14

# Unfair competition and passing off

## Introduction

14.1

The Common Law enables traders to protect their reputation by suing in tort for passing off. This is a form of action found only in the common law countries; continental jurisdictions have unfair competition laws which often do a similar job. Indeed, recent cases indicate that UK passing off law is developing into a kind of unfair competition regime.

The action for passing off is particularly useful in protecting unregistered trademarks, including trademarks which are not registered for the goods or services to which the other mark is applied. Section 2, TMA 1938, specifically preserves the action, while stating that there is no action for infringement of an unregistered trademark.

---

*Example*

In *Reckitt & Coleman v Borden* (1990), the House of Lords held that the producers of *Jif* lemon juice successfully sued another producer who had sold its products in a similar plastic lemon-shaped container. The container shape could not have been registered as a trade mark: *Re Coca Cola's Application*.

---

Passing off has always applied equally to goods and to services. Before service marks became registrable in 1986, the action was of great importance to service industries.

## General formulation of passing off

14.2

In *Erven* Warnink *BV v J Townend & Sons (Hull) Ltd* (1979) – the 'Advocaat case' – Lord Diplock laid down the classic formulation of the passing off action. He stated that it consists of:

- A misrepresentation;
- Made by a trader in the course of trade;
- To perspective customers or ultimate consumer; which is
- Calculated to injure the business or goodwill of another trader (in the sense that this is reasonably foreseeable consequence); and
- Which does cause such damage.

### Misrepresentation

14.2.1

Passing off is committed by a trader's misrepresentation in

course of their trade

Nobody has any right to represent his goods as the goods of somebody else: *per* Lord Halsbury in *Reddaway v Banham* (1896).

Such a representation is, however, rarely expressly made.

The tort is no longer anchored, as in its nineteenth-century formulation, to the name or trade mark of a product or business. It is wide enough to encompass other descriptive material, such as slogans or visual images, which radio, television or newspaper advertising can lead the market to associate with a plaintiff's product, provided always that such descriptive material has become part of the goodwill of the product. And the test is whether the product has derived from the advertising a distinctive character which the market recognises: *per* Lord Scarman in *Cadbury Schweppes Pty Ltd v The Pub Squash Co Ltd* (1981).

A representation may amount to passing off even though it is an accurate description of the goods.

*Example*

*Reddaway v Banham* (1896) concerned 'Camel Hair Belting', which accurately described the product but which the market understood as meaning the plaintiff's goods. The court, however, did not prevent the defendant describing his goods as camel hair, it only stopped him describing them in a confusing manner.

The principle extends to traders representing 'seconds' as goods of the manufacturer's usual quality (*Spalding & Bros v A W Gamage Ltd* (1915)), and to passing off their business as another's, or as being connected or associated with another's: *Office Cleaning Services Ltd v Westminster Windows and General Cleaners Ltd* (1946) (HL).

*Note*

In *Mirage Studios v Counter Feat Clothing Ltd* (1991) – the 'Teenage Mutant Ninja Turtles case' – it was held that a passing off action would lie despite the fact that the plaintiffs did not make T-shirts but merely licensed others to do so. The fact that copyright licences were granted by the plaintiff established the necessary connection.

**14.2.2    Goodwill**

The basis of all passing off actions is the protection of goodwill. The plaintiff must have sufficient goodwill in the 'get up' of their goods or distinguishing features used when supplying services.

In *Star Industrial Coy Ltd v Yap Kwee Kor* (1975) (PC) Lord Diplock stated that goodwill:

has no existence independent of the business to which it relates. It is local in character and divisible; if the business is carried on in several countries a separate goodwill attaches to it in each. So when the business is abandoned in one country in which it has acquired a goodwill, the goodwill in that country perishes with it although the business may continue to be carried on in other countries.

There must be a business or trading presence in this country. A 'spill-over' reputation is not enough: *see Anheuser-Busch Inc v Budejovicky Budvar NP (1984) (CA)*, 'the Budweiser case'; *Bernadin v Pavilion Properties Ltd (1967)* – the 'Crazy Horse case'. If there is no reputation in the UK, there can be no damage.

The get-up must denote the plaintiff's goods or business exclusively, or with a limited number of others.

*Example* _____

In *J Bollinger v Costa Brava Wine Co Ltd (1960)* – the 'Spanish Champagne case' – 12 champagne producers were allowed to prevent the sale of 'Champagne'. This has now been followed in cases involving sherry and scotch whisky, but not at first instance in a case involving elder flower champagne where the judge found that the plaintiff had suffered no substantial damage.

_____

Infringement is more easily shown with invented words or 'fancy names'. Traders are well-advised to avoid descriptive names.

*Note* _____

No-one has the right (necessarily) to the use of their own name: *Parker-Knoll Ltd v Knoll International Ltd (1962) (HL)*.

_____

## Deception                                           14.2.3

The defendant's actions must be likely to and/or have actually caused deception. There is, however, no need to prove fraud (an *intention* to pass off), but if none is present a common field of activity is required.

This does not mean that the parties have to be competitors. All that is needed is sufficient similarity so traders or members of the public think the goods or services are from same source. But in *Derek McCulloch v Lewis A May (Produce Distributions) Ltd (1954)*, where the plaintiff was a radio presenter ('Uncle Mac') and the defendants made breakfast cereal, it was held that the lack of a common filed of activity was fatal to the case. Such a requirement is now less likely to be imposed: *see* the '*Ninja Turtles* case' above.

Geographical names (which generally may not be registered as trademarks) may acquire secondary meanings, so users may protect their reputation by suing for passing off.

*Example*

1   In *Whitstable Oyster Fishery Co v Hayling Fisheries Ltd* (1901) (CA) the defendant was permitted to describe oysters which reached maturity at Whitstable as 'Whitstable Oysters'.

2   In *Wotherspoon v Currie* (1872), where the plaintiff had made his Glenfield Starch at Glenfield but moved his factory, he could still prevent the defendant calling his starch which he made in Glenfield by the same name.

Comparative advertising, ie. a statement that A's goods are the same as B's, can be passing off, but not statements that they are similar or superior.

### 14.2.4    Damage or injury

The plaintiff must have suffered or be likely to suffer damage or injury to their business or goodwill as a result of the defendant's misrepresentations. Inconvenience or annoyance is *not* enough.

Once evidence is established of deception or likely deception, injury to reputation or goodwill is readily presumed (but *see* the 'Elderflower Champagne case' – *Tattinger v Allbev* (1992)). In classic passing off cases, custom is diverted and injury naturally follows.

In *Stringfellow v McCain Foods (GB) Ltd* (1984) (CA) no damage to the night-club of the same name (falling attendances, etc) was found to result from sales of 'Stringfellows chips'.

## 14.3    False trade descriptions

Cases have extended passing off law so that it has become a weapon against false trade descriptions. The public, when it bought Spanish 'Champagne', was not given to believe it was the French product but it was *misled* into thinking that it was genuine Champagne.

In the 'Advocaat case', the product complained of was 'Keelings Old English Advocaat', a mixture of Cyprus sherry and dried eggs. No-one would think it was actually the same as the plaintiff's advocaat, but the House of Lords was satisfied that the plaintiff had established that the defendant's product was being passed off as the genuine article.

## 14.4    Passing off by others

The tort covers the supply of goods to someone else, who

then passes them off as another's.

When a manufacturer sells to a wholesaler, or a whole-saler supplies a retailer, the chances are that there is no deception because the buyer is familiar with the various goods on the market. Passing off occurs here when they are sold to inexpert consumers and the manufacturer who originally applied the misleading get up is liable.

This rule applies even where the actual passing off takes place overseas. In two cases, suppliers of whisky to South America, where it was mixed with local spirits and sold as Scotch, were successfully sued by Scotch distillers. In one – *John Walker & Sons Ltd v Henry Ost & Co Ltd* (1970) – bottles and labels were also supplied to complete the deception, but in the other, though this extra feature was absent, the action still succeeded.

A passing off action may also lie against a defendant who puts into circulation an instrument of fraud such as a fake Rolls-Royce motor car: *Rolls-Royce v Dodd* (1981).

## Self-assessment questions

1  What are the essential elements for a passing off action?
2  Can an accurate description of goods be passing off?
3  Does passing off apply to services?
4  Why is it necessary for the plaintiff to have a reputation in the UK?
5  What is goodwill?
6  Is it necessary to show an intention to deceive to success-fully sue for passing off?
7  Can geographical names be protected by passing off?
8  Is it passing off to supply wrongly marked goods to another trader?

# Chapter 15

# Commercial exploitation of intellectual property rights

## Introduction                                                    15.1

Intellectual property is worth nothing unless it can be exploited commercially. In this chapter we describe first the rules which govern the initial ownership of IP rights. The following chapter considers how they can be transferred, licensed and used as security. We also set out the considerations that apply on a corporate sale or purchase.

## Ownership issues: the general rule                              15.2

The general rule is that the *creator* of intellectual property is its owner. However, this general rule is very often displaced:

- In the case of a trademark, it is the owner of the unregistered mark who is the rightful owner of the mark on registration;

- The provisions of a *contract* can override the statutory rules about ownership of intellectual property – the contract may pre-date the creation of the intellectual property concerned;

- Where the intellectual property is created by an *employee* there are statutory rules which determine whether the employee or employer will be the owner (these are set out below);

- There are also statutory rules governing the ownership of intellectual property where the creation of the property has been *commissioned* (these are also set out below).

Where the rights are registered, ownership is generally dealt with by the first application to register the right. The applicant for registration will have to declare as part of the formality in filing the application that they are the owner.

## Patents                                                         15.3

Inventions belong to their *inventors*, unless the rights have been given to someone else. This can happen either by a specific assignment or by a contract of employment. Even after a patent application has been filed it can be assigned to someone else. Where the inventor is an employee special rules apply (*see* 15.1.1).

The patent will be granted to the inventor or the inventor's successor in title.

### 15.3.1    Joint inventors

If two or more people collaborated in making the invention, each of them may be entitled to a share in the ownership of the patent and will be able to work the invention (though not to assign their rights, or grant licences) without reference to the other co-owners.

All joint applicants should be named in the application. There are provisions to enable someone who should be entitled to an invention to insist on being registered as the owner or a co-owner.

## 15.4    Trademarks

Registration of a trademark will only be granted to the *owner of an existing common law mark*. This means someone who already uses the trademark, or at least has a *bona fide* intention of using it. If the applicant has no *bona fide* intention of using the mark, it may be cancelled on the application of an interested party, eg. someone else who wants to use it.

### 15.4.1    Registered users

The owner of a registered mark may allow someone else to use it for certain goods or services. The user's name may be entered on the register provided that the registrar approves the arrangements as not being contrary to the public interest: s.28, TMA 1938.

There must be a connection in the course of trade or business between the registered user and the goods or services for which the permitted use is exercised.

*Note*

Application for the recordal of a registered user is made on Form TM50 with payment of the prescribed fee. The Trade Marks Bill will abolish registered users.

An application to register a trademark may be accompanied by an application to record a registered user agreement: s.29(1)(b). This is sufficient to establish the necessary intention to use the mark.

## 15.5    Registered designs

There is no question of ownership of a registered design until it has been registered. The person entitled to apply is the *proprietor*, and the original proprietor – the person entitled to apply for registration – is the author, or creator, of the design.

A person who acquires rights in a design may be treated as the proprietor and be entitled to apply for registration.

## Copyright                                                         15.6

### Authorship and ownership                                        15.6.1

Generally, the *author* of a work is the person who created it: s.9(1), CDPA 1988. However there are some special rules: s.9(2). If the work is computer-generated, the author is taken to be the person who made the arrangements for the work to be created. A work may have joint authors: s.10 and *see Wiseman v Weidenfeld & Nicholson* (1985).

The author of a *sound recording* or *film* is the person who undertook the arrangements necessary for making it, and the author of a *broadcast* is the person responsible for the content of the programme and who either transmitted it or made the arrangements necessary for transmitting it.

The author of a *cable programme* is the person who provides the programme service in which the cable programme was included.

The author of a *typographical arrangement* is the publisher of the edition which incorporates it.

Generally, the first owner of copyright in a work is the author: s.11(1). There are exceptions for employee authors and commissions (*see* 15.11.2 and 15.9.2 respectively).

## Unregistered design right                                        15.7

Generally the first owner of unregistered design right will be the designer. However, if the first marketing rule (*see* Chapter 9, para. 9.4.2) is the only way a design can obtain unregistered design right protection, the owner of the right is the person who first markets articles made to the design.

## Joint ownership                                                   15.8

Intellectual property statutes contain specific provisions regarding joint ownership of intellectual property rights.

### Patents                                                          15.8.1

The joint owners of a patent generally each have an equal and undivided share in the patent. Each may make and sell the product or use the process which is protected by the patent but they cannot assign or licence their rights without the agreement of the other owners. This situation leads to unequal results in research and development agreements where one party may be a large industrial concern and the other may be a research organisation or university.

The joint proprietors of a patent may agree otherwise. If one party takes an interest in the patent after grant, the terms of their relationship will be determined by the document of transfer. This will usually indicate whether the proprietors are joint tenants or tenants in common. The latter will be implied if the parties are in a business relationship or where co-owners contribute unequally to the costs of the patent.

### 15.8.2    Copyright

A copyright work may be created by joint authors. Their contributions must be impossible to distinguish; if they can be told apart, the work is a multi-author, collective work, not a work of joint authorship, and they have distinct rights in their contributions.

The joint owners of copyright can only exercise their rights together. They cannot grant permission to use the copyright material independently, nor may they sue separately.

Section 173, CDPA provides that references to the copyright owner are to all of the joint owners.

### 15.8.3    Unregistered design right

By s.259, CDPA a design produced by the collaboration of two or more authors whose contributions are not distinct from each other is a joint design. References to the designer in Part III of the Act are to be construed as references to all the designers of a joint design. The same rules as apply to copyright are therefore applicable to unregistered design right.

### 15.8.4    Registered designs

There are no provisions in the Registered Designs Act 1949 on joint ownership. There must, however, be situations in which joint authors create a registrable design, in which case both would be entitled to apply for registration. Form 2A, used for applying for registration, is couched in terms which permit joint applications.

An assignment of a part interest in a registered design could also give rise to joint ownership. In the absence of any express provision in the Act, it is best to assume that designs will be treated in the same way as patents.

### Trademarks                                             15.8.5

In the nature of a trademark it is impossible for identical rights
to be jointly owned. However, there is no reason why different
parties may not own rights in the same mark registered for
different goods or in different classes of goods.

## Commissions                                            15.9

### Designs                                                15.9.1

If a designer is commissioned to make a design then the law
provides that any registered design or unregistered design
right will belong to the commissioner: s.2 (1A), RDA; s.215,
CDPA.

### Copyright                                              15.9.2

There is no provision in copyright law about the ownership
of commissioned works, so copyright in such a work will
continue to belong to the author. Under the 1956 Act there
was specific provision which vested copy right in a portrait
or photograph in the person who commissioned its making,
but this was removed from the legislation in the 1988 Act.
Commissioners are now given a right to control the subsequent exploitation of such works (*see* Chapter 13, para.
13.2.5) but no economic rights in them.

### Inventions                                             15.9.3

Where someone is commissioned to produce an invention
it is the inventor not the commissioner who is entitled to
apply for a patent.

## Directors                                               15.10

Directors of companies are under a fiduciary duty which
requires them to disclose any information known to them
which affects the company. They must avoid any conflict
between their fiduciary duty and their personal interests,
which means that they have to disclose all relevant intellectual property which they create.

The law concerning the ownership of patents belonging to
employee directors is slightly different. An invention made in
the course of a director's duties will belong to the company
under the Patents Act 1977, but in addition to that an invention
made other than in the course of the director's duties may
belong to the company because of the general duties imposed
upon directors. A director who fails to observe these requirements may commit a breach of a constructive trust.

## 15.11    Employees

### 15.11.1    Inventions

The Patents Act 1977 contains specific rules concerning inventions by employees. Note that this applies to *inventions*, not just matters which are protected by patents. The rules apply to any invention made after 31 May 1978.

> *Note*
>
> Such inventions may have design and copyright aspects which are not dealt with by the rules of the Patents Act. If this is the case, it may be necessary to obtain separate assignments of those rights.

Section 39, 1977 consists of a self-contained code for determining the ownership of an invention made by an employee who works wholly or mainly in the UK. The basic rule is that such an invention belongs to the employee unless one of two situations set out in the legislation applies. The Act makes no provision for joint ownership in such a case and the rules are based on the consideration of the employee's duties. This means more than just their duties under their contracts of employment; consideration of *actual* duties performed by the employee is necessary.

**Categories of employee**
For *'normal' employees* – those not of a particularly high status within the organisation – the two-stage test to determine ownership of an invention is:

- What are the employee's *normal duties*?
- Would the invention reasonably be expected to result from the *discharge* of those duties?

The test is an *objective* one. The Court will consider whether the employee has made other inventions; and, if so, whether the employee has done so recently and whether they are in a similar technical field. The Court will also consider whether equivalent employees are also in the habit of making inventions.

For *higher status employees* – those of relatively high status in the organisation – the two-stage test is:

- Was the invention made in the performance of the employee's duties?
- Would the responsibilities of the employee render it inconsistent for the employee to hold the invention for themselves?

*Note*

This second stage raises the question of whether the employee has a special obligation to further the interests of the employer's business: *Reiss Engineering v Harris* (1987).

Disputes over the ownership of an invention may be dealt with by either the Patents Court (part of the High Court) or the Patent County Court which may issue a declaration. Alternatively the Patent Office has a mechanism for resolving such disputes.

Where the invention in question has been patented, claims of ownership are limited after two years from the grant of the patent.

### Right to payment
Where a patent has been granted and it turns out to be of *benefit to an employer*, the Patents Act 1977 makes provision for the employee to receive some sort of financial reward for it. The rules apply not only to patents granted in the UK but also to foreign patents and to the lesser protection afforded by the foreign laws, eg. the German utility model system.

### Benefit
The question of whether a benefit accrues to the employer may be difficult to determine. Clearly, where the invention protects a product it restricts competition and there is a readily identifiable benefit to the employer. Where the invention has been licensed and the employer has enjoyed a flow of royalties as a result the answer is also reasonably clear cut. The same is true of a situation where the patent has a blocking effect, excluding others from the market.

The Act lays down two rules depending on the original ownership of the patent, but both are subject to collective agreements to the contrary: s.40.

- Where the employee's invention has always belonged to the employer under the terms of the Patents Act 1977, compensation will be paid if the benefit to the employer was 'outstanding'.

- Where the rights belonged to the employer because they had been assigned or licensed by the employee (and if licensed, the license must be exclusive) the employee's entitlement to reward depends on the relative benefits of the patent. It may be that the employee is already receiving royalties or has been paid some consideration for the assignment of the patent, but whether or not this is the case, the law will ensure that the employee gets a 'fair share of the benefit'.

By s.42(2) any terms in the contract which conflict with these provisions are void. Terms which pre-date the invention and which diminish the employee's rights in that invention are unenforceable.

This does not apply if the invention had already been made and belonged from the beginning to the employer. But where it belonged initially to the employee and was sold or licensed exclusively to the employer the rights to compensation may not be ousted by the contract of employment.

### 15.11.2  Copyright

Copyright in a literary, dramatic, musical or artistic work made by an employee in the course of their employment will belong to the employer. This (like other ownership provisions) is subject to agreement to the contrary: s.11(2).

Copyright in works made by officers or servants of the Crown belongs to the Crown, as does copyright in Acts of Parliament and measures of the General Synod: s.163.

Copyright in works made by or under the direction of either House of Parliament, or a bill introduced into either House, belongs to the House of Commons or House of Lords as the case may be: s.165.

Copyright in a literary, dramatic, musical or artistic work made by certain international organisations (for example, the United Nations) will belong to the organisation: s.168.

### 15.11.3  Designs

Unregistered design right in a design made by an employee in the course of their employment belongs to the employer. If the design is made otherwise than in the course of the employee's duties, the right belongs to the employee.

The right to apply for registration of a design which has been made by an employee belongs to the employer.

These rules do not apply if the design has been *commissioned*. If they have, the rules on commissioned designs will apply.

## Self-assessment questions

1   Who is the correct proprietor of a trademark?
2   Who may be granted a patent?
3   Who is the author of a work, and why is this concept important?
4   What rights do joint owners of a patent have?

5   Distinguish works of joint authorship from collective works.

6   Who owns copyright in commissioned work?

7   Who owns an invention made by an employee?

8   When is an employee entitled to payment for an invention?

9   By whom is copyright in a parliamentary Bill owned?

# Chapter 16

# Dealings in intellectual property rights

## Assignment

Although in equity a court may enforce an assignment of intellectual property rights irrespective of whether or not it is in the prescribed form, statute does require formalities for certain types of assignment. These are that:

- An assignment of a patent or copyright must be in writing;
- An assignment of copyright must be signed by the assignor;
- An assignment of a patent must be signed by both the assignor and the assignee.

In the case of a *patent*, infringement proceedings can only be taken by the registered proprietor, so the assignment must be registered promptly at the Patent Office. Failure to do so for more than six months may result in the loss of the right to claim damages for infringement for the period between assignment and recordal.

Only the registered proprietor of a *registered design* may bring infringement proceedings. An assignment of a *registered design* is deemed also to assign any overlapping unregistered design rights.

### Trademarks

Assignments of trademarks raise a number of particular problems. If only part of a business is sold the connection between the goods which bear the mark and a single source of those goods may be broken. This would undermine the value, and possibly the validity, of the registered trademark.

If there are *associated* trademarks, one cannot be assigned alone. If the business is being divided so the purchaser only gets some of the associated marks, it may be necessary to settle for a long-term licence instead. This may be considered undesirable from the buyer's point of view.

UK law provides that similar marks registered for use on similar goods be associated with each other. This prevents them from being assigned separately where this would result in confusion. But even with unregistered marks, the concept of splitting goodwill between two businesses is fraught with difficulty.

The goodwill of a business should always go with the trademarks. Ultimately, their value lies in the fact that they represent the goodwill of a company to its customers. But trademarks are sometimes assigned without the goodwill which attaches to them, and in such cases definite steps have to be taken to detach the goodwill from the mark to avoid confusion.

Where an assignee seeks to register an assignment of the trademark without goodwill, the Registrar will make directions that the fact of the assignment is advertised, usually in an appropriate trade journal.

Anyone who becomes entitled to a registered mark, whether by assignment or by other means, must apply to the Registrar to register the fact. If an assignment or other document transferring ownership of a trademark is not registered, it will not generally be admitted as evidence in a court.

### 16.1.2     Associated rights

An assignment of a registered design must also transfer the corresponding and registered design right. By contrast, an assignment of unregistered design right automatically transfers any registered designs which subsist in the same article.

In the case of a trademark, where the trademark consists of a device there may well be copyright in that as an artistic work, which will have to be dealt with separately.

### 16.1.3     Stamp duty

The basic principle is that intellectual property is a species of property so that an assignment of it has to be stamped. (The usual threshold value applies.) In principle, a license to use intellectual property does not need to be stamped even it is made by deed.

**Assignments**
Stamp duty is therefore payable on an assignment of copyright, trademarks, patents or designs. An agreement for the provision of know-how is not subject to stamp duty if the agreement is executed in the UK in writing. A know-how agreement executed by deed is liable to a fixed duty of 50p.

**Exclusive and non-exclusive patent licences**
The grant of an *exclusive license* to use a UK patent (even if it is restricted as to territory) for as long as the patent continues, made for a monetary consideration is normally chargeable to stamp duty *ad valorem*. However, it is not treated as a transfer of property if it contains a power of revocation.

Non-exclusive licences are not chargeable to *ad valorem*

stamp duty at all but if they are made in consideration of a lump sum payment and executed by deed then they attract 50p fixed duty.

### Copyright

Any irrevocable assignment of the exclusive rights of a copyright holder, whether or not limited as to period or to territory, will be liable to duty. This includes irrevocable copyright licences.

Instruments assigning copyright for consideration are chargeable to *ad valorem* duty. Where the agreement is in effect an executory contract to sell copyright and to bring into being the work so as to create the subject of sale, that is treated as a contract for the sale of property and the amount of the purchase price attributable to copyright is chargeable to stamp duty.

## Joint ventures                                   16.2

Joint ventures raise particular ownership problems, especially if their purpose is to create intellectual property. The ownership of intellectual property created in this way has to be dealt with in an agreement, because the statutory provisions are seldom appropriate.

Patents, for example, will belong to the parties as tenants in common, each having an equal undivided share. This means that one of the parties cannot licence the exploitation of the invention without the agreement of the other and this may be a significant problem to a party which is unable to work the invention itself.

The agreement should also set out in detail who brought what intellectual property to the venture. In the event of a break-up of the arrangement, which may be for a limited period or purpose anyway, it is likely to be crucial to know who owns what.

## Charges                                          16.3

Intellectual property (including future rights) may be used to secure lending, though this is a technique which many lenders will find novel. The process of creating a charge is not difficult in itself, although problems arise from the volatility of IP rights – they are constantly developing – and their infinite divisibility.

From a lender's point of view, a charge which catches not only specific IP rights (which are easily identified and readily valued) but also all other present and future rights is the best form of security. Fixed charges are also preferred by lenders, though the possibility of creating one over present and future IP rights remains untested in the courts.

Where intellectual property rights are used to produce articles for sale, or in providing services, the rights remain intact. Where the business of the borrower consists in disposing of interests in the intellectual property, however, difficulties may be encountered – granting licences is precisely how, for example, computer software houses earn their living. If an exclusive licence is granted, that can have a serious deleterious effect on the value of the security and the documentation which creates the charge should therefore address what the borrower may do with the rights.

### 16.3.1    Creating the charge

#### Copyright

A charge or mortgage over copyright must take the form of an assignment to the lender with a provision for re-assignment on redemption.

Where the mortgage is made by deed the mortgagee has the power, once the contractual date for repayment has passed, to sell the mortgaged copyright either in whole or in part or to appoint a receiver of income due under the copyright, unless a contrary intention is expressed in the mortgage deed. These powers may not be exercised until a demand has been made for the mortgage money and default has been made in whole or in part for three months after the demand or there is at least two months interest in arrears or the mortgagor is in breach of any its obligations under the mortgage deed.

*Note*

Banks will *invariably* exclude this postponement by making the debt repayable on demand and by excluding s.103.

On exercising the power of sale the mortgagee can assign the copyright free of the mortgagor's equity of redemption.

*Note*

In the case of a charge in favour of a bank there is no equity of redemption because it is *repayable on demand*.

The mortgagee must not act negligently in the conduct of the sale and is almost certainly under a duty to obtain the full price for the copyright. The duty would extend to a guarantor: *Standard Chartered Bank v Walker* (1982).

There would seem to be no reason why an unpaid

mortgagee should not itself go into the possession in the sense of exploiting the copyright itself until the capital and interest have been recovered through the profits received by its exploitation of the rights.

The mortgagor has a sufficient interest in the copyright to sue for damages for injury to their reversion. Conversely, a mortgagee would have an insurable interest in the property.

### Patents

Again, an assignment with a proviso for redemption is the correct form. This will be treated as a mortgage: certain dealings by the mortgagor will be permitted by implication (*Re Florence Land Public Works Co, ex parte Moor* (1878)) unless restricted by the mortgage. A mortgage of a patent must be executed by the mortgagee and the mortgagor (s.30(6), PA 1977, which also applies to other dealings in patents). Where there are joint proprietors, all must consent to the mortgage: s.36(3).

If a patentee sells its patents to a purchaser who needs to raise finance to pay for the purchase price, and the patentee itself agrees to take a mortgage charge over the patents to secure the sum payable, the patentee cannot be sure of recovering the patents if the purchaser fails to discharge the mortgage. The danger of not recovering the patents arises where the mortgagor has paid a sufficient sum to make it inequitable that the mortgagee shall recover the patents. The reason is that the law will not order foreclosure where a sale of the property mortgaged is a more appropriate way of securing for the mortgagee the balance of the sum due leaving the mortgagor with what may be left over from the sale.

A preferable arrangement is to grant to the purchaser an exclusive licence under which they pay off the purchase price by a substantial annual sum paid as a royalty for use, coupled with an option to purchase the patents for a nominal sum after the appropriate sum has been paid. Failure to pay will carry a penalty of termination of the arrangement. No court order is called for, and the patentee recovers the patents on default.

Provisions may be included whereby for each completed year fully paid, an allocated sum is deemed to represent a capital repayment, and some credit for this may be recoverable by a defaulting purchaser.

### Registered designs

Security over a registered design is virtually identical to that over a patent. Note that the Registered Designs Act 1949 contains no provisions equivalent to ss.30(6) and 36(3), PA 1977.

### Trademarks

The Trade Marks Act 1938 does not mention charges over trademarks. Assigning the mark with a proviso for redemption is not appropriate, because problems will arise maintaining the mark; specifically, if it is not to become vulnerable to a challenge for non-use the lender will have to enter into a registered user agreement with the borrower, and the necessary quality control provisions entailed in that makes it an impracticable course.

The correct approach seems to be to use a straightforward charge. For reasons set out below (*see* 16.3.2) the charge should restrict the right of the borrower to take infringement proceedings, or licence or cancel the mark without the lender's consent.

## 16.3.2    Registration

### Companies Act 1985

Where the borrower is a company incorporated under the Companies Acts, s.395, CA 1985 provides that a charge created by it must be registered at Companies House within 21 days after it is created. Failure to register the charge makes it void against any liquidator or creditor or any one who acquires an interest in the property charged of the company.

Section 395 specifically mentions charges over copyright, patents, goodwill and trademarks. Prudence would suggest that registered and unregistered designs should be treated as if they are included, though they are in fact omitted.

### Patents

Registration at the Patent Office of a charge over a patent is not mandatory but it may be done at any time. Failure to register will allow a person who claims an interest under a later transaction which *is* registered to gain priority over it, unless that person knows of the earlier charge: s.33, PA 1977.

### Registered designs

Section 9, Registered Designs Act 1949 makes similar provision to patents for registered designs.

### Trademarks

A charge over a trademark can be registered by requesting the Registrar to enter a memorandum on the register: s.34(1)(e), Trade Marks Act 1938. This is at the discretion of the Registrar, who will normally require that the charge impose conditions on the use of the trademark.

In *Svenska A/B Gas Accumulators Trade Mark* (1962) it was held that a memorandum should be entered where the agreement modified the proprietor's statutory rights of assignment.

*Note*

The lender would be well-advised to ensure that it is appointed the agent of the borrower, so that it can attend to the formalities of registration on behalf of itself and the borrower. A bank would ensure that it has a power of attorney (by definition irrevocable) if it takes an equitable mortgage.

### No registration at IP Office

Lenders are often tempted to do without this registration at the appropriate IP office. With a large portfolio of rights in different countries, it could be a very expensive and time-consuming exercise. They should, however, insist on reserving the right to seek registration at a later date.

## Licensing intellectual property rights        16.4

Granting licences for others to use intellectual property rights is a very useful way of exploiting the rights. The proprietor may not have the resources to exploit the rights properly, or the licensee may be involved in a different economic activity and therefore able to use the rights in a way which the owner would not be able to do themselves.

### Copyright        16.4.1

The CDPA's provisions on licensing copyright works through licensing schemes are among the Act's most complicated provisions. Putting in place the machinery for blanket licensing was one of the purposes of the Act.

The Act applies to licensing schemes. These are arrangements whereby the operator of the scheme grants licences on standard terms: s.116(1). It all covers 'one off' licences issued by licensing bodies. 'Licensing bodies' are organisations which grant licences on behalf of more than one copyright owner.

The Copyright Tribunal is given jurisdiction over disputes arising in the operation of certain licensing schemes. These are:

- Schemes for licensing the use of literary, dramatic, musical or artistic works or films, which are operated by licensing bodies;
- Any schemes for licensing copyright in sound recordings, broadcasts, cable programmes and typographical arrangements;
- Any schemes for licensing the rental or lending of sound recordings, films or computer programs.

The Act also provides for licensing schemes to be certified, which results in some of the acts permitted by the 1988 Act, eg. certain copying by educational establishments, being disapplied to works covered by the scheme.

### 16.4.2      Franchising

Business format franchising involves the use of a business method and name, get up, image and identity. The business method information is confidential information belonging to the franchisor.

The franchisor sells the right to use the confidential information and know how and other material. The consideration is normally a lump sum plus a royalty on the franchisee's turnover.

Franchisees agree to conform to common requirements about maintaining the franchises image and reputation. They must use the marks, logos and get up in the same way as other franchisees.

Franchise agreements will contain territorial restrictions (in the absence of which the franchisee would be disinclined to invest in the franchise) and restrictions on where supplies of the goods can be obtained. They may therefore contravene Article 85 of the Treaty of Rome and the Restrictive Trade Practices Act 1976. There is, however, an EC block exemption regulation for franchising agreements (*see* Chapter 19, para. 19.3.4).

Franchise agreements raise the problem of use of trademarks. The applicant for registration of a trademark has to have a *bona fide* intention of using the mark, or support the application with a registered user agreement. Since the franchisor will not be using the mark itself, it will have to register registered user agreements with each of the franchisees to whom it grants the right to use the mark.

Where the mark is not registered, there is a problem about the ownership of the goodwill which is protectable by action for passing off. The reputation accrues to the franchisees who actually trade under the mark, not the franchisor. The franchise agreement should therefore include an acknowledgement by the franchisee that the rights belong to the franchisor.

## Self-assessment questions

1 What formalities apply to assignments of:

(a) patents; and

(b) copyright?

2 Who may bring proceedings for infringement of a patent or registered design?

3 How can a trademark be assigned without goodwill?

5 How should problems about ownership of IP by a joint venture be addressed?

6 How may copyright be charged as security?

7 How can a charge be created over a patent?

8 What registration requirements must be observed when charging:

(a) a patent;

(b) a trademark?

9 What is a licensing scheme in copyright law?

10 What IP is involved in franchising?

**Chapter 17**

# Intellectual property in mergers and acquisitions

## Introduction

17.1

Many commercial practitioners never encounter intellectual property rights except in the context of corporate deals and it is with these that IP specialists are likely to find that they will spend a great deal of their time. This chapter explains the particular considerations applying to such transactions, and describes the operation of the legal rules set out in this companion to this area.

Because they are intangible, intellectual property rights are easily overlooked. But they exist in every business, and often they will be the most valuable assets a business owns.

The questions to be answered when acquiring a business which has valuable intellectual property are:

- What are the intellectual property rights used in the business and who owns them;
- What intellectual property is being sold; and
- How is it to be transferred?

The procedure on acquisitions and mergers is essentially similar. We will confine ourselves to considering acquisitions, but the following applies also to mergers.

*Note*

These questions may also have to be answered for several different jurisdictions. Investigations overseas, and the advice of local counsel, may be needed.

## What are the intellectual property rights used in the business?

17.2

A business is likely to use not only intellectual property rights it owns, but also rights owned by third parties. In both cases information about them must be acquired by the seller's disclosure and by the purchaser's own due diligence investigation. This should also reveal who owns the rights.

The seller's *disclosure* is backed up by a warranty in the acquisition agreement that there are no intellectual property rights owned or used by the business except for those specifically disclosed by the seller.

The purchaser's *investigation* should only be used as a 'back up' for the disclosures. Its value is limited because only the seller is able to identify unregistered intellectual property rights which it owns or uses.

## 17.3    What intellectual property rights are being sold?

Businesses in all sectors are likely to own industrial property rights. The level of detail with which the rights should be investigated will, however, vary according to the type of business involved and the type of acquisition which is contemplated.

Intellectual property rights are almost always important, and in some businesses they are a vital revenue generating asset. A pharmaceutical company's patents, a confectionery company's brands, and a software house's copyright are all central to their business activities. As well as simply ascertaining what rights there are, in cases like this it will often be necessary to consider matters such as the validity of the rights and their enforcement.

As far as the type of transaction is concerned, there is a significant difference between an *asset sale* and a *share sale*.

*Note*

In an asset sale, individual items of intellectual property are being transferred from own owner to another. In a share sale, the owner remains the same, but *its* ownership changes. In each case, however, the buyer will want to be sure that it knows what intellectual property is involved so its value can be assessed and any problems dealt with.

Where only part of a business is being acquired the inter-relationship of the various intellectual property rights in the business will require thorough consideration.

The nature of the vendor will also be a relevant consideration. It may determine what representations and warranties are available (they are particularly restricted where the disposal has been made by a receiver) and the ability of the vendor to meet a claim.

### 17.3.1    Registered rights

The subsistence of registered rights is determined conclusively by the state of the register (though this does not guarantee their validity). In the UK records are kept by the Patent Office, the Trade Marks Registry, and the Designs Registry. The contents of these registers can be searched by computer, so it is perfectly feasible in the course of an acquisition to obtain a listing of all registered intellectual property rights belonging to a business. Similarly, it is possible to establish who owns a particular intellectual property right.

Searches can be done on the same basis throughout much of the world. Several databases, accessible to subscribers, enable interested parties to perform such searches. Manual searches can also be carried out where computerised searches are either unavailable or inadequate.

If time does not permit such an investigation, or if the cost is too great, the enquirer may be content with information provided by the business and by its trademark and patent agents. This information could be made subject to appropriate warranties. However, this is very rarely an adequate substitute.

## Unregistered rights                                              17.3.2

Unregistered rights are by their nature a great deal more difficult to identify. This applies equally to rights which are protected automatically (copyright, design right) and rights which could have been registered but have not been (trademarks, unpatented inventions).

Many businesses will be the proprietors of designs, and evidence of the existence and ownership of designs will probably be available in the shape of technical drawings and similar information. Usually these bear an indication of when they were made and by whom, matters which are crucial to the question of ownership and the duration of protection. If the information is not disclosed on the document itself, appropriate efforts should be made to obtain it from the business and to have it warranted. Similar considerations apply to copyright works.

Businesses which depend to a large extent on exploiting their intellectual property rights are likely to be able to give a good idea of what they own. Publishers will keep lists of their titles, software houses will keep records of programs which they have written (and many computers record the information automatically), and fashion designers and photographers have portfolios of their work.

But documentary material concerning know-how is notoriously difficult to come by, and it may simply reside in the heads of the employees (*see* Chapter 10). A purchaser may attach such value to the know-how that they will refuse to proceed unless the seller produces comprehensive documentary records. The information provided by the seller should, however, only be regarded as a starting point for an investigation. Information about ownership and date of creation may have to be found, and purchasers will also want to know about any challenges which have taken place to a business's intellectual property rights.

## 17.4    Who owns the intellectual property?

The target of the acquisition may own intellectual property rights which have been transferred to it by others – perhaps in similar deals. If so, the chain of title may have to be investigated. Where the right is registered, this may not be a problem, but look out for rights which have been retained by, or licensed to, third parties, and also beware of acquired rights the transfer of which has not been registered.

Assignments of trademarks without goodwill raise particular difficulties. In some jurisdictions this is not allowed, while in others (including the UK) formalities have to be observed.

Intellectual property rights may also be charged as security (*see* Chapter 16, para. 16.3). This normally entails an assignment of the rights, with a provision for re-assignment on payment of the sum secured. Since assignments have to be in writing (and where appropriate, registered), they should not be too difficult to discover and if intellectual property has been mortgaged or charged the agreement must contain a warranty that any encumbrances will be discharged prior to completion.

## 17.5    How are intellectual property rights transferred?

Different considerations apply to *asset sales* and *share sales*. But in either case the object is to ensure that the purchaser is able to use all those rights which were used in the business before the acquisition took place. The purchaser will also wish to ascertain whether the rights are properly protected and whether the business is going to be able to continue using them.

Intellectual property rights used by a business may be owned by it or by a third party. The third party may be part of the same group as the business, or it may be wholly independent. If it is independent the use by the business may or may not be authorised. A purchaser of the business will want to be able to continue using those rights; if the business has to stop using any of them, it will have to stop doing something which it was doing before the acquisition took place.

### Asset sales                                              17.5.1

In asset sales the transfer is effected item by item. Each type of intellectual property owned by the vendor company will have to be separately transferred, and the purchaser will have to make sure that it can continue to use all the third party intellectual property rights used in the business which it is acquiring.

Separate assignments should be drawn up for each of the relevant rights. For registered rights, the assignment itself will have to be registered and any stamp duty due on the assignment will have to have been paid.

It is likely that there will be further documents which will have to be executed by the parties, particularly where the transfer of foreign rights also has to be registered. A suitable further assurance undertaking is therefore an essential part of the acquisition agreement.

Assignments of *copyright* and *unregistered design rights* will take as their starting point whatever schedule of rights it has been possible to construct. The transfer can be effected by the actual sale and purchase agreement. A separate document of assignment is unnecessary, nor does the assignment have to be by deed. It does, however, have to be in writing and signed by the assignor. It must also be stamped, if appropriate.

In the event, there may be occasions when a specific assignment of certain rights is needed. A further assurance clause in the agreement will ensure that this can be obtained. This is likely to be important, for example, if unspecified rights have been transferred by the sale agreement and the purchaser needs to take infringement proceedings on some of them. A specific assignment may also be appropriate where the parties do not wish to disclose the terms of the acquisition agreement.

*Note*

An assignment must carry with it an assignment of any accrued rights of action. If this right is not transferred, the purchaser will not be able to sue for any infringement taking place before the acquisition.

Remember that copyright can be, and often is, assigned in part. The video rights in a film may be assigned separately from the right of public performance (which enables it to be shown in the cinema), and the television rights may be assigned separately again.

The problem with assigning know-how is that it is not

property. It cannot therefore be assigned, a fact which does not always prevent assignments of it from appearing in business acquisition agreements. In fact, the only way of transferring know-how is for it to be imparted to the purchaser.

To maintain the exclusivity of the know-how, covenants will have to be taken from the vendor not to use the information or disclose it to others.

Purchasers of valuable know-how should always ensure that they take the employees with the business. Leaving them behind means leaving some of the know-how with the vendor, raising problems of monitoring any subsequent use of the know-how by the employees either in their own business or as continuing employees of the vendor.

If it is necessary to leave key employees behind, consideration should be given to obtaining their services as consultants to ensure the complete transfer of the know-how. The purchaser should also satisfy themselves that their contracts of employment give the necessary degree of security. If necessary, the vendor can be required in the agreement to put in place the necessary safeguards.

Finally, all documents which relate to the know-how must be delivered to the purchaser at completion. Any copyright or any intellectual property rights in them must also be transferred in the agreement to the purchaser.

## 17.5.2   Third party rights

### Intra-group arrangements

Intellectual property rights used by the business which is being acquired may be owned by another company in the same group as the vendor. Often this will be a holding company or a parent, or it could be a subsidiary of the company which owns the business or another trading subsidiary of the same parent. If the trademark is that of a foreign manufacturer, registration in the UK may well be in its name but the mark may be used by its UK distributor.

The product now made by the business being acquired may have been originally developed and sold by another company in the same group, and patent and trademark rights may still be owned by that other company. If this is the case, an assignment from the company which actually owns the rights will be needed.

Some groups deliberately put their intellectual property rights into the hands of one company in the group and other members of the group who wish to use them may be licensed to do so. If the business being acquired has exclusive right to use certain intellectual property rights, an assignment should be obtained from the holding company; if not, it may be possible to obtain a partial assignment, or otherwise the acquirer will have to be satisfied with a licence.

Licensing arrangements will need to be made to regulate the continued use by the purchaser and any other companies in the group which use the same intellectual property rights. It is often the case that intra-group licences are unwritten, which makes it difficult to settle the terms of the licence to the outsider. A detailed investigation may be necessary to establish on what terms the licence should be given.

### Independent third parties

All businesses use intellectual property rights owned by independent third parties. At the very least, they will have computer programs the copyright in which belongs to the software house which has licensed the purchaser to use them.

Businesses in fields such as broadcasting use other people's copyright material all the time, without actually acquiring the rights in the material outright. Many third party licences will be of vital importance to the business and the purchaser will have to consider the transferability of the licence and its terms.

### Licences

17.5.3

A licence is nothing more than a contract, and whether the licensee can transfer the benefit of the licence to the purchaser will depend on its terms. All such agreements must be very carefully renewed, and where appropriate (as in the case of patent licences) the purchaser should check that they have been registered.

### Trademark licences

A licence of a trademark requires a registered user agreement, otherwise the licensee's use of the mark does not count if the registration is challenged for non-use. The Register will show whether this has been done. Registered user agreements are necessary in the UK and many other jurisdictions.

Licences must also be checked for validity under EC and domestic competition laws. A surprising number of patent licences, for example, contain provisions 'black-listed' by the relevant block exemption, such as requirements to pay royalties on non-patented matters as well as patented ones. These may predate the block exemption and not have been reviewed when it came in, or they may have been made in ignorance of it.

### Consent

The licence may provide that the licensor's consent must be

obtained before the benefit of the licence may be transferred. This will have to be checked out by the purchaser.

**Transfer**

The benefit of a licence can be transferred by:

- Novation;
- Assignment; or
- Sub-licensing.

*Novation* is where the purchaser is substituted for the original licensee under the contract. A novation agreement, being tripartite by nature, must be made between the original licensor and licensee, and the purchaser. If an acquisition is being carried out in an environment of secrecy, or if time is tight, it may be impossible to involve the original licensor and novation would therefore be impossible.

The benefit of a contract is, unless it is expressly prohibited, *assignable*. The burden of a contract cannot, however, be transferred without novation. For the vendor, assignment has the disadvantage that it remains primarily liable to the original licensor and the only protection available to it will be what it can get in the way of indemnities.

Licences sometimes prohibit assignment but allow *sub-licensing*. Where the vendor retains part of its business and wishes to retain rights under the licence itself, it will be an appropriate solution anyway.

*Note*

The purchaser must bear in mind that if novation is unobtainable and assignment and sub-licensing are prohibited the benefit of the licence cannot be transferred. This may have a disastrous effect on the value of the business.

If the purchaser has to take a licence rather than obtain an assignment of some intellectual property rights, this may affect the business. Whether the licence is exclusive, sole or non-exclusive, any limitations, eg. as to territory, may make it less valuable. The rights given by copyright may be licensed separately, and other intellectual property rights may be split between different licensees.

A licence is inherently fragile. Breach of its terms may result in termination. If the purchaser is required to take a sub-licence they will be at the mercy of its sub-licensor's compliance with the terms of the head licence and it would be well advised to try to get a new (possibly parallel) licence from the head licensor. You should insist on, at least, an undertaking from the licensor to grant a new licence if the head licence is terminated.

### Licensees and infringers

Licensees generally do not enjoy such extensive rights to sue for infringement as those possessed by the owner of intellectual property rights. The purchaser should, if they have to take a licence, insist on provisions to oblige the seller to take prompt action.

If the duration of the licence is limited the effects of its termination will have to be assessed by the purchaser. The same applies if there is an express right of termination contained in it.

Consideration will have to be given to the royalties payable for the use of the rights. The extent to which the licensor retains the right to supervise and inspect the products produced under the licence will also be a matter which the purchaser will want to consider carefully.

The licensor should be obliged to maintain and enforce the licensed rights. If the licensor allows the rights to lapse, the business may be able to continue using them without paying the royalty, so there is some advantage to there being no such provision. Conversely, competitors would also be free in those circumstances to use the rights. Moreover, the licensee usually has no right to take action for infringements.

Finally, if the business being acquired uses third party intellectual property rights without permission, the purchaser could be taking on a liability for an infringement. Careful enquiries will be needed to detect whether this is happening, and indemnities against liability for infringement would be needed.

### Share sales

In a share sale the situation is very different from that of an asset sale. The business which owns or uses intellectual property rights remains the same, only the ownership of its shares changes. IP rights do not have to be transferred

However, licenses may contain provisions dealing with change of ownership, management or control of the licensee, providing for the termination of the licence on one of these events, especially where a competitor is acquiring the shares. If so, the licensor will have to be approached for any necessary consent.

Where consents have to be obtained, a frequent short cut is for the vendor to undertake to use their best endeavours to secure them. Although best endeavours are pretty onerous, they fall well short of a guarantee, so the purchaser would be well-advised to resist any such undertaking. If the consents prove impossible to get, the value of the acquisition may be dramatically reduced.

Even if the purchaser is in a position to sue for breach of contract where the vendor fails to deliver the necessary consents, acquisition agreements frequently contain *de minimis* provisions. This could mean that no action would lie unless the value in issue was perhaps 5% of the purchase price.

*Note*

An obligation to put in place the necessary consents before completion usually results in the vendor pursuing the matter with a greater degree of urgency.

The purchaser should always ensure that the agreement contains a warranty that the terms of any licence, the benefit of which is being acquired, have been observed, and that the licensor would not have reason to terminate it.

## 17.6    Warranties and disclosures

Warranties are contractual obligations which the vendor undertakes and which relate to the circumstances of the business. They constitute a statement of facts on which the purchaser has based the offer, and they give the purchaser the right to bring an action for breach of contract if they are not observed.

They also encourage the vendor to disclose any problems before the purchase is completed. The purchaser will not be able to take action over matters brought to their attention before the acquisition. These matters are usually set forth in a disclosure letter.

### 17.6.1    Content of IP warranties

Intellectual property warranties in either share sale or asset sale agreements should include:

- Details of all registered intellectual property rights owned or used by the business (disclosed in a schedule to the agreement), and confirmation that all renewal fees have been paid;
- Details of unregistered rights (also disclosed in a schedule);

*Note*

The seller should make it plain that the list is not exhaustive – because it is impossible to be sure that it is.

- Disclosure of details of all licences granted to the company;
- Disclosure of details of licences granted by the company;
- Confirmation that there has been no breach of any term of these licences – this may be limited to breaches which

would give the licensor the right to terminate;

- Confirmation that the business is not using any intellectual property rights which infringe the rights of a third party;
- Confirmation that no third party is infringing any of the business' intellectual property rights;
- Confirmation that the business is entitled to unrestricted use of all information in its possession;
- Confirmation that the business has not disclosed any of the know-how transferred under the agreement to third parties or, if it has, that this has been done under the terms of confidentiality agreements which have been disclosed to the purchaser.

*Note*

The first disclosure above will not cover the validity of the rights. The fact that a right is registered is not conclusive of its validity, and if it is a particularly important right the purchaser should satisfy themselves that it is valid.

Warranties may be limited to circumstances within the actual knowledge of the seller. Any matters which would amount to breaches of the warranties should be disclosed, in which case the purchaser would be well-advised to insist on suitable indemnities to cover possible third-party claims.

## The value of rights                                17.6.2

The purchaser should make sure that they have an idea of the value of the intellectual property rights they are buying. The rights should at least be examined in detail by appropriate personnel within the purchaser's organisation. Alternatively, specialist intellectual property valuers should be commissioned to carry out the work.

Consideration will have to be given to the ownership of rights which have been created by third parties. While generally any intellectual property created by an employee will belong to the employer, the same is not true of intellectual property created by a consultant, even if that person is commissioned to produce it. In the absence of an agreement to the contrary, the third party will remain the owner of the intellectual property rights.

*Example*

A frequent example concerns commissioned software. A company may pay a software house to write computer programs for its use, tailor-made to its requirements, but unless copyright in the programs is specifically transferred to the commissioner it will remain with the writer. This may well mean that the company which commissioned the work in the first place finds that programs written for it have also been supplied to its competitors.

Every licence granted diminishes the value of the intellectual property, and a perpetual exclusive royalty free licence to a competitor would make the licence rights absolutely worthless.

On the other hand, if the company has some intellectual property which it is not using, but which it has been able to licence against payment of a royalty, it can be a valuable asset. This is the basic principle of franchising, whereby a trading style and business system is licensed to third parties. It also offers a method of extending the exploitation of the business's intellectual property rights to parts of the world where it is not already established.

### 17.6.3     Licenses-out

Licences-out should be checked by the purchaser as carefully as licences-in. They may also contain termination clauses which are actuated by change of control of the licensor. The purchaser will want to know that there is no subsisting breach, and that there are no other potential problems.

Sole and exclusive licences require particular care because of the restrictions which flow from them or the licensor using the rights themselves (in the case of exclusive licences) or licensing others to use the rights (in both cases).

The purchaser will also be interested to know to whom licences have been granted. They may be competitors.

### 17.6.4     Litigation

Litigation over intellectual property rights can be very expensive and damaging to the business. The same applies whether the business is the infringer or the owner of the rights. An adverse judgment in the infringement action could mean that the company has to stop making a product immediately. A major redesign, or the launch of a new brand, may also be necessary.

Litigation started by the business indicates that the right to use that intellectual property may well be in doubt. It is therefore essential that all intellectual property litigation is disclosed.

Confidential information is nebulous by its nature and can easily be disclosed and therefore lose its confidential nature. The warranty must ensure that adequate steps have been taken to preserve confidentiality.

### Knowledge                                                    17.6.5

Common limitations in intellectual property warranties
will exclude liability if the fact which causes loss was not
known by the vendor at the time. A warranty may also be
worded so that it requires disclosure only if a third party has
notified the vendor of something happening, eg. a challenge to the validity of a patent.

Intellectual property warranties may also be limited if
the purchaser has knowledge of the matters covered by the
warranty. This would particularly be the case in a management buy-out. The purchaser may also be deemed to have
knowledge, since information about intellectual property
rights is held on public registers. The vendor may therefore
limit their liability to information not available to the purchaser from these public sources.

Warranties are all about apportioning risk, and there is
no reason on the face of it why the vendor's liability should
be excluded just because they had no knowledge of something. The chances are that neither party would know about
a hidden liability; one of them has to bear the risk.

## Commercial matters                                           17.7

Any problems with the intellectual property rights being
transferred may well be reflected in the purchase price.
However, if this is not possible, an indemnity may prove to
be an acceptable alternative.

An indemnity will be more appropriate where the risk
which it is designed to cover is more speculative. In such a case
a reduction in the purchase price will be difficult to negotiate.

It may also be possible to work out a practical solution to
an intellectual property problem. For example, a computer
program which cannot be used without infringement could
be replaced by a proprietary one, or a replacement could be
commissioned. At the end of the day, the way a solution is
arrived at will depend very much on the relative bargaining
power of vendor and purchaser.

## Ancillary obligations                                         17.8

### Seller's change of name                                      17.8.1

Particularly where the goodwill of a business is transferred
in an asset sale, the purchaser will want to ensure that the
seller changes their name on or shortly after completion.

### 17.8.2        Confidentiality

Valuable know-how is only protected by obligations of confidentiality. The seller should be obliged to preserve confidentiality, preferably (from the buyer's point of view) without limit of time. In any case, the obligation may not continue if the know-how falls into the public domain. The seller's obligation should also cover customer lists and other non-technical information.

### 17.8.3        Non-competition

The value of the purchaser's acquisition will need to be protected by a prohibition on the seller competing with it. There are three elements to such an undertaking:

- The seller will not for a given period of time be involved in any business which competes with that of the business sold;
- The seller may not solicit customers of the business; and
- The seller will not entice away the business's employees who have transferred over to the purchaser.

These restrictions are an important method of protecting valuable know-how which would otherwise be free for the vendor to use. Very careful drafting is needed because they will be unlawful under the doctrine of restraint of trade if the restrictions go too far.

### 17.8.4        The doctrine of restraint of trade

The Courts will not enforce contracts which are in unreasonable restraint of trade. To do so would be against public policy. Many restraints of trade are now governed by statute (such as resale price maintenance) but the common law doctrine remains important, especially for restrictive covenants.

Every restraint is presumed void unless it can be proved valid. The validity of a contract which restrains trade depends basically on three factors:

1   The restriction must be necessary to *protect some legitimate interest of the covenantee.* It is legitimate for the purchaser of a business to protect its goodwill by requiring the vendor to agree not to solicit its customers, and for an employer to prevent former employees from soliciting customers and from using or divulging know-how acquired in the course of their employment.

2   Restrictions must be *reasonable as between the parties.* They must go no further than is necessary to protect the interest of the covenantee. What is reasonable depends on the facts of the case and on the nature of the interest

requiring protection. The burden of proof is on the plaintiff.

Restrictions must be *properly limited in time, geographical extent and subject matter*, and the courts have been sympathetic to arguments based on inequality of bargaining power (*see Schroeder Music Publishing Co Ltd v Macaulay* (1974) (HL)).

3   They must be *reasonable in the public interest*. Restraints which have a wide economic effect are more likely to run into difficulties under this head.

Restrictive covenants are commonly found in employment contracts, where there is well-developed case law on their extent. Here, however, we are concerned with business transfers and the protection of intellectual property.

The courts are more ready to uphold restraints on trade in business transfers than in employment contracts. They are necessary to protect the buyer's investment. However, they must go no further than necessary to protect the acquired business. The seller could not, for example, be prevented from competing with other businesses owned by the buyer elsewhere.

**Interpretation**

The Court will not rewrite a restraint clause; if it is void it will remain void, even though it would be valid if the territorial scope were reduced by a small amount. But if it covers different activities, the Court may delete one or more of those activities. This is not interfering with the restriction, merely 'blue pencilling' a restraint. Put another way, the Court may 'cut out' but will not 'cut down' a void restraint.

*Example*

In *Nordenfelt v Maxim Nordenfelt Gunds and Ammunition Co* (1894) the vendor of a munitions business agreed not to compete with any activity of the company anywhere in the world for 25 years. The House of Lords held that in the circumstances there were two restrictions. The first was limited to munitions, where because of the vendor's importance (he was also an inventor in the field) it was reasonable. The second purported to embrace all the other activities of the company, and was too wide to be upheld.

However, the Court will sometimes give a commonsense meaning to the words of the clause.

*Example*

In *Clarke v Newland* (1991) a doctor accepted a restriction on his practising locally for three years after leaving a partnership. The court held that the agreement was meant to apply to general practice only, and was therefore valid to this extent only, and could not be invoked to prevent him working as a hospital doctor, which would not compete with the former partnership.

## Self-assessment questions

1 What is the importance of the seller's's disclosure?

2 Why should the purchaser investigate the target's intellectual property rights?

3 What difference is there between a share sale and an asset sale?

4 How are registered IP rights identified?

5 How are unregistered IP identified?

6 Can the benefit of a licence be transferred?

7 What problems relating to IP may be encountered in a share sale?

8 What should an IP warranty contain?

9 What ancillary obligations may be needed to protect intellectual property on an acquisition?

10 How far is it lawful to include a restraint of trade clause?

# Chapter 18

# Restrictions on exercising intellectual property rights

## Introduction
18.1

The rights given by intellectual property laws cannot be exercised without restraint. Apart from the effect of external restraints, there are limitations placed on the exercise of rights by the statutes which grant them. These are the subject matter of this chapter.

## Patents
18.2

### Licences of right
18.2.1

Section 46, Patents Act 1977 allows the proprietor of a patent to apply to the Comptroller for an entry to be made in the Register to the effect that licence is to be available under the patent as of right. The patent is referred to subsequently as being endorsed 'licences of right'.

The *effect* is that the proprietor gives away the monopoly nature of the patent. They cannot thereafter (unless the endorsement is cancelled under s.47) withhold a licence from anyone who wants one. The *benefit* to the proprietor is that the renewal fees become significantly less.

The terms of the licence, particularly relating to royalties, are to be settled by the parties. If agreement cannot be reached, it falls to the Comptroller to settle the terms. Existing licence holders may benefit from a decision to have the patent endorsed; they may apply to have the terms of their licences changed to match those of licences of right.

If the patent has been endorsed, in most infringement actions the defendant can avoid having an injunction granted against them by undertaking to take a licence on the terms so settled. This does not apply, however, where the infringement consists of importing goods from outside the EC.

### Compulsory licences
18.2.2

The Comptroller may also order compulsory licences to be made available in certain circumstances: s.48. The power also allows the Comptroller to endorse the patent with the fact.

The grounds are set out in s.48(3). They cover:

● Non-working of the patent in the UK;

- (Where the patent is for a product) unsatisfied demand in the UK (or demand met by imports);
- Import substitution preventing the patent being worked in the UK;
- Refusal to licence on reasonable terms, leading to loss of exports, problems with working a dependent patent, or prejudice to the establishment or development of commercial or industrial activities in the UK;
- Specified conditions imposed in licences.

Section 50 sets out the purposes for which the Comptroller should exercise the power to order compulsory licences. The Comptroller is charged with securing that patents which can be worked in the UK are worked there and that the proprietor of the patent receives a reasonable remuneration. The Comptroller also has to ensure that the interests of any person working or developing a patent in the UK under the protection of a patent are not unfairly prejudiced.

*Note*

In *Commission v UK* (1993), the validity of s.48(3) was called into question. In so far as it hinders imports from other EC countries, it is prohibited by Article 30 of the Treaty of Rome.

### 18.2.3    Monopolies and Mergers Commission reports

The Monopolies and Mergers Commission (MMC) may report that certain matters operate against the public interest. This may occur on a monopoly reference, on a merger reference or on a competition reference.

If the Comptroller concludes that the matters complained of include the terms of licences granted by the proprietor of a patent, or the refusal of the proprietor to grant licences, the Comptroller may cancel or modify any offending condition in a licence and make licences available as of right: s.51.

## 18.3    Trademarks

There are no licensing of right or compulsory licensing provisions relating to trademarks. Since the whole point of them is that they identify the goods or services of the proprietor, it would be inappropriate for there to be such provisions.

In the course of registering a trademark it may be necessary to accept certain conditions, or to agree with the owners of conflicting rights how a mark will be used. So, whatever goods the registration might cover, it is possible that the use of the mark is limited by an agreement with the owner of a similar mark.

## Registered designs                                          18.4

### Licences of right for registered designs                    18.4.1

Licences of right for registered designs may be ordered to be made available. The terms of existing licences granted by rights owners may also be varied. Where the equivalent powers in respect of design right are exercisable by the Secretary of State, under the Registered Designs Act 1949 they are exercisable by the Registrar upon application by the Secretary of State following an MMC report.

The application must be advertised and representations made within 30 days of publication of the notice must be considered before the application is made. Thereafter, the Registrar may exercise much the same powers as the Secretary of State has in respect of patents, including cancelling and modifying conditions in existing licences, and entering on the Register the fact that licences are available as of right in respect of the design.

## Copyright                                                   18.5

The Copyright, Designs and Patents Act 1988 contains the equivalent of compulsory licensing provisions. It permits many acts which would otherwise be restricted by copyright. The following acts are permitted:

- Fair dealing with a literary, dramatic, musical or artistic work for research or private study: s.29(1);
- Fair dealing with a work (of any type) for criticism or review: s.30(1);
- Fair dealing with a work for reporting current events: s.30(2);
- Incidental inclusion of copyright material in an artistic work, sound recording, film, broadcast or cable program: s.31;
- A variety of acts done for educational purposes: ss.32–5;
- Making the three-dimensional object depicted in a design, unless that object is itself an artistic work: s.51.

### Literary, dramatic, musical or artistic work for research   18.5.1
### or private study

An act is fair dealing in relation to a literary, dramatic, musical or artistic work for research or private study if it does not prejudice the exercise by the copyright owner of their rights. In other words, provided making a copy does not substitute for buying a book (which means it must be of a relatively small extract) it will not infringe copyright. Multiple coping is not permitted under this provision: s.29(3).

*Note*

Copyright in the typographical arrangement of a published edition is not infringed by fair dealing for research or private study: s.29(2). This closes a loophole which existed under the old Copyright Act 1956.

If the work is a computer program (a type of literary work, remember), it is *not* fair dealing to convert it into a higher level language or to copy it incidentally while converting it: s.29(4), added by the Copyright (Computer Programs) Regulations 1992. These acts are, however, permitted by s.50(B) (also added by the Regulations) which lays down the following conditions before the acts are permitted:

● It must be necessary to decompile the program to obtain the information needed to write an independent program which will interoperate with another program; and

● The information must not be used for any other purpose.

### 18.5.2    Criticism or review

In the case of fair dealing with a work (of any type) for criticism or review, a sufficient acknowledgement must be given: s.36(1). The criticism or review may be of a different work, or of a performance. For example, a reviewer can quote the lyrics of a song performed in a concert in a review of the concert.

### 18.5.3    Reporting current events

Fair dealing with a work for reporting current events applies to any works except photographs: s.30(2). Again a sufficient acknowledgement must be given, except where the current events are reported by sound recording, film, broadcast or cable programme.

### 18.5.4    Incidental inclusion

Incidental inclusion of copyright material in another artistic work, sound recording, film, broadcast or cable program is not an infringement. Nor is it an infringement to issue copies of the other work which includes the copyright material to the public, playing, showing or broadcasting it or including it in a cable programme.

### 18.5.5    Educational purposes

A variety of acts done for educational purposes is permitted. These include:

- Copying in the course of instruction: s.32;
- Including copyright works in anthologies intended for educational use: s.33;
- Performances before audiences of pupils and teachers: s.34(1); and
- Recording a broadcast or cable programme for educational purposes: s.35. The permitted act in this case extends to any work included in the broadcast or programme.

*Note*

If there is a licensing scheme for such purposes this provision does not apply.

## Design documents                                           18.5.6

It is not an infringement of copyright in a design document, eg. an engineering drawing, to make the three-dimensional object depicted in the design, unless that object is itself an artistic work: s.51.

*Note*

Other permitted acts cover certain activities of libraries and archives and public administration.

# Unregistered design right                                    18.6

## Exceptions                                                   18.6.1

The Act provides that certain acts which would otherwise infringe design right are permitted. There are also exceptions to the monopoly right under the Registered Designs Act 1949. So by no means are all original 'designs' protected.

## Infringement of copyright                                    18.6.2

A design for an article may well be first recorded in a copyright work such as a design drawing. Section 51 limits the effect of copyright by providing that in certain circumstances no infringement of copyright takes place if articles are made to the design, or if articles made to the design are themselves copied.

Section 51 therefore defines where copyright finishes; s.236 defines where the design right starts. It provides that where copyright subsists in a work consisting of or including a design in which design right subsists, design right is not infringed by an act which is an infringement of the copyright in the work. This means that, if the article depicted in a design is an artistic work, such as a sculpture or a work of artistic craftsmanship (so that making the article would infringe copyright and design right in the design), only action for infringement of copyright can be taken.

### 18.6.3 Licences of right

**Licences of right in the last five years**

During the last five years of the period for which design right subsists licences to do anything which would otherwise infringe design right are available as of right to any person. The terms of the licence, including royalties payable, are left for the parties to agree between themselves. If they are unable to agree they will be determined by the Comptroller General of Patents, Designs and Trade Marks.

The factors to which the Comptroller may have regard are those which the Secretary of State prescribes by order, such as quality standards and the investment made by the owner of design right in creating the design in the first place.

The design right owner may not refuse a licence, but anyone wishing to have a licence must apply to the owner initially in order that negotiations on the terms can be undertaken. Licences will automatically cover all the acts restricted by design right so that the terms cannot prevent a licensee performing any of the acts which, but for the licence, would be infringing acts.

Even though licences are available as of right to do acts which would otherwise infringe, if they are done without any attempt being made to obtain a licence they will constitute an infringement.

**Licences of right before the last five years**

Licences of right may also be made available if the Monopolies and Mergers Commission (MMC) considers that certain matters may be expected to operate or have operated against the public interest. This power applies to conditions in licences granted by a design right owner restricting the use of the design by the licensee or the right of the design right owner to grant other licences, or a refusal of a design right owner to grant licences on reasonable terms.

If the MMC reports that matters which it considers may be expected to operate or have operated against the public interest include these matters then the Secretary of State's powers under Part I, Schedule 8, Fair Trading Act 1973 are said by s.238(1) to include the power to cancel or modify those conditions and, instead or in addition, to provide that licences in respect of the design right shall be available as of right. In default of agreement between the parties, the terms of the licence available by virtue of this provision are to be settled by the Comptroller.

If a prospective licensee of right cannot identify the owner of the design right on reasonable enquiry, the Comptroller may settle terms which provide for no payment to be made. The design right owner may apply for the terms to be varied, but only from the date on which they become identifiable. If it transpires that licences were *not* available as of right at the time (and the section applies to licences of right available either in the last five years or by order following an MMC Report), the licensee is not liable in damages for, or for an account of profits in respect of, anything done before they became aware of the rights owner's claim that licences were not available.

## Undertakings to take licences                        18.6.4

Where a licence of right is available either in the last five years of design right or by order of the Secretary of State or the Registrar respectively, but a defendant in an infringement action has:

- Made no attempt to negotiate terms with the owner of the design right or the registered proprietor; or
- The parties have negotiated but failed to agree terms and no application has been made for the Comptroller to settle the matter;

the defendant may undertake to agree to a licence. If they do so no injunction or order for delivery up will be granted by the court and the amount which the plaintiff may recover in damages or on an account of profits will be not more than twice the amount which would have been payable had the defendant taken up the licence which was available to them as of right. This amounts to a restriction on the penalty which may be imposed on a defendant for their failure to take up a licence of right.

The undertaking may be given at any time before the court makes its final order in the proceedings. It is unnecessary for the defendant to make any admission of liability. Consequently, a defendant who denies having infringed design right may limit their liability while still being able to defend the proceedings.

The plaintiff's remedies for infringements committed before licences became available as of right remain unaltered.

## Licensees of right                        18.6.5

Licensees of right under design right are prevented from claiming that they are licensed by the owner of design right, either in trade descriptions which they applied to goods or in the course of their advertising.

The meaning of a trade description is the same as that used in the Trade Descriptions Act 1968. This includes any indication, direct or indirect, and by whatever means given, of the conformity of goods with a type approved by any person. This provision is necessary because the owner in fact has no choice over who may take out a licence to manufacture the goods, nor have they any control over the products produced under such a licence. Any breach of the provision is actionable by the design right owner.

### 18.6.6    Crown use

#### The Crown's rights

The Crown – or more accurately government departments – has extensive powers to do anything for the purposes of defence (including foreign defence) or the health service which would otherwise infringe a patent, registered design or design right.

#### Payment for Crown use

The owner of the rights is entitled to payment for the use of the design by the Crown. They may be able to strike an agreement with the government (subject to the approval of the Treasury); if not, the terms on which the rights may be used are to be determined by the court, including the County Court. If the owner cannot be identified upon reasonable enquiry the government department concerned may apply to the court for an order that the Crown use shall be free of any payment unless and until the owner of the right subsequently claims their right to payment.

#### Third party rights

Any existing agreements between the owner of the rights and any third party (including another joint owner) will not restrict the Crown in its use of the rights and of associated materials and information. Nor may such an agreement oblige the Crown to pay the third party for such use.

### 18.6.7    Compensation for use

The owner of design right in a design and the proprietor of a patent or registered design of which the Crown makes use are entitled to compensation for loss of profit arising from the fact that they are not awarded contracts to supply articles made to their designs.

The owner can claim compensation both for lost trading profit and for losses in respect of underused capital assets. However, they must be in a position to supply the Crown from their existing capacity. They would not be able to claim losses by arguing that, if they built a new factory, they would be able to supply the Crown. If due to other circumstances they are ineligible for the award of such a contract, they will still be entitled to compensation.

If the owner also loses out on further contracts for the supply of articles, but these contracts are not for the services of the Crown, no compensation will be payable. For example, where a foreign government orders from the same source as the Crown has used, the claimable loss will not include lost profits in respect of foreign orders which go elsewhere because the Crown has previously gone elsewhere.

The amount of compensation may be agreed between the right owner or licensee and the government department concerned with the approval of the Treasury. If not, it is to be determined by the court and the Act makes it clear that any compensation payable under these provisions is in addition to any amount payable for Crown use of the designs, including any amounts payable to third parties.

## Self-assessment questions

1   Why might a patent owner permit licensing of right?
2   When are compulsory licences of a patent made available?
3   What acts are permitted to be done to copyright works?
4   When is copyright in a design document infringed?
5   Explain the licensing of right provisions relating to unregistered design right.
6   What is the effect of an undertaking by an infringer to take a licence of design right?
7   What is the Crown permitted to do with IP rights?
8   When must the owner of IP rights be compensated for Crown use?

# Chapter 19

# Restrictions imposed by competition laws

## Introduction 19.1

Competition laws impose significant restraints on the exercise of intellectual property rights – which by their very nature are anti-competitive. This chapter describes how EC and UK laws have dealt with the problem.

## Restrictive Trade Practices Act 19.2

### Horizontal agreements 19.2.1

The Restrictive Trade Practices Act 1976 (RTPA) has limited applicability to horizontal agreements about IP rights. Bilateral licences in which the relevant restrictions relate only to the patented goods or process or, as the case may be, registered design are outside the scope of the legislation entirely, notwithstanding that the agreement may contain all sorts of restrictions on the parties' conduct: Sched. 3, para. 5.

There is also a limited exception for horizontal agreements where two firms exchange know-how and accept restrictions on the type of goods to be produced with it, and no further restrictions are allowed: Sched. 3, para. 3.

Copyright pooling agreements are also exempt: Sched. 3, para. 5A, added by the Competition Act 1980. There is also a limited exemption for agreements relating to certification trademarks.

### Vertical agreements 19.2.2

Careful drafting will ensure that vertical agreements fall entirely outside the scope of the RTPA.

#### Patent licences

In *Ravenseft Properties Ltd's Application* (1977), the Restrictive practices Court held that a restriction is only accepted where a pre-existing freedom is abandonment. A newcomer to a lease (in that case) or other arrangement usually has no such freedom to give up. So restrictions in IP licences will frequently not be restrictions at all.

Restrictions on the licensor granting *further licences* are not relevant restrictions and may therefore be ignored when determining registrability. If the agreement does contain relevant restrictions, it is still only registrable if *two or more parties* accept restrictions; even then the agreement may be exempt from registration if the restrictions relate solely to the patented goods.

There are other provisions in UK law which govern patent licences:

- Section 44, Patents Act 1977 prohibits certain tie-in and no-competition clauses;
- Section 45 gives a statutory right to terminate a licence agreement after the last of the licensed patents has expired;
- Licence terms can be modified following an adverse finding by the Monopolies and Mergers Commission (MMC);
- The Resale Prices Act 1976 prevents patentees imposing minimum prices after the goods have left the hands of their licensees.

*Note*

No-challenge clauses are not only permitted in UK law, but there is also a common law obligation on a licensee not to challenge the patent under which the licence is granted. They are, however, not allowed in EC law.

### Know-how licences

The RTPA contains no specific exemptions for one-way licences of know-how, only exchanges, and the *Ravenseft* doctrine has no application as know-how is only a right *in personam*, not a property right as such. Careful drafting can still secure immunity from the Act, eg. by ensuring that only one party accepts restrictions under the agreement. Bilateral exchanges benefit from the provisions of Sched. 3, paras. 5 and 8.

### Copyright and design right licences

These normally fall outside the scope of the RTPA, being exempted by Sched 3, paras. 5A and 5B respectively. These exemptions are not limited to bilateral agreements.

### Trademark licences

These also will normally fall outside the RTPA. Sched. 3 para. 4 of the Act exempts two types of agreement:

- *Certification trademark agreements* if they contain nothing more than the regulations for the certification mark which the Secretary of State has approved.
- *Licence agreements* where the only restrictions accepted by the licensee relate to the *types of goods* bearing the mark which are to be produced or the process of manufacture to be applied to the goods. Pricing restrictions are not permitted.

# Article 85                                                    19.3

### Application to licences                                      19.3.1

A licence which gives the licensee the right to do something
which formerly they could not might appear to raise no
competition issues under Article 85, Treaty of Rome 1957. This
is the 'rule of reason' approach in EC antitrust law, and was
applied in *Nungesser and Eisele v Commission* (1982) – the 'Maize
Seed' case. Indeed the European Court of Justice held there
that exclusive rights for a national territory within the Community could be granted without infringing Article 85 –
because without such protection no licensee would be prepared to take on the risk of investing in an unknown product
– but attempts to partition the common market, by hindering
parallel imports, would not be permitted.

However, additional ancillary restrictions might bring
the agreement within Article 85.

*Example*

In *Windsurfing International v Commission* (1986) clauses
governing quality control and other matters were caught by
Article 85(1). Exemption under Article 85(3) was unavailable
because the agreement had not been notified, although the
Commission doubted that it would have been given anyway.

### Patent licensing block exemption                             19.3.2

Regulation 2349/84 (which expires at the end of 1994) grants
exemption to patent licensing agreements. It covers agreements between two parties relating to the licensing of patents.

*Note*

Licences of associated know-how and trademarks do not
remove the agreement from the regulation's scope.

### Permitted restrictions

Article 1 sets out a 'white list' of permitted restrictions. The
licensor may agree not to grant further licences for the
contract territory for as long as the patent remains in force,
nor to exploit the patent themselves within the territory.

The licensee may agree:

● Not to exploit the product in the licensor's territory as
  long as the patent remains in force;

● Not to manufacture or use the product in other licensees'
  territories;

● Not actively to sell the product in other licensees' territories;

- Not to sell into other licensees' territories at all during the first five years after the product is first marketed in the Community; and
- To use only the licensor's form of presentation (usually a trademark) for the product.

Article 2 contains a list of restrictions which are generally unobjectionable but which are exempted 'just in case', for the sake of legal certainty. These include clauses regarding minimum royalties, field of use restrictions (the invention may only be used in one field of activity), obligations to mark products with the name of the patentee, and minimum quality standards.

**Prohibited restrictions**
Article 3 is the list of provisions which can never be permitted. These include:

- Royalties charged on non-patented products (though an obligation to carry on paying even after the patent has expired is permissible, so long as the licensee can get out of the agreement by reasonable notice: *see Ottung v Klee and Weilbeck* (1989));
- Price restrictions;
- Product ties which have no objective justification;
- Export restrictions greater than those permitted by Article 1; and
- Acts designed to curtail opportunities for parallel importers.

No-challenge clauses (where the licensee agrees not to challenge the validity of the licensor's rights) are also prohibited; the ability to deal with invalid rights, which distort the market by their very existence, must be preserved.

The regulation contains what is known as the opposition procedure. This permits agreements which contain clauses not expressly permitted by Articles 1 and 2 (and none expressly excluded by Article 3) to be notified and to obtain exemption if they are not opposed by the Commission within six months.

### 19.3.3    Know-how licensing block exemption

Regulation 556/89 is a similar block exemption regulation for non-patented know-how licences. It also covers patented technology, provided the licence includes some know-how which is 'substantial, secret and identified.'

The structure of the regulation is very similar to that of the patent licensing regulation, but the 'white list' and 'black list' permit more than the older block exemption does. It is therefore attractive to take advantage of the know-how regulation wherever patents and know-how are licensed together (and the two normally go hand-in-hand, for a patent itself rarely contains everything a licensee needs to know for commercial exploitation of the invention).

The restrictions between licensor and licensee may last for 10 years from the first licence in the territory. The restrictions on manufacturing and active sales between licensees may last for 10 years from the first licence in the common market. Under the patent licence regulation, restrictions may last longer since they depend on the duration of the patent protection.

Passive sales – where the buyer approaches the licensee unsolicited – may be prohibited for five years from the first licence in the common market.

Article 1(4) provides that where there is a patent for the licensed know-how, territorial protection (excluding that for passive sales) may last for the duration of the patent.

### Improvements

The main reason for preferring the patent licensing regulation would be where there is a stream of technology resulting from improvements to be passed on to the licensee. The patent licensing block exemption allows the territorial protection to be extended in this situation provided that each party has the right to 'resile' (withdraw) every three years after the expiry of the last of the patents.

If a customer requires a second source of products made according to the know-how, the block exemption allows a licence to be granted for the manufacture of a limited number of products. Usually, limitations on manufacture are 'blacklisted'. In this situation the agreement has to be notified but can be granted exemption under an accelerated procedure.

Provided the technology remains secret, the 'white list' permits a restriction on using the technology after the licence has expired. There are limitations, however, to the extent to which the licensee may be required to grant back licences covering improvements; such a grant back may not be required to last for longer than the period for which the licensee has the right to use the technology. A licensee who has made useful improvements is therefore in a strong position to seek an additional term, since the licensor can only rely on getting the right to use the improvements as long as the licensee has the right to use the original know-how.

### 19.3.4　Franchising

Regulation 4087/88 is the franchising block exemption. Franchising agreements contain trademark and know-how licences, along with other matters, and are an increasingly important (though highly variegated) method of doing business.

The regulation applies to agreements which contain obligations relating to:

- The use of a common name or shop front or sign and a uniform presentation of contract premises and/or means of transport;
- The communication by the franchisor to the franchisee of know-how; and
- The continuing provision by the franchisor to the franchisee of commercial or technical assistance during the life of the agreement.

The know-how must be secret, substantial and identified.

#### Permitted restrictions

Article 2 lists the restrictions which are permitted in a franchise agreement. The franchisor may grant an exclusive territory and agree neither to grant a franchise nor itself to exploit the franchise in that territory or supply the goods to third parties there.

The franchisee may be required:

- To exploit the franchise only from the contract premises and not to seek customers outside its territory; and
- To buy the franchisor's goods only from nominated sources and not to buy competing goods except spare parts and accessories.

Article 3 contains a 'white list' of provisions which are permitted if they are necessary to protect the franchisor's intellectual property or to maintain the common identity or reputation of the franchised network.

#### Prohibited restrictions

The 'black list' comes in two parts. Article 4 sets out the conditions that must be satisfied for exemption to be granted and Article 5 lists clauses that may not be included.

The conditions are that:

- Franchisees must be free to obtain goods from other franchisees; and
- Guarantees which the franchisee is obliged to give must apply to goods bought from other franchisees or suppliers.

### Outside the block exemptions      19.3.5

No-challenge clauses in trademark licence agreements are permitted so far as they relate to the ownership of the mark, but not to its validity. These are a different story; they have a clear effect on competition (*see Moosehead/Whitbread* (1990)).

## Article 86      19.4

The owner of intellectual property rights has to beware of Article 86. Since IP rights are concerned with granting monopolies, they can easily put (or help put) their owner in a dominant position which must not be abused.

*Example*

1 In *Ministere Public v Tournier* (1989) the French national copyright management society was accused of charging excessively high and arbitrary rates to discotheques which wanted to use the recordings in which it owned copyright. The Court agreed that this was possible and suggested that a comparison of rates in other Member States might show that there was an abuse. However, the point was also made that the differences might turn out to have objectively valid reasons.

2 In *Volvo v Veng* (1988) the right owners refused to licence third parties to manufacture replacement panels for motor cars which were protected by UK registered designs. The Court held that this was part of the 'substance of the exclusive right' granted by the legislation and there was no abuse. However, the Court observed that there could be an abuse if, for example, the right owner refused to supply independent repairers, charged excessively high prices or stopped supplying parts for which there was still demand.

3 In *RTE, BBC and ITP v Commission* (1991) the Court confirmed that a dominant right owner may not have the luxury of choosing with whom to do business. A publisher of a television guide, who wished to produce a single comprehensive guide to all the programmes shown in Ireland, was thwarted by the refusal of the owners of copyright in the listings (protected under copyright law as compilations) to licence their reproduction even for a fee.

The Commission, responding to a complaint from the independent publisher, decided that the rights owners were preventing the creation of a new market (for a single programme guide) which consumers would find attractive. This was an abuse, and the Court of First Instance upheld this decision.

The Court held that marketing weekly listings constituted a distinct market from the daily listings available in the newspapers. It considered the geographical market which it had to consider to be the whole of the island of Ireland and that within that market the exercise of copyright secured dominance on the part of the three television companies' publishing arms. Preventing the production and marketing of a new product for which there is potential consumer demand went beyond the essential function of copyright protection and therefore amounted to an abuse.

4   *Tetra Pak Rausing SA v Commission* (1989) provides an illustration of the way the extension of economic strength by a dominant company may be an abuse. In a merger, the dominant firm gained an exclusive licence to exploit IP. The Court of First Instance held this to be a violation of Article 86. The fact that the exclusive licence, the benefit of which was acquired, was within the block exemption made no difference; the Court was concerned with the anti-competitive implications of the acquisition in the dominated market.

## Self-assessment questions

1 What affect does the RTPA have on horizontal agreements relating to IP?

2 What does the *Ravenseft* doctrine say?

3 Are no-challenge clauses permitted in patent licences?

4 Why does *Ravenseft* not apply to know-how licenses?

5 Distinguish *Maize Seed* from *Windsurfing International*.

6 What restrictions does the patent licensing block exemption permit?

7 What is the opposition procedure?

8 How long may know-how licenses last under the block exemption?

9 What are the features of a franchising agreement?

10 When will it be an abuse of a dominant position to exercise IP rights?

# Chapter 20

# Restrictions imposed by EC rules on free movement

## Introduction

Intellectual property rights can have the effect of dividing up the common market. They are usually granted on a national basis, though (as we saw in Chapter 12) this is gradually changing. The rules on free movement of goods, in the meantime, have a considerable effect on the exercise of intellectual property rights.

Article 30 prohibits qualitative restrictions on trade between Member States 'and measures having equivalent effect'. Intellectual property laws are such measures. Article 36 contains exceptions to Article 30, including one for 'industrial and commercial property'.

## Fundamental principles

The European Court of Justice (ECJ) has developed three fundamental principles which seek to reconcile the competing interests of free movement of goods and intellectual property law. These principles have played a central part in the application of these rules to intellectual property and all of them had their origin in *Deutsche Grammophon v Metro* (1971).

1   While the Treaty does not affect the *existence* of intellectual property rights, there are nonetheless circumstances in which the *exercise* of such rights may be restricted by the prohibitions laid down in the Treaty.

2   Article 36 permits exceptions to the free movement of goods only to the extent to which such exceptions are necessary for the purpose of safeguarding the rights that constitute the specific subject matter of the type of intellectual property in question.

*Note*

Perhaps the main advantage of this formula, apart from the fact that it narrows the scope of the exceptions permitted by Article 36, is that it allows subtle distinctions to be made depending on the type of intellectual property in issue.

3   The exclusive right conferred on the owner of intellectual property is *exhausted* in relation to the products in question when they put them into circulation anywhere

within the Common Market. The proprietor of national intellectual property rights may not rely on national IP legislation to oppose the importation of a product which has lawfully been marketed in another Member State by, or with the consent of, the proprietor of the right itself or persons legally or economically dependent on him.

### 20.2.1 Industrial and commercial property

The expression 'industrial and commercial property' clearly embraces patents and trademarks. It also extends to such specialised areas as plant breeders' rights. The ECJ has held that copyright can also be a form of industrial or commercial property because it:

... includes the protection conferred by copyright, especially when exploited commercially in the form of licences capable of affecting distribution in the various Member States of goods incorporating the protected literary or artistic work: *Musik-Vertrieb Membran v GEMA* (1981).

### 20.2.2 Existence and exercise

The principle that the Treaty does not affect the *existence* of industrial and commercial property rights is derived from Article 222. This provides that:

... the Treaty shall in no way prejudice the rules in Member States governing the system of property ownership.

The distinction between existence and exercise is criticised as artificial: if a right cannot be exercised, does it truly exist? But the distinction serves a purpose.

## 20.3 Intellectual property and the Treaty of Rome

Intellectual property rights are unaffected by the provisions of the Treaty unless they *hinder free movement* or *offend the rules of competition*. The impact of the competition rules is covered in Chapter19.

### 20.3.1 Free movement

Merely because national intellectual property laws differ does not mean that they contravene the Treaty. Article 36 will still save them in many cases, but as intellectual property laws become harmonised and community-wide rights become available (*see* Chapter 12) this will less often be the case.

*Example*

In *Keurkoop v Nancy Kean* (1982) the design of a handbag which was manufactured in Taiwan was registered in the Benelux countries but without the authority of the actual author. Benelux law permitted registration of a design by a third party but gave the actual author the right within five years to claim proprietorship of the design. Keurkoop began importing infringing handbags and Nancy Kean sued. The court referred the case to the ECJ under Article 177, asking whether these peculiarly liberal provisions concerning registration were justified under Article 36.

The court held that:

'in the present state of Community law and in the absence of Community standardisation or the harmonisation of laws, the determination of the conditions and procedures under which protection is granted is a matter for national rules and, in this instance, for the common legislation established under the regional union between Belgium, Luxembourg and the Netherlands referred to in Article 233 of the Treaty.'

This approach was confirmed in *Thetford v Fiamma* (1988) where the plaintiffs were the owners of UK patents for portable lavatories. The defendants imported infringing portable lavatories from Italy and the plaintiffs sued. The invention the subject of the patent had appeared in a patent specification filed more than 50 years previously but which had not been published. The Patents Act 1949 (the governing statute at the time) expressly stipulated that this sort of rediscovery of an old invention is no bar to patentability.

The defendants argued that because of its history the invention lacked an inventive step and sufficient novelty to be patentable and therefore could not be considered to be industrial or commercial property within the meaning of Article 36. The court, however, followed the *Nancy Kean* doctrine.

## Copyright

The application of the doctrine to copyright has been more recently considered in the case of *Warner Brothers v Christiansen* (1988). That concerned videos purchased in England, where at the time there was no rental right, and imported into Denmark. The purchaser hired them out from his shop, a restricted act under Danish copyright law. The Court followed the doctrine that it is for national laws to define the scope of commercial and industrial property rights and in the absence of harmonisation the Danish law stood.

In *EMI Electrola v Patricia* (1989) the Court applied a similar logic to sound recordings. The term of protection for sound recordings (unharmonised at that time under EC law) differed between Germany and Denmark. A Danish CD manufacturer made commercial recordings of old Cliff Richard records, which were out of protection in Denmark, and sold them in

Germany, where they were not. He prayed in aid the Treaty of Rome as a defence against copyright infringement but the Court did not accept this. German law was perfectly entitled to protect such works for longer than Danish law did.

### 20.3.2        Discriminatory provisions

Restrictions on the ownership of intellectual property rights to nationals of a particular Member State, and requirements that the holder of the patent manufactures in that Member State, would be considered unlawful. The same principle applies to national provisions which govern the transfer or extinction of intellectual property rights, including compulsory licensing.

*Example*

In *Allen and Hanburys v Generics* (1988) Salbutamol was subject to licences of right in the UK under the transitional provisions of the Patents Act 1977. Generics imported the drug from Italy where it was not patented and Allen and Hanburys sued. The case went to the House of Lords which referred several questions to the ECJ including:

- Could UK law distinguish between infringement by manufacturing in the UK (against which a plaintiff cannot obtain an injunction if the defendant offers to take a licence) and an infringement by importation (where an injunction remains available)?

- Can the authorities prevent the licensee of right from importing products from other Member States?

The ECJ held that a prohibition on imports could only be justified under Article 36 if:

... that prohibition is necessary in order to ensure that the proprietor of such a patent has, vis–à–vis importers, the same rights as he enjoys against producers who manufacture the product in the national territory, that is to say the right to a fair return from his patent.

The court found that no such prohibition was necessary for this purpose.

The treatment of compulsory licences will be similar to the treatment of licences of right, so it emerges that compulsory licences for the importation of a product may not be withheld if they are available for the manufacture of the same product.

*Note*

The grounds in UK patent law for granting a compulsory licence, namely that demand in the UK is being met substantially by imports, are unlawful under Article 30: *Commission v UK* (1993).

## Exhaustion 20.4

The doctrine of exhaustion of rights was first laid down in *Deutsche Grammophon v Metro* (1971). In that case, Deutsche Grammophon manufactured records in Germany and sold them to their French subsidiary. They then came into Metro's hands and the plaintiff sought an injunction to stop Metro from selling them in Germany. Such sales would infringe the plaintiff's rights in the sound recordings. The court held:

If a right related to copyright is relied upon to prevent the marketing in a Member State of products distributed by the holder of the right or with his consent in the territory of another Member State on the sole ground that such distribution did not take place on the national territory, such a prohibition which would legitimise the isolation of national markets, would be repugnant to the essential purpose of the Treaty which is to unite national markets into a single market.

To determine when the rights protected by IP laws have been exhausted, you first have to identify what these rights are. Under Article 36, national IP laws will only be tolerated to the extent that they are necessary to protect the property mentioned in that article. This, which the ECJ calls the 'specific subject matter' of the right, is what is not prohibited by Article 30. But once it has gone, having been exercised, that is the end of that particular right.

The cases are therefore concerned with the search for the specific subject matter of the various IP rights.

The same principle applies even where no protection is available in the Member State where the goods are first marketed.

*Example*

In *Merck v Stephar* (1981) the plaintiff marketed in the Netherlands a patented pharmaceutical product which it also sold in Italy. Pharmaceutical products were not at that time capable of being patented in Italy (although the law has now changed). The defendant acquired the product in Italy and sold it in the Netherlands.

The ECJ held that the patent was exhausted when the goods were sold in Italy and no action would lie for infringement of the patent in the Netherlands. If the patentee chooses to market their product in a Member State where it is not patentable they must bear the consequences of their decision. (Had the product been sold in Italy without Merck's authorisation, the outcome would have been rather different; unauthorised sales would not have exhausted Merck's rights.)

### 20.4.1    Exhaustion of patent rights

The first exhaustion case dealing with patents was *Centrafarm v Sterling Drug* (1974). The price of the drug Negram differed between the UK and the Netherlands by a factor of some 50% and Centrafarm bought it in the UK for resale in the Netherlands. The drug was patented in both countries and the patents belonged to Sterling Drug who commenced proceedings in the Netherlands. The Dutch Court referred the matter to the ECJ which held that Sterling Drug could not use its patent rights to stop parallel imports when the goods were marketed in the UK with the patent owner's consent, the rights given by the patent were exhausted. The court held:

In relation to patents, the specific subject matter of the industrial property is the guarantee that the patentee, to reward the creative effort of the inventor, has the exclusive right to use an invention with a view to manufacturing industrial products and putting them into circulation for the first time, either directly or by the grant of licences for third parties, as well as to oppose infringements ...

*Example*

In *Pharmon v Hoechst* (1984) a licence of right to make the products in question in the UK was granted, but with a ban on exports written into it. Pharmon nevertheless exported the product to the Netherlands and Hoechst sought an injunction to stop the sale of the drug in that country. The ECJ held that Hoechst had not consented to the manufacture of the product by the compulsory licensee. The exclusive right of first marketing must be protected, therefore the patentee could prevent the marketing of parallel imports in such circumstances.

The Advocate General added a proviso which was not adopted by the court that this would be different if the patent holder had expressly or impliedly consented to the grant of a compulsory licence. This might, for example, be the case where there were links between the patent holder and the compulsory licensee such as where they were parent and subsidiary.

### 20.4.2    Exhaustion of trademark rights

The first case on the exhaustion of trademark rights was *Centrafarm v Winthrop* (1974) which arose on the same facts as the *Sterling Drug case*. There the court defined the specific subject matter of trademarks as:

... the guarantee that the owner of the trademark has the exclusive right to use that mark, for the purpose of putting products protected by the trademark into circulation for the first time, and is therefore intended to protect him against competitors wishing to take advantage of the status and reputation of the trademark by selling products illegally bearing that trademark.

It was therefore incompatible with the Treaty to exercise a trademark in one Member State so as prohibit the sale there of a product which has been marketed by the trademark owner under the same trademark in another Member State, or which has been so marketed with the consent of the trademark owner.

*Example*

In *Hoffman-La Roche v Centrafarm* (1978) the defendant purchased tablets in the UK and repackaged them for the German market affixing the plaintiff's trademark to them. The court held that the plaintiff was entitled to use its trademark rights to prevent these parallel imports. The mark guaranteed the identity of the origin of the trade marked product to the consumer or ultimate user, who could distinguish that product from products which have another origin. This also means that the consumer or ultimate user can be certain that a trade marked product has not been subject at a previous stage of marketing to interference by a third person, without the authorisation of the proprietor of the trademark, such as to affect the original condition of the product. The right attributed to the proprietor of preventing any use of the trademark which is likely to impair the guarantee of origin so understood is therefore part of the specific subject matter of the trademark right.

The court went on to explore the circumstances in which the use of a trademark in this way would nevertheless amount to a disguised restriction on trade. The prevention of marketing repackaged products would constitute such a disguised restriction where:

● It is established that the use of the trademark right by the proprietor, having regard to the marketing system which he has adopted, will contribute to the artificial partitioning of the markets between Member States; and

● It is shown that the repackaging cannot adversely affect the original condition of the product; and

● The proprietor of the mark receives prior notice of the marketing of the repackaged product; and

● It is stated on the new packaging by whom the product is being re-packaged.

This proposition was refined in *Pfizer v Urim-Pharm* (1981). The case arose from the different prescribing practices of doctors in Germany and the UK. Urim-Pharm repackaged pharmaceuticals into different quantities more appropriate for the German market. The tablets concerned were contained in blister packs so there was no question of any tampering with the products.

The new packages into which the drugs were put had windows through which the original trademarks were clearly visible. The outside of the packaging identified the repackager. Urim-Pharm had clearly done their homework on the Hoffman-La Roche case and took the step of informing Pfizer of what they were doing. The court consequently found in their favour.

### 20.4.3        Exhaustion of copyright

The application of the exhaustion doctrine to copyright was first addressed in *Deutsche Grammophon* . It was refined in *Musik-Vertrieb Membran v GEMA* (1981), back into Germany. The royalty rates were lower in the UK than in Germany and GEMA, the German collective licensing body, sought the difference between the two rates. The question for the court is whether exhaustion operated to stop them doing so and the court held that it did. The owner of copyright was free to choose where to the sell the product and could have withheld it from the market when royalties were lower.

In both these cases, however, the court managed to avoid defining the specific subject matter of copyright. That omission was redressed in *Coditel v Cine Vog* (1979), where rights to the film *Le Boucher* were assigned to Cine Vog on condition that it would not be shown on television in Belgium for 40 months after its release in the cinemas. The rights in Germany were assigned to someone else but on different terms and the film was broadcast on German television before it was allowed to be shown in Belgium under the terms of Cine Vog's assignment.

Coditel, a Belgium cable television operator, picked up the German transmission and re-transmitted it in Belgium. Cine Vog sued for infringement of its rights and the matter was referred to the ECJ which held that:

... the right of the copyright owner and his assigns to require fees for any showing of a film is part of the essential function of copyright in this type of literary and artistic work.

The Court concluded:

The exclusive assignee of the performing right in a film for the whole of a Member State may therefore rely upon his right against cable television diffusion companies which have transmitted that film on their diffusion network having received it from a television broadcasting station established in another Member State, without thereby infringing Community law.

Note that the specific subject matter of the right to restrict performance of a copyright work may well differ from the specific subject matter of other acts restricted by copyright. This distinction was brought out in *Basset v SACEM* (1985), where the plaintiff was the owner of a discotheque in France. He failed to pay the agreed royalties to the collecting society which sued him. (In France, the fees payable to the collecting society include a 'supplementary reproduction royalty' which is not matched by any similar charge in any other Member State, although it does not have the affect of making the total royalty payable necessarily any higher than which prevails in other Member States.)

The ECJ, to which the matter was referred, decided the case on the basis that the supplement was outside art. 30. As far as the court was concerned, charging the supplementary reproduction royalties was merely a normal exploitation of copyright.

## Self-assessment questions

1  What is the effect of Article 30?

2  How does Article 36 deal with intellectual property rights?

3  Why is the existence of national intellectual property not affected by the Treaty?

4  What is the importance of the specific subject matter of an IP right?

5  Explain the doctrine of exhaustion.

6  Why are differences between national IP laws tolerated?

7  What did the court decide was the specific subject matter of patents in *Centrafarm v Sterling Drug*?

8  Does first marketing under a compulsory licence exhaust patent rights?

9  What is the specific subject matter of a trademark?

10  In *Coditel v Cine Vog*, what was held to be the specific subject matter of the performing rights in a film?

Chapter 21

# Enforcement of intellectual property rights

## Avoiding litigation

### The cost of litigation

It is trite to say that litigation is best avoided. In the IP field in particular it can be enormously expensive. Large patent cases may easily cost £1 million, and an average IP case in the High Court may cost the participants £250,000 each. On top of this there are internal costs to the clients' businesses such as lost employee time and diverted management energies. So the starting point for a discussion of IP litigation has to be how to avoid it!

### Discouraging infringers

Many infringements of IP rights arise from simple ignorance, of the existence of the other person's rights or of IP law in general. Education is an important part of the enforcement process. Putting a notice of your rights on products which are protected by them is a good way of discouraging infringement and also has the desirable effect of making it difficult for a defendant to argue that the infringement was innocent (a statutory defence under s.62, Patents Act 1977; ss.97 (copyright) and 233 (design right), Copyright, Designs and Patents Act 1988; and s.9, Registered Designs Act 1949) and therefore avoid a claim for damages.

**Patents**
The words 'patent applied for' or 'patent pending' may be added to goods covered by a patent application. It is an offence under s.110, Patents Act 1977 to do so, or otherwise to represent that an application has been made, or the goods are protected, if there is no such application.

After grant, the goods should be marked to show that they are protected. The patent number should be shown to ensure the s.62 defence is excluded.

**Registered designs**
These are covered by provisions very similar to those which apply to patents, including making it an offence to make a false representation.

**Copyright**
Copyright law in the UK imposes no marking requirements.

However, a notice is required in some countries and may be required under the Universal Copyright Convention.

*Note*

No notice is required in the USA but an appropriate notice removes the defence of innocent infringement. Such a notice must comprise the word 'Copyright' (abbreviated to 'Copt' or replaced by the familiar ©), followed by the date of first publication and the name of the copyright owner.

## Design right

There is no conventional way of marking a design protected by design right. A copyright notice will not serve the purpose because the rights (though related) are not the same. Care must be taken to ensure that any mark used does not falsely imply registered design protection.

## Trademarks

There are no innocent infringement provisions in trademark law. Notices are commonly used (look in particular at any computer advertisement) and the usual form is 'TM' next to the mark. A notice describing the ownership of the trademark is frequently included in advertising material. By s.60, Trade Marks Act 1938 it is an offence falsely to represent a mark as registered; the 'TM' notice does not imply this (it may refer to common law protection) but the word 'registered' does. If the only registration is foreign, this must be explained.

*Note*

The ® symbol which is often seen is reserved under US law for trademarks registered with the US Trademark Office.

## Confidential information

Confidential information is protected by taking care not to divulge it except under conditions of confidentiality. Breach of such a condition is actionable as a breach of contract. Confidential information should always be marked as such, perhaps even on every page.

## Other general methods

Information about the subsistence of intellectual property rights can also be spread in publicity material, by educating employees and the public about IP in general, and by establishing a reputation as a vigorous defender of intellectual property rights. A company which is well known for suing infringers will find in time that its rights come to be respected.

The threat of litigation is often enough to stop a potential defendant doing something. The cost of IP proceedings

makes the threat of them particularly potent, but the consequences to the threatened party (which may well entail
discontinuing a whole product range) are so great that the
law prohibits *threats* of proceedings for infringements of
patents, design rights and registered designs.

A right owner who thinks their patent or design rights
have been infringed is obliged to expose the validity of
those rights to court proceedings rather than relying on the
effect of a threat: s.70, PA; s.293, CDPA; s.26, RDA. A letter
before action must be limited to drawing the other side's
attention to the existence of the rights thought to be infringed, leaving the prospective defendants to draw their
own conclusions.

## Negotiating 21.1.3

At an early stage in any enforcement of IP rights, the clients
must decide what end result they desire. If a royalty would
be acceptable, there are good reasons for trying to negotiate
licence terms before going to Court (although it may be
necessary to issue proceedings to bring the other side to the
negotiating table).

The infringer, or the infringing act, may be very small.
Only a few articles may have been made, or the prospective
defendant may not be good for costs and damages. A
royalty arrangement is probably also best in this situation.

Any negotiated settlement will have to deal with unsold
goods. These could be sold to the plaintiff at cost, or the
infringer may be allowed to sell them if the profit is turned
over to the plaintiff.

A final possibility is where the infringer is either in a
different, non-competing, field, in which case the rights owner
will benefit from licensing the offending use, or has intellectual property rights of their own which would be valuable to
the plaintiff, in which case cross-licences may be attractive.

## Resolving disputes out of court 21.1.4

Alternative dispute resolution (ADR) procedures and arbitration may provide convenient ways of resolving IP cases.
A neutral mediator in ADR proceedings may be able to
assist the parties to arrive at a licensing deal, something
beyond the powers of a judge (or arbitrator).

Arbitration is usually only available where there is a
contract which provides for it, eg. a licence. However, the
parties to an infringement action may agree on arbitration,
although it can be as expensive as going to Court.

Questions of infringement or validity of a patent may be

referred to the Comptroller-General if both parties agree, although this procedure is little used. The Comptroller has discretion to refuse a reference if it ought to be dealt with by the Court, and an appeal lies from the Comptroller's decision to the Patents Court (and thence to the Court of Appeal) in any event.

### 21.1.5    The importance of prompt action

Intellectual property litigation is often decided by the outcome of interlocutory proceedings. Obtaining an interlocutory injunction or an *Anton Piller* order is usually of great importance to the plaintiff and frequently disposes of the case altogether. But such relief will only be granted by the Court if the plaintiff has applied promptly.

More generally, delay in asserting rights may be fatal.

**Limitation Act 1980**
The Limitation Act 1980 precludes any action for infringement more than six years after the infringement was committed. If the infringement started seven years ago but ended five years ago, an action will lie and an injunction to stop the infringement may be obtained but damages will only be awarded for infringing acts committed during the second year.

**Estoppel**
If there has been a long delay during which the defendant had been led to believe that the rights owner did not object to the infringing activities the rights owner may be estopped from asserting their rights. The prospective defendant must be able to show good reason for their believe and also that they had made significant investment to set up to produce the goods.

Infringers must therefore be put on notice that the rights owner objects to their activities.

**Loss of rights**
Infringements can sometimes lead to the loss of IP rights.

1 *Abandonment of trademark rights.* Inaction in the face of numerous open infringements may amount to abandonment of a registered or unregistered trade or service mark, although the level of inaction required is high. Delay may result in the infringer's use ceasing to be deceptive.

*Example* _____

In *Vine Products v MacKenzie* (1969) sherry producers had waited a century before taking action against producers of 'British Sherry' and the Court held that they had lost the right to stop it.

2 *Confidential information.* Confidential information is no longer confidential the moment it is disclosed, unless the recipient is bound to respect the confidence. Prompt action against an unauthorised disclosure is necessary if confidentiality is to be maintained.

## Preparing to sue                                21.2

### What are the benefits of suing?                21.2.1

Before entering into litigation, the client must consider very carefully what is going to result. A cost-benefit analysis is usually essential to a rational decision, although there may be other goods reasons for litigating – to start, or break a deadlock in, negotiations, for example.

The costs of litigation depend on its duration. If interlocutory relief is likely to be granted the costs will be much reduced.

The benefits of litigation depend on the effect the infringer is having on the client's business.

- The *profit on lost sales* will be the lowest measure – if the infringer is undercutting the client, the client's selling price will be reduced, and if the infringer's goods are inferior the client's reputation may be suffering;

- If the client contemplates licensing the infringing use, the *anticipated royalties* should be placed in the balance;

- If licences have been granted to others for the same rights, the *existing licensees* will be unwilling to keep paying if they face competition from a free-riding infringer – the licence agreement may also require the rights owner to protect the IP.

### The right to sue                               21.2.2

Before instituting proceedings, a prospective plaintiff must make sure they have the right to sue. This will not be a problem if the plaintiff was the first owner of the IP concerned but if they have acquired rights by assignment or they are a licensee this question will need answering.

It is essential that the formalities for the assignment of the rights concerned have been followed (*see* Chapter 16, para. 16.1).

Where the rights concerned are registered, the assignment should be registered too. This amounts to evidence of ownership of a patent (s.32(9), PA) and failure to register in such a case leads to loss of damages. Registration of a trademark assignment is evidence that the assignment is valid: s.46, TMA. Assignments of registered designs must be registered: s.19(5), RDA.

The assignee of copyright may sue if the appropriate right has been assigned: s.90(2), CDPA. This sounds obvious, but copyright compasses so many separable rights that it is an important issue. The same applies to unregistered design right: s.222, CDPA. If there is an exclusive licensee of design right, they must be joined as a party: s.238, CDPA.

### Co-owners

There are special rules for co-owners:

- *Patents*: co-owners must be joined as plaintiffs if they consent, defendants if they do not: s.66, PA;
- *Design right and registered designs*: co-owners can sue without condition: s.258, CDPA and s.2(2), RDA;
- *Copyright*: co-owners must be joined to the action: s.102(1), CDPA;
- *Trademarks*: the 1938 Act permits joint ownership but says nothing about who may sue. Probably co-owners would have to be joined.

### Exclusive licensees

Special rules also apply for exclusive licensees:

- *Patents*: owner must be joined: s.67, PA;
- *Copyright*: same rights as owner: s.101, CDPA;
- *Design right*: owner must be joined: ss.234–5, CDPA;
- *Registered designs*: the statute says nothing, but an exclusive licensee would be well advised to join the owner if the owner will not take action.

Except in the case of the registered user of a trademark (who may be an exclusive or non-exclusive licensee), non-exclusive licensees have no right to sue. Registered users may sue if the owner refuses or neglects for more than two months to do so: s.28(3), TMA. However, licence agreements usually contain specific provisions requiring the owner to take action to protect the licensed rights.

### 21.2.3     How watertight are the IP rights?

The strength of the IP rights in issue must be checked carefully before starting litigation. This involves not just checking the legal rights themselves but also a search of the prospective plaintiff's files for anything which might on discovery hinder the action.

Almost invariably, the defendant in an IP action will challenge the validity of the plaintiff's rights. The plaintiff must therefore check on the validity of the rights in question and explore the possibility of strengthening them if necessary.

### Patents

A granted patent may be revoked for several reasons, in particular that the invention is not patentable or that the specification does not disclose the invention in sufficient detail. If this happens in litigation the owner may not only lose the case but also face a large order for costs. In litigation resources far greater than those at the disposal of the Patent Office examiners will be brought to bear on the issue of validity, and the examination will therefore be much more detailed than that which preceded the grant of the patent. A plaintiff should therefore commission a thorough prior art search and an examination of the patent in the light of that search.

*Note*

It is *not* a good idea to get the patent agent who originally handles the application to do this: an objective opinion is what is needed. Such an opinion from a patent agent will be privileged and therefore safe from discovery.

If gaps in the protection given by the patent are identified, it can be amended. The procedure for doing so depends on a number of factors:

- *Before* there has been a challenge to the patents's validity, application may be made to the Patent Office: s.27, PA.
- *After* a challenge, application may be made to the Office or to the Court: s.75, PA.

The offered amendment may in each case be refused (unlike the situation before the patent is granted).

The amendment may neither:

- Bring in matter which extends beyond the matter disclosed in the original patent application as filed; nor
- Extend the protection given by the patent as originally filed.

Obtaining an amendment which breaks either of these rules is grounds for revocation of the patent in its entirety. Pre-litigation amendments may be found by the Court to have been wrongfully allowed. Thus, there is some danger in following the pre-litigation amendment procedure.

Applications to amend are advertised to permit others to oppose, and this could add dramatically to the cost and duration of the proceedings. Delay may also be fatal to the success of an application. Early amendment is advisable because the Court must be satisfied that the original patent was 'framed in good faith and with reasonable skill and knowledge' before it can award damages where the patent has been amended, and if amendment takes place after the patent has been held invalid (or partially so) there may be no right to damages at all.

### Copyright and design right

A plaintiff must prove entitlement by showing:

- Admissible evidence of the chain of title, eg. proof of the status of an employee who created the work or design, or a valid assignment;
- That the work or design is original;
- That the qualification requirements are met; and
- That protection was still running at the material time.

### Registered designs

If the design was not original when the application to register it was filed, or it was not registrable, it will be invalidly registered. A validity search and examination similar to that needed before starting a patent action would be advisable.

### Trademarks

In a passing off action the plaintiff must show sufficient use of the mark before the defendant's use or registration.

In an infringement action where the mark is registered, non-use may make the mark vulnerable to removal (or partial removal) from the register. Non-use may arise either from the applicant having no *bona fide* intention of using the mark when it was registered, or not having used the mark for five years up to a month before its validity is challenged; this is to prevent a trademark proprietor who becomes aware of a possible challenge quickly resuming or starting use (*see* Chapter 7, para. 7.10.1).

*Note*

1   Use by a licensee who is not a registered user will not save a mark which is not being used by its registered proprietor.

2   The use of the mark must be on the goods (or services) for which it is registered, or goods (or services) of the same description, and the mark as used must be the same as or very similar to the mark as registered.

The validity of a registered trademark may also be challenged on the grounds that the original registration was not valid, ie. the Registrar was wrong to register it, or that it has become descriptive, eg. through generic use.

### Confidential information

A plaintiff must be able to show that the information is confidential and that the 'chain of confidentiality' between it and the defendant is unbroken.

## Other considerations

### Information about the infringement

Before suing an infringer a great deal of evidence has to be collected. Expert evidence about the infringing articles may have to be obtained, particularly where the subject matter is highly technical, eg. a computer program. In the case of a trademark, evidence of deception or confusion has to be shown and market research evidence may be needed.

### Whom to sue

It may be possible not only to sue a company which has infringed IP rights but also to sue employees or directors of the company who were responsible for the act.

*Employees'* actions are normally covered by the principle of vicarious liability, so the employer is responsible for their wrongful acts, but if the employee commits the act otherwise than in the course of their employment the principle may not assist them. A *director* may be personally liable if they have personally ordered or directed the infringing acts.

*Note*

In *C Evans & Sons Ltd v Spritebrand Ltd* (1985), a case concerning copyright infringement, the judge refused to hold that it was necessary that a director knew that acts they had ordered were infringing acts, or that the directors were reckless.

It may be useful to be able to sue an employee or director if the company is not financially sound and the officer will be more able to meet an award of damages.

There may be several infringers all doing the same thing, or there may be several infringers at different levels in the chain of distribution. In either case, the plaintiff should take action against the one against which the case is clearest, although a judgment against a retailer will not necessarily stop infringing acts higher up the chain. If a quick result is needed, the plaintiff should select the defendant against whom it is most likely interlocutory relief will be available. (It is more likely that an interlocutory injunction will be given against a defendant who has not made preparations to start manufacturing infringing articles than against one who is already in production.)

### Where to sue

The Brussels Convention lays down rules for determining

where jurisdiction lies against an EC defendant:

- Where the IP rights are registered in the UK, the UK courts will have jurisdiction;
- Where the rights in question are non-registrable ones, the defendant should be sued in the country where the harm occurred – and it will be the law of that country which will determine whether an infringement has been committed and the remedies available to the plaintiff.

Where the defendant is *not* a citizen of or resident in an EC country:

- If they can be served with proceedings in England or Wales they can be sued here (unless they were tricked into entering the jurisdiction); the defendant may later be able to establish that there is another jurisdiction where it would have been more appropriate to bring the action.
- In any other case the Court's leave must be obtained before serving the defendant outside the jurisdiction.

## 21.3     Preparing to be sued

Infringers rarely get the opportunity to do much preparation, especially if the first they know is when the writ arrives. If they have advance warning, there are several things they can usefully do.

Potential defendants should check on the validity of the other side's intellectual property rights in just the same way as a plaintiff should. However, it might reveal scope for attacking their validity.

### 21.3.1     Patents

A patent may be attacked by:

- A threats action;
- An application to the Patent Office for revocation; or
- A petition to the Court for revocation.

In a *threats action* the patentee will usually counterclaim for infringement, in which case the action becomes a full-blown infringement action; the advantage to the defendant is that the initiative in starting the action has been taken away from the plaintiff.

An *application for revocation* may be made at any time by filing the appropriate form and a statement of case, setting out the grounds on which revocation is claimed. The statement of case is sent to the patentee, who may file a counterstatement. There is usually no discovery and evidence is usually given in written form. A hearing takes place before a hearing officer who decides the matter. An appeal lies to the Patents Court.

A *petition* is the equivalent to an application for revocation, but in the High Court infringement issues cannot be raised, so it is not particularly attractive to the prospective defendant, but there may be more scope than there is in proceedings before the office to adduce evidence of invalidity. Validity can also be put in issue in infringement proceedings, actions for threats and actions for declarations of non-infringement.

### Copyright 21.3.2

There is no threats action in copyright law, although it is possible to sue for *slander of title* to much the same effect. If threats are made to a customer, distributor or licensee an action for *inducing breach of contract* may lie. The recipient of threats of action for infringement of design right may sue (s.253, CDPA) seeking a declaration that the threats are unjustified, an injunction to stop them and damages.

### Groundless threats 21.3.3

Anyone aggrieved by groundless threats of infringement proceedings (except where the alleged infringement consists of making or importing an article) may bring proceedings against the threatener. The court may declare that the threats are unjustifiable, grant an *injunction* against the continuance of threats, and award *damages* in respect of any loss which the aggrieved person has sustained as a result of the threats. Similar provisions apply to design right and to the monopoly right. The use of the word 'threat' should not be taken to imply menace; any indication, however innocently phrased, that legal proceedings are contemplated is capable of being a threat.

The person aggrieved need not be the person against whom the threats are made; where, for example, the owner of design right coerces the trade customers of a competitor into ceasing to buy the competitor's allegedly infringing goods they must be prepared to put their design right and their allegation of infringement to the test of court proceedings. In that case, the competitor will be able to bring proceedings before the court for the groundless threats.

Relief will be available if the plaintiff proves that the threats were made and that they are a person aggrieved by them. It is, however, open to the defendant to show that the acts over which proceedings were threatened did constitute, or if done, would have constituted, an infringement of the right concerned. The mere notification that a design is registered or protected by design right does not constitute a threat of proceedings.

In the case of a registered design, a threats action is possible. Also, anyone prejudiced by a wrongful registration may apply to the High Court to have the design removed from the register. This is useful if the defendant has a weak case on non-infringement but thinks that the invalidity argument is strong.

There is no provision in trademark law for a threats action although one for *slander of title* may lie. If the use requirements of the Act have not been met an application may be made to the Registrar or the Court to rectify the Register. This also covers the situation where the mark is wrongly on the Register (because it should never have been registered, or it has become descriptive).

*Note*

Where a mark has been on the Register in Part A for seven years it is almost impossible to attack it unless registration was obtained by fraud or the mark is confusing, contrary to law or morals, or scandalous: s.13, TMA 1938.

### 21.3.4    Strength of the argument

The strength of a non-infringement argument should also be assessed at this stage. A declaration of non-infringement may be obtained from the High Court in the case of a patent. It is essential that such an application is preceded by a request to the patentee for a written acknowledgement of non-infringement.

There is no similar specific provision in other areas of IP law, but the Court has jurisdiction to grant declarations of legal or equitable rights which may be used to the same effect.

### 21.3.5    Other possible defences

The prospective defendant should also consider other possible defences, including:

- That the claim is statute barred (*see* Limitation Act 1980);
- Acquiescence or estoppel;
- That the owner of the rights granted the defendant a licence; and
- That the exercise of the IP rights contravenes EC law (*see* Chapters 19 and 20).

**Statutory defences**

In addition there are statutory defences particular to the different IP rights.

1  *Patents.*   Exempted acts include (s.60, PA):
- Private, non-commercial use and use for experimental purposes;
- Use before the patent was filed;
- If the patent had been allowed to lapse and before it was restored the defendant made serious preparations to use the invention, that use can be continued;
- Repair of patented products;
- Licences of right;
- Innocent infringement.

2  *Copyright.*
- Permitted acts (*see* Chapter 18, paras. 18.5);
- Objectionable works – the court may occasionally refuse to allow copyright to be protected in a work which is particularly undeserving;
- Innocent infringement;
- Spare parts: *BL v Armstrong* (1986).

3  *Design right.*
- Design right is not infringed by an act which infringes copyright in something which is also a copyright work (*see* Chapter 18, para. 18.6.2);
- Licences of right;
- Innocent infringement;
- 'Must fit' and 'must match'.

4  *Registered designs.*
The only statutory defence is *innocent infringement.*

5  *Trademarks.*
- An earlier unregistered user may have better rights to a trademark than the registered proprietor;
- Use of own name;
- Part B marks – there is no infringement of a Part B mark if the defendant can show that there is no confusion or deception and that the use is not likely to be taken as indicating a connection in the course of trade: s.5(b), TMA.

## The courts        21.4

### Patents        21.4.1

Jurisdiction in patent matters is shared between the Patents Court (a part of the Chancery Division of the High Court) and the Patents County Court.

## Patents Court

The Patents Court is constituted under s.52, Supreme Court Act 1981. Its function is:

... to take such proceedings as are within the jurisdiction conferred by the Patents Act 1977 and such other proceedings related to patents, or other matters as may be prescribed.

The Patents Court also has jurisdiction over registered designs, other than appeals from the Registrar of Designs (which are heard by the Registered Designs Tribunal).

The judges of the Patents Court are puisne judges nominated by the Lord Chancellor. At present there is one (Aldous J).

By s.14, the whole jurisdiction of the High Court may be exercised by any judge of that court: but in practice any patent matter should (unless there are special circumstances) be brought before the Patents Court rather than any other branch of the High Court.

## Patents County Court

The Patents County Court was established under the Copyright, Designs and Patents Act 1988. Section 287 gave the Lord Chancellor power to designate any county court a Patents County Court and to confer on it a special jurisdiction. The Patents County Court (Designation and Jurisdiction) Order 1990 (SI 1990 No 1496) designates Edmonton County Court.

The ordinary jurisdiction of the court as a county court remains unaffected by the designation, so other causes of action, eg. contractual disputes and passing off actions, may also be brought before it.

Every county court has general ancillary jurisdiction to give the same relief, redress and remedies as the High Court: s.38(1), County Courts Act 1984. They can therefore grant interlocutory relief (*ex parte* or on notice) including injunctions and *Anton Piller* orders.

Unlike other county courts, the Patents County Court is allowed to entertain proceedings within its special jurisdiction notwithstanding that no pecuniary remedy is sought: s.287(3), CDPA.

## Transfers

The High Court may order that actions within the special jurisdiction of the Patents County Court be transferred to it, on its own motion or on the application of any party to the proceedings. Likewise, the Patents County Court may order the transfer of proceedings to the High Court. In considering whether to make such an order, either court must have regard to the financial position of the parties.

The High Court may make, and the Patents County Court may refrain from making, an order for a transfer notwithstanding that the proceedings are likely to raise an important question of law or fact.

The High Court has no power to order the transfer of proceedings *from* the County Court.

### Patents Court                                   21.4.2

All proceedings under the Patents Acts 1949–61 and 1977 and the Registered Designs Act 1949 must be assigned to the Chancery Division and taken by the Patents Court. So too must all proceedings for the determination of a question or the making of a declaration relating to a patent. Documents relating to such actions must be marked 'Patents Court' in the top left-hand corner.

Interlocutory motions in matters assigned to the Patents Court are to be made to the Court. Except in an emergency, a notice of motion must specify the relief sought and must be issued and served on the other party. Summonses (except summonses for directions, *see* below) are dealt with similarly.

Appeals from the Patents Court lie to the Court of Appeal (RSC O.59) subject to restrictions concerning appeals to the Patent Court from the Comptroller (RSC O.104 r.45). The Comptroller must be served with notice of any appeal from a revocation order and may appear on the appeal (O.59 r.17).

Patent agents may represent parties and may instruct counsel to appear before the Comptroller and on appeal in the Patent Court. Their costs may be taxed: *Reiss Engineering v Harris* (1987). Section 280, CDPA governs confidentiality of communications between a client and the agent.

#### Proceedings in the Patents Court

Infringement proceedings are begun by writ. The plaintiff must serve particulars of the infringement (showing which claims are alleged to be infringed) with the statement of claim. One instance of each type of infringing act must be included.

Each type of infringement is a separate cause of action and must be separately particularised: *Sorata Ltd v Gardex Ltd* (1984).

Applications for *revocation* under s.72, PA are made by petition, unless they are made by a defence or counterclaim in pending proceedings. The respondent has 21 days after service of the petition in which to serve an answer on the petitioner. Particulars of the objections to the validity of the patent must be served with the petition.

Where validity is challenged by defence or counterclaim, the challenging party must serve the defence or counterclaim and particulars of objections to the validity of the patent within 42 days after service of the statement of claim.

Particulars of objections to validity must state every ground on which validity is challenged. In particular, O.104 r.6 sets out matters which must be detailed if want of novelty or of an inventive step are alleged.

### Procedure

A party may within 21 days after service of a reply or answer (or after the period allowed for service) serve on the other party a notice requiring it to admit the facts specified in the notice for the purposes of the proceedings. The party on whom the notice is served has 21 days in which to serve on the other a notice of admission stating for each of the facts whether it is admitted or not.

The general rules on discovery (O.24 rr.1 and 2) apply in an infringement or revocation action, except that the lists of documents must be served within 21 days after the service of the notice of admissions or the close of pleadings. Where a defendant claims that an allegedly infringing process is a trade secret it may claim limited discovery.

A party may wish to establish facts by experiment. If so, that party must serve notice of the experiments. The notice must state the facts that the party wishes to establish and give full particulars of the experiments proposed. The other party must respond with a notice of admissions relating to those facts within 21 days. If any facts are not admitted, the party seeking to establish them by experimental proof may ask for directions at the hearing for the summons for directions.

Not later than 14 days before the hearing of the summons for directions any party which proposes to call oral expert evidence must give notice of the name of each expert it proposes to call to every other party and to the court.

The summons for directions must be taken out by the plaintiff or petitioner within 21 days after the expiration of all the periods in the provisions concerning discovery, admissions and experiments. It must be returnable in not less than 21 days. Minutes of the order proposed, specifications of any patents in issue and copies of pleadings and documents referred to in them must be provided.

The court has wide powers. It must bear in mind the need to define issues, limit expense and avoid surprise (*per* Scarman LJ in *Polaroid Corporation's patent – Sufficiency Appeal* (1977).

### Patents County Court 21.4.3

#### Proceedings

All actions in the Patents County Court within its special jurisdiction are begun by *summons*, using the prescribed form (NP4) or following its text and layout.

The *statement of claim* must be endorsed on the summons or accompany it. It must be full but concise and set out all the facts, matters and arguments relied on to establish the allegations made and justify the relief sought. It must be signed by the plaintiff (if suing in person) or the plaintiff's solicitor or registered patent agent. If drafted ('settled') by counsel, it must also be signed by counsel.

Every *defence* and *counterclaim* must be accompanied by a statement of case.

High Court practice is followed to cover service of a *reply to a counterclaim*.

*Interrogatories* may only be served with the leave of the Court. The same applies to a *notice to admit* unless served within 14 days of the close of pleadings. *Applications for leave* may only be made on notice at the preliminary consideration of the case by the judge.

*Discovery* is not ordered automatically and should only be requested if reasonably necessary for disposing fairly of the action.

The Court may appoint scientific advisers or assessors to assist it. The appointment of an assessor is normally on the application of one of the parties. Notice must be given to the other parties and the party making the application must deposit a reasonable sum to cover the assessor's fee.

### Interlocutory proceedings 21.4.4

Justice often demands that the court stop the defendant causing further damage to the plaintiff pending trial, or doing something which would interfere with the plaintiff's chances of getting the relief to which they are entitled. Given that it may take years for an IP action to get to trial, the importance of interlocutory relief becomes plain.

#### *Ex parte* injunctions

Where the plaintiff shows that there is real urgency which makes it impossible to give the usual notice, and there has been no delay, the court may grant an injunction *ex parte*. The writ will normally have been issued (though not necessarily served), though this is not in fact necessary. Emergency applications may be made to judges anywhere and at any time, and if a writ has not been issued a promise to do so as soon as possible will suffice.

*Ex parte* injunctions last for a short time. As soon as the matter can be brought to court with notice to the defendant this should be done, and the interlocutory injunction will only last that long.

Opposed *ex parte* applications are where notice is given informally to the defendant, enabling them to attend and to argue at the hearing but giving no chance to gather evidence. If the court grants an injunction at such a hearing, it will normally set a timetable for the full motion hearing and the injunction will remain in place (without the need for a series of appearances to secure short-term injunctions) in the meantime.

### Interlocutory injunctions

Interlocutory injunctions prevent the defendant continuing with the acts which are alleged to infringe the plaintiff's rights until the matter is determined at trial.

Application is by *notice of motion*, which is served on the defendant. The plaintiff will be required to give an undertaking in damages (to compensate the defendant if at trial it becomes apparent that the injunction should not have been given) and must also provide sufficient evidence to establish a *prima facie* case on each of the requirements for an injunction, specifically:

● There must be a *serious question to be tried* – the claim must be neither frivolous nor vexatious and must have some prospect of succeeding;

● The *balance of convenience* must favour the grant of an injunction. The key question is, would it hurt the plaintiff more to go without the injunction pending trial than it would the defendant if it were granted: *American Cyanamid v Ethicon* (1975)? This question is answered by considering:

    – whether damages would be an adequate remedy for the plaintiff, and if the defendant could pay them;

    – whether the undertaking for damages is adequate protection for the defendant, and whether the plaintiff could honour it;

    – the maintenance of the status quo:

    – other factors, such as whether the injunction would result in factories being closed; and

    – the relative strength of the parties' cases.

If the injunction will dispose of the action – as will often be the case in IP actions – the court will want to see a strong *prima facie* case rather than just an arguable one.

The defendant may contest the motion, and may file

written evidence in reply. The plaintiff normally then has the chance to serve further evidence. If the defendant does not intend to contest the motion, they will probably agree the form of an undertaking with the plaintiff. Once all the evidence has been submitted there will be a hearing.

The plaintiff must give a cross-undertaking in damages. If it turns out at trial that the injunction should not have been given, or that it should not have been given in such broad terms, or if the defendant has given an undertaking it need not have given, the plaintiff must pay damages to the defendant. Where the plaintiff is not a UK resident or British company, security for this undertaking may be needed, eg. by placing funds in a bank account under the joint control of the parties' solicitors.

### *Anton Piller* orders

If following the normal litigation procedures would mean that there is a real chance that the defendant would destroy vital evidence, an *Anton Piller* order may be useful. This is a draconian measure, ordering the defendant to allow the plaintiff's representatives to enter their premises, to remove certain specified documents and goods, and to answer specified questions. The plaintiff must have strong evidence that the defendant is committing an infringement, and that if the defendant receives notice of the action infringing articles and evidence are likely to disappear.

*Anton Pillers* are therefore most effective where the goods in question can easily be moved. They have been particularly effective against pirate video and audio tapes and T-shirts.

The plaintiff must begin by issuing the writ, but before it is served an *ex parte* application is made to the court. The hearing is in camera.

The plaintiff's evidence must contain a full disclosure, including disclosure of facts which are unfavourable to its case. If the plaintiff fails in this duty the order may be discharged, notwithstanding that it was justified, and damages may be awarded against the plaintiff.

The defendant has no privilege against self-incrimination, though answers given to questions which it is obliged by the order to answer may not be used in subsequent criminal proceedings.

The order will be limited to specified premises (which may be abroad, provided the defendant is personally within the jurisdiction) and must specify exactly what the defendant has to do. The plaintiff's solicitor is usually required to attend, to serve the order and copies of the evidence and to ensure that the proper procedures are followed. The solicitor is also responsible for taking care of the seized items.

Force may not be used to gain entry, though the defendant's refusal to let the plaintiff in is a contempt of court. The defendant is, however, usually allowed to contact their solicitor before submitting to the search and may apply immediately to have the order discharged. The defendant also has the protection of the plaintiff's undertaking in damages and a further undertaking that the material seized will be used only in the case in which the order is obtained.

*Mareva* injunctions

A *Mareva* injunction prevents a defendant transferring assets outside the jurisdiction of the court to avoid a money judgment. The court may freeze specified assets pending the conclusion of the trial. It may also require the defendant to make an affidavit giving details of their assets and preventing them from leaving the country in the meantime.

The order can be made any time after the writ has been issued, or (in urgent cases) with an undertaking to issue as soon as possible. Application is usually *ex parte* so the defendant does not have an opportunity to thwart the order's operation by disposing of the assets. The plaintiff must have enough evidence to establish each of the requirements for the grant of the injunction, and must give a cross-undertaking in damages.

If the defendant has a history of paying their debts a *Mareva* injunction will not be available, and if it would be likely to put the defendant out of business it will not be given. If the defendant is an individual they must be left with sufficient assets to live on and to pay to defend the action. No order can be granted over assets which are outside the jurisdiction of the court.

## 21.5        Remedies

### 21.5.1        Introduction

In intellectual property infringement actions, the plaintiff will generally be entitled to:

● Damages or an account of profits;

● An injunction ordering the defendant to cease the infringement;

● An order for delivery up or destruction of infringing items, and in some cases their forfeiture.

The right to sue usually belongs to the owner of the intellectual property right but in certain circumstances an exclusive licensee has the same rights.

### Damages                                                             21.5.2

Damages for infringement are generally available to the owner of intellectual property rights. Usually they are calculated on the basis of putting the plaintiff in the position they would have been in had the tort not been committed. Damages will compensate the plaintiff for the actual loss suffered, provided it is not too remote, and might be based on a royalty which should have been paid or on lost profits.

Damages are *not* available against an innocent infringer, that is an infringer who does not know and has no reason to suppose that the intellectual property right which has been infringed existed.

There is a six-month period of grace for the renewal of a patent, and if an infringement is committed during this time the court has a *discretion* to award damages.

Where an amendment to a patent specification is allowed, damages will often not be awarded for an infringement committed before the amendment was allowed. However, the court may award damages in such a case if it thinks that the specification as published was framed in good faith and with reasonable skill and knowledge.

An applicant for a patent may sue for infringements taking place between publication and grant. The infringement must be of both the granted patent and the claims as originally drafted (so anything which changes between filing and grant may not be sued upon).

Where a patent is endorsed 'licence of right', or a registered design is subject to licences of right, and the defendant undertakes to take a licence, no injunction will be granted and the damages will be limited to twice what the royalty would have been under the licence. The undertaking may be given at any time before the final order in the proceedings.

The owner of a trademark will be entitled to nominal damages, and may recover substantial damages if loss has been suffered, eg. through loss of sales. Damages for injury to the plaintiff's reputation may also be awarded.

### Additional damages                                                  21.5.3

By ss.97(2) (copyright) and 229(3) (design right), CDPA the Court may award additional damages having regard to all the circumstances and particularly the:

- Flagrancy of the infringement; and the
- Benefit accruing to the defendant as a result of the infringement.

### 21.5.4    Account of profits

As an alternative to damages, the court may order an account of profits. The defendant has to show what profits were made from the infringement and the court awards this sum to the plaintiff.

This is an equitable remedy, so the court will use its discretion in awarding accounts.

### 21.5.5    Injunction

An injunction is an order of the court which prohibits the defendant from doing, or continuing to do, something, or requiring them to do something. It might compel a person to stop making infringing copies, or to destroy an article they have in their possession.

Injunctions are *discretionary* remedies, and are not given if damages will be an adequate remedy. However, this is often not the case in an intellectual property matter, so injunctions are frequently granted.

*Interlocutory* injunctions are interim or temporary injunctions granted pending full trial. In case the defendant should eventually win, the plaintiff who seeks an interlocutory injunction must undertake to pay the defendant damages resulting from the interlocutory.

In *American Cyanamid Co v Ethicon Ltd* (1975) Lord Diplock said:

> The object of an interlocutory injunction is to protect the plaintiff against injury by violation of his right for which he could not be adequately compensated in damages recoverable in the action if the uncertainty were resolved in his favour at the trial; but the plaintiff's need for such protection must be weighed against the corresponding need of the defendant to be protected against injury resulting from his having to be protected against injury resulting from his having been prevented from exercising his own legal rights for which he would not be adequately compensated under the plaintiff's undertaking in damages if the uncertainty were resolved in the defendant's favour at the trial. The court must weigh one need against the other and determine where the 'balance of convenience' lies.

### 21.5.6    Delivery up

A copyright or design right owner can obtain an order for delivery up of infringing articles and certain other things designed or adapted for making articles to a particular design or copies of a particular copyright work. Likewise, the owner of a patent can obtain an order for the delivery up of infringing articles.

The court will grant such an order where a person has such an item in their custody or control for commercial purposes, and in the case of a thing for making articles to a design, where that person has reason to believe that it has been or is to be used to make an infringing article.

Unless the right owner was under a disability for part of the time, such an order will not be given more than six years after the article or thing in question was made. The Court must also make (or have grounds for making) an order as to the disposal of the article or thing.

### Right to seize infringing copies and other articles          21.5.7

A copyright owner may seize an infringing copy of a work which is found exposed for sale or hire. This power is expressed to be subject to the provisions about disposal of infringing copies.

Notice of the time and place of the proposed seizure must be given to a local police station. A person seizing such copies may enter premises open to the public, but may not seize anything a person has at their business premises. The power is directed against street traders, if the infringer has a permanent place of business the correct course is to use an Anton Piller order.

At the time anything is seized the copyright owner must leave a notice in the prescribed form.

### Disposal of infringing articles          21.5.8

An application may be made for an order that an infringing article or copy or thing delivered up to the design right or copyright owner be:

- Forfeited to the right owner; or
- Destroyed or otherwise dealt with as the court thinks fit;

or for a decision that no such order be made. The court must consider what other rights which are available to the right owner would be adequate compensation.

The Act provides that notice be given to anyone with an interest in the articles, etc, which are the subject of the application, enabling them to appear or to appeal against the order.

In a trademark infringement case, the court may order erasure of the mark.

### Innocent infringement          21.5.9

If at the time of an alleged primary infringement the infringer did not know, and had no reason to believe, that design right subsisted in the design in suit, the plaintiff is not entitled to damages.

In the case of a secondary infringement, if the defendant can show that they (or a predecessor in title) acquired the article innocently, the rights owner's remedy is limited to damages not exceeding a reasonable royalty.

## Self-assessment questions

1 How may a product be marked to show the existence of:
   (a) a patent;
   (b) a registered design;
   (c) a trademark?
2 Why is prompt action particularly important in IP cases?
3 What rules govern actions by exclusive licensees?
4 When may a patent be amended?
5 What is the effect of the Brussels Convention?
6 What is the significance of a groundless threat of an infringement action?
7 What statutory defences are provided in a patent infringement action?
8 Which courts have jurisdiction in:
   (a) patent;
   (b) copyright;
   (c) registered design; and
   (d) trademark cases?
9 How is an infringement action started in the patents Court?
10 How are damages assessed in infringement actions?

# Chapter 22

# Intellectual property and competition: particular issues

## Biotechnology and plants 22.1

Developments in the field of biotechnology raise problems for the patent system and two questions in particular:

- What should be patentable;

and if biotechnology inventions are to be patented,

- What will the patent office granting the patent hold on its record if the invention is something which effectively replicates itself?

Patent law in the EC currently gives little protection for plants and animals. The provisions of the European Patents Conventions (EPC) on what is patentable can be traced back to 1964, when the possibility of an invention in this field was pure science fiction. It excludes from patentability:

... any variety of ... animal or plant or any essentially biological process for the production of ... animals or plants, not being a microbiological process or the product of such a process.

This raises formidable difficulties of interpretation. Although the EPC has been sufficiently flexible to find ways round the absolute prohibition on patenting new life forms, so that for instance 'OncoMouse' has been protected (see Chapter 5, para. 5.4.2, a comprehensive answer to the problem still has to be found.

The EC Commission has proposed a directive to harmonise the laws of the Member States on biotechnology patents. It has also drafted a regulation on plant breeders' rights, to create a Community system for protecting plant varieties.

### Plant variety protection 22.1.1

Protection of plant varieties is governed at the international level by the Union for the Protection of Plant Varieties (UPOV) Convention 1961. In the UK the requirements of this treaty are given legal effect in the Plant Varieties and Seeds Acts 1964 and 1983.

#### Subject matter
The expression plant variety is not usefully defined. To be protected it has to be capable of reproduction when the inventor's instructions are followed.

It must also fall within one of the prescribed 'schemes' under the Act. These are tailor-made to suit the biological and commercial requirements of plant varieties and the term of protection can be varied to meet the particular requirements of a category of varieties. Protection runs for between 30 and 40 years.

### Conditions for protection

The variety must be new in the limited sense of not having been the subject of 'prior commercialisation'. This is a very weak notion of novelty, further diluted by the fact that once a scheme has come into force for the variety in question the only prior commercialisation which can count against the variety is that done by the inventor.

The variety must also be distinct. It must be distinguishable from other varieties whose existence is a matter of common knowledge.

The variety must also be uniform and stable. Uniformity does not mean that all examples have to be the same, but they must resemble each other. Stability is a longer-term consideration of much the same thing; a variant must remain true to its description even after repeated propagation or reproduction.

### Scope of protection

The owner of plant breeder's rights has the exclusive right to sell or offer or expose for sale the reproductive material of the variety, and to produce this material for sale in the UK. The exclusive use of the registered generic name also comes with the right. Sale for non-reproductive purposes, eg. food, does not infringe, nor does the retention by a farmer of a proportion of the year's crop for use as seed next season.

Schemes for categories of varieties may give varieties within them further peculiar privileges.

### EC Regulation

The draft EC regulation will create a Plant Varieties Office. It would not replace national offices but there will be no cumulation of national and community protection. Patent protection for the subject matter of a Community plant variety will also be ousted.

The right would be available for all botanical taxa (or categories) and hybrids. It is proposed to last for 30 years, 50 in the cases of vines and trees. The variety will have to be distinct, homogeneous, stable and new, and an appropriate classification must be possible.

## Patentability of biotechnology inventions                    22.1.2

The draft directive seeks to resolve problems about the patentability of living matter and also addresses ancillary matters.

### Patentability of living matter

The directive will require that Member States' patent laws must provide that an invention shall not be considered unpatentable just because it relates to living matter. This is intended to ensure that differences in national laws do not create barriers to trade, and the directive is made under the harmonising provisions of Article 100A.

Article 7 provides that a process which requires human intervention consisting of more than merely choosing an available biological function under natural conditions shall potentially be considered patentable subject matter. The mere fact that something existed in a mixed form in nature does not make it unpatentable. This will open the way to patents for isolated plasmids which have formerly only existed in microbiological cells.

### Scope of protection

The draft directive also sets out limitations on the scope of protection to be given by biotechnology patents. Where a patent protects a process relating to the production of living matter or matter containing genetic information such as a strand of DNA, the progeny of the living organism produced by the process must be considered. The direct product of a patented process is an infringement of the patent under general principles of patent law and the directive will make it clear that so too will naturally resulting replicas of that product. This is important because left to its own devices in the right conditions, the product will multiply of its own volition.

*Example*
_____

BioTech Ltd invents a process for synthesising a micro-organism which it has identified. If it patents the inventions, it will be protected not only against others using the process to synthesise the same micro-organism, but also against others producing the micro-organism by natural means.
_____

### Dependency licences

The draft deals with potential overlaps between biotechnology patents and plant breeders' rights. Where the holders of PBRs can exploit the national rights given to them only by infringing a prior national patent, that plant breeder will be granted a non-exclusive licence under the patent to the extent needed to exploit the PBRs. A reasonable royalty will be payable. These licences will not be available until three years from the grant of the patent or four years from the filing date.

**Deposit**

Patents are granted against a disclosure of the invention sufficient to enable the invention to be worked. This concept runs into difficulties where biotechnology and micro-organisms are involved. Such an invention involves the use of a micro-organism which is not available to the public and which cannot be described in such a way as to enable the invention to be carried out by someone skilled in the art; or it may consist of the organism itself.

The directive lays down provisions governing the deposit of the micro-organism itself and its release to the public. This ensures that the invention has been disclosed and that it can be worked, in the sense that what is needed to replicate the organism is available to the public, after the patent has expired.

The question of burden of proof is tied up with this. If the subject matter of a patent is a process for obtaining a new or known product, the Directive provides that the same product produced by someone else will be presumed to have been obtained by the patented process. This rule will apply provided that the necessary means to carry out the process were deposited as required by the directive, and they had been released to a third party.

## 22.2     Computer programs

### 22.2.1     Introduction

Computer programs are treated for copyright purposes as a type of literary work. Since they begin life in written form, as a functional specification on a piece of paper, which is worked up into an algorithm which is finally translated into a series of commands for the computer, this has a certain logic. Much of the design and writing can now be carried out using computer programs, or at least using computers, but essentially the process remains the same.

A program's source code is a series of commands converted into a computer language which can be translated into a set of binary digits and then into a stream of electrical impulses – 'bits' – which the computer's electronic brain can understand. The source code, though incomprehensible to a human reader, is therefore apt also to be regarded as a literary work.

The earliest cases on computer programs assimilated them to literary works. In 1985 the Copyright (Computer Software) Act provided that they were to be *treated as* literary works; in the 1988 Act the approach was changed slightly, to provide that they are a *type* of literary work.

### The EC Directive                                                22.2.2

As part of its programme for harmonising certain areas of copyright law to help complete the internal market, the EC Commission proposed a draft directive on the protection of computer software (programs plus preparatory material) in 1988.

In the directive, the competition issues associated with protecting programs were starkly highlighted. Programs contain pieces of code which are intended to enable a program to inter-operate with another program, or with the hardware on which it is to run; it is therefore hard, if not impossible, to avoid literal copying of such items. Furthermore, codes are not commonly published by the authors of computer programs, so the only way a subsequent programmer can possibly determine how to make a program inter-operate with the first one is to *decompile* it and print out the code in human-readable form.

*Note*

The directive became law in 1991 (Directive 91/250/EEC) and has now been implemented in the UK by the Copyright (Computer Programs) Regulations 1992 (SI No 3233), which came into effect on 1 January 1993. The Regulations, made under the powers contained in s.2(2) of the European Communities Act 1972, amend the Copyright, Designs and Patents Act 1988 and apply to computer programs created before that date as they do programs created afterwards.

### Amendments to UK law

**Literary work**  The definition of a literary work, contained in s.3(1) of the 1988 Act, is amended expressly to include preparatory design material for a computer program (which may already have been included anyway).

**Distribution right**  The directive strengthens the distribution right of copyright owners in the UK, subject to the exhaustion of those rights by first distribution in the EC and requires a special definition of what amounts to issuing copies of a work to the public. A new sub-section (3A) is inserted in s.18 to cover this point. The definitions of adaptation and infringing copy contained in the Act are also amended to comply with the directive.

**Decompilation** Decompilation of computer programs is excluded from the fair dealing provisions in s.29, but the directive permits the lawful user of a program to decompile it under certain conditions. Decompilation is dealt with in a new s.50(B), one of three new sections which set out what lawful users may do with computer programs. Section 50(A) covers making back up copies and s.50(C), other acts which lawful users are permitted to perform. These include copying and adapting a program for limited purposes, including error correction. What amounts to a lawful user is set out in s.50(A)(2), which says it means someone who has a right to use the program. Such a right may, and usually will, be acquired under a licence.

Decompilation is allowed where it is necessary to do so to create an independent program which can be operated with the decompiled program or with another program. The information obtained by decompiling the program may not be used for any other purpose. This new permitted act, being limited to situations where decompilation is 'necessary', will not apply where the information is available to the user.

**Copy-protection** Section 296 of the Act already deals with devices designed to circumvent copy-protection. The directive requires a small extension of its scope: possession of such a device in the course of a business is added to the list of acts which are actionable by an owner of copyright whose copy-protection the device is designed to circumvent.

**Licenses** Section 296(A) is a new provision which will make void certain prohibitions or restrictions which may be contained in software licenses. These include any prohibition or restriction on making back up copies, decompiling where the conditions in s.50(B)(2) are met, or the use of any device or means to study the functioning of the program.

### 22.2.3          Computer programs and competition

**Copying the 'look and feel'**

In addition to the obvious matter of literal copying of a computer code, the courts have had to wrestle with problems of non-literal copying, as where a programmer writes a program to do the same as an existing program but on a different type of computer. It is often said that the 'look and feel' of a computer program may be protected in this way.

The purpose of copyright is to protect original expression, not the ideas which are thereby expressed. This problem is particularly acute when the object of the copyright protection has some functional purpose. This is the case with computer programs; the ability to stop others copying essential elements of a program could result in much broader protection than that normally given by copyright.

*Note*

A similar problem is encountered in the field of spare parts, in particular for motor vehicles (*see* 22.5).

The Courts' approach to programs case law in the UK is still relatively undeveloped (though it is getting more sophisticated all the time). Questions about copyright protection for computer programs are almost invariably asked first in the American courts, whose decisions are often cited in UK judgments.

US law protects computer programs in their own right, though it was clearly the intention of Congress that they should be protected like literary works US copyright law also contains an express exclusion from copyright protection of

... any idea, procedure, process, system, method of operation, concept, principle or discovery, regardless of the form in which it described, explained, illustrated or embodied in such work: 17 USC s.102(c).

In *Whelan Associates Inc v Jaslow Dental Laboratory Inc* (1986) the Third Circuit Court of Appeals held that the defendant's program, a re-write of the plaintiff's program, infringed copyright notwithstanding a complete lack of literal similarity between the two. The court held that copyright extends beyond the program's literal code to its structure, sequence and organisation. The court found substantial similarity between the programs' complex data-file structures, screen outputs and five important sub-routines. The 'look and feel' of the programs was similar.

*Note*

The Federal courts of the USA are divided into 13 Circuits, each of which has its Court of Appeals. The highest Federal court is the Supreme Court. The first instance courts are the District Courts. Most computer cases arise in a limited number of jurisdictions – the District Court for Northern California, covering Silicone Valley, hears many of them. The Third Circuit covers Pennsylvania, New jersey and Delaware. New York is in the Second Circuit and California, the Ninth.

### Idea and expression

In determining the scope of the protection given by copyright, the *Whelan* Court defined the idea of the program as its task (assisting in running a business supplying dental equipment) and excluded from copyright the idea and anything necessarily incidental to it. What remained was (in American parlance) copyrightable, and because quite a lot remained the decision has been seen to favour plaintiffs.

Cases after *Whelan* applied the idea/expression merger doctrine to software copyright. Where there is only one way (or a limited number of ways) to express a particular idea, this doctrine holds that idea and expression merge.

The doctrine's origins lie in the (US) case of *Morrisey v Proctor and Gamble* (1967), where the First Circuit (whose area includes Massachusetts) held that the rules of a promotional game could not be copyrighted (a verb which exists in America but not in the UK). There were only a few ways in which the rules could be expressed, and it would be a simple matter to secure protection for each of them. To avoid monopolisation of the idea of the game itself, copyright was denied to the rules on the grounds that idea and expression merged in them.

There is no clear line between idea and expression. It is impossible to disentangle them completely from each other. At any given level of abstraction, different matter constitutes the idea. In an infringement action, the court must choose an appropriate level of abstraction after weighing all the circumstances.

As the Second Circuit Court of Appeals stated in *Nichols v Universal Pictures* (1930):

Upon any one work ... a great number of patterns of increasing generality will fit equally well, as more and more of the incident is left out. The last may perhaps be no more than the most general statement of what the [work] is about, and at times may consist only of its title; but there is a point in this series of abstractions where they are no longer protected, since otherwise the [author] could prevent the use of his 'ideas', to which, apart from their expression, its property is never extended.

### The *Lotus* cases

*Lotus v Paperback Software* (1990) concerned copying of the user interface of a program (*Lotus 1-2-3*). Keeton J in the District Court (Federal Court of first instance) held that copyright would only protect elements of a program that go beyond all functional elements of the idea itself and beyond the obvious, and then only if there are other ways of expressing the idea and if the expression is original and substantial.

In *Lotus* the defendant's 'clone' was held to infringe Lotus' copyright. The judge accepted that the bulk of the work involved in making a program is in 'conceptualising' it, relatively little effort goes into encoding it. Creating the user interface requires greater creativity, originality and insight than converting it into instructions to the machine.

The judge also concluded that *1-2-3's* menu command structure was capable of being expressed in many (though not an unlimited number of) ways. The menu structure was therefore capable in principle of copyright protection, and was certainly substantial enough to be protected.

The same judge gave a similar judgment in *Lotus v Borland* (1992). There the defendants were the makers of another spreadsheet program, QUATTRO. In most respects an original creation, QUATTRO contained an 'emulation interface' which the user could select and which was designed to be compatible with *1-2-3*.

Keeton J held that the selection of functional operations which the spreadsheet would perform must be considered part of the program. To be protected, there would have to be expression distinct from this selection.

The idea underlying 1-2-3 was an electronic spreadsheet with a user interface involving a system of menus. These were arranged hierarchically, forming a tree of which the trunk was the main menu and the branches sub-menus.

The English Courts have deliberated on the matter – most recently, in *Total Information Processing Systems Ltd v Daman Ltd* (1992) – and the EC directive on software protection has attempted to bring some direction to this area of copyright law (see 22.2.2).

### How useful is the 'structure, sequence and operation' model

The future application of *Whelan* is now in question following the decision of the Second Circuit in *Computer Associates International Inc v Altai Inc* (1992) and in *Apple Computer Inc v Microsoft Corporation and Hewlett-Packard Company* (1992).

### The *Computer Associates* case

This case concerned a program called CA-SCHEDULER which creates a schedule specifying when a computer should run certain tasks, then controls it as it executes the schedule.

Altai produced a program which did a similar job and which in its first version included large portions of code which were identical to CA's. This situation arose because a former CA employee was responsible for writing that part, and without the knowledge of Altai he simply copied it. Altai re-wrote the offending parts of the program, but CA still claimed that it infringed their copyright. At issue was the degree of protection afforded to the non-literal elements of the program. The District Court ruled that the *Whelan* test was too simplistic, and cited Nimmer on Copyright:

... the crucial flaw in this reasoning is that it assumes that only the 'idea', in copyright law terms, underlies any computer program and that, once a separable idea can be identified, everything else is expression.

CA argued that the District Court erred by failing to find that copyright protects expression contained in the non-literal elements of computer software. Despite the rewrite, CA claimed, the defendant's program remained substantially similar to theirs, although all literal similarities had been purged. The Court of Appeals was therefore asked to determine the extent to which technical material obtained from operating systems could be protected by copyright.

In *Whelan*, the Court took the view that the purpose or function of utilitarian work (such as a program) is the work's idea, and everything not necessary to that purpose or function is part of the expression. Where the purpose can be achieved in various ways, the means chosen is not necessary to it and is therefore protectable expression.

This approach has, the Court noted, been much criticised. The appreciation of computer science evidenced by the decision is, moreover, outdated. In *Computer Associates* the Court defined an approach which it said emphasised practical considerations more than the metaphysical.

Drawing on familiar copyright doctrines, the Court proposed a three-step procedure for determining whether non-literal aspects of programs are 'substantially similar' and therefore whether one infringes copyright in the other. In doing so, the Court warned that computer technology is a dynamic field, and even this approach may need modification.

The Court's procedure was to break down the allegedly infringing program into its constituent parts. Each could be examined for incorporated ideas, expression necessarily incidental to those ideas, and elements taken from the public domain. A Court may thus sift out all the non-protectable material, leaving only the creative expression which copyright will protect. This can then be compared with the structure of the allegedly infringing program to determine whether the two are substantially similar.

To elaborate – in *step one*, the abstractions test enunciated in *Nichols v Universal Pictures Corp* (1930) is applied. The test has the advantage over the Whelan approach that it recognises that any given work may comprise a mixture of numerous ideas and expressions. As if reverse-engineering the program, the Court's job is to dissect the structure of each level of abstraction within it. The process begins with the code and ends with an articulation of the program's ultimate function.

In *step two*, the inquiry moves (as the Court said) from the conceptual to the concrete. For each level of abstraction, the structural components must be tested to determine whether their inclusion there was 'idea' (or necessarily incidental to the idea – *see Baker v Selden* (1879), which concerned a book-keeping system); or required by factors external to the program; or taken from the public domain.

This process of 'analytic dissection' was endorsed by the Ninth Circuit Court of Appeals in *Brown Bag Software v Symantec Corporation* (1992). Well-developed copyright doctrines are applied to leave a core of protectable material.

In the third step it remains only for the Court to compare the residue with the defendant's program. If any of this 'golden nugget' has been copied, the Court must assess its importance in the plaintiff's program, to establish substantial similarity. On this basis, the Court found that the Altai program did not infringe CA's copyright.

### *Apple v Microsoft*: **protecting screen displays**
In *Apple v Microsoft* copyright in screen displays, in particular the desktop metaphor well-known to users of Apple computers and more recently also to users of Microsoft's immensely successful Windows program, was considered.

The plaintiff claimed to own not literary copyright in a computer code but rights in an audio-visual work. The Court disposed of the matter by determining that almost all the features which Apple claimed had been copied did not in fact have copyright protection. Either they were unoriginal or they were nothing more than ideas or processes, containing no protectable expression.

The Court, adopting the *Computer Associates* approach, examined each feature in which copyright was claimed – the icons, the overlapping windows, and all the other bits and pieces which made up the screen display. It specifically declined the Apple's:

... invitation to use the advent of the microcomputer and its interface to abandon traditional standards which govern copyrights and invent some new law based on highly indefinite constructs such as 'look and feel'.

To the Judge, the material which Apple pointed to as meriting protection was just like the instruments and controls of a car. They were purely functional items, and they (and arrangements of them) were wholly beyond the realm of copyright. Similarities between the way the programs operated were due to standardisation for functional reasons, not to copying. User expectations – market forces – required the incorporation of similar features in most graphical user interfaces.

Citing with approval the *Computer Associates* judgment, the Judge agreed that the *Whelan* test was too facile; viewing only the purpose of a program as its 'idea' extended copyright protection too far. A simple program may contain a number of non-protectable ideas, not just one.

### Application by the UK courts

In *John Richardson Computers Ltd v Flanders and Chemtec Ltd* (1993) Ferris J applied the *Computer Associates* approach to a case involving programs for assisting with running pharmacies. However, although judicial authority is therefore given for the application of these American concepts, the result is far from satisfactory, as the judge used the process at a late stage (assessing the substantiality of the infringing act) instead of employing it as the main analytical tool.

The facts involved a rewritten version of a program originally created to run on a BBC micro. The same programmer had written both programs, and the case turned on the extent to which the second program reproduced parts of the first.

The judge's view was that the correct approach was to decide first whether the plaintiff's program as a whole merited copyright protection, and then to determine whether any similarity in the defendant's program attributable to copying amounts to the copying of a substantial part of the plaintiff's program. He also added another step, looking at the matter as a whole and assessing whether there was any part of the non-substantial copying which could be added to the copying already found to be substantial so that the global amount of copying was therefore greater. The test set out by Ferris J can be reduced to five steps:

- Decide if the plaintiff's program as a whole is entitled to copyright protection;
- Decide whether there are similarities between the defendant's program and the plaintiff's;
- Decide whether any of those similarities are attributable to copying;
- Decide whether any copying is of a substantial part of the plaintiff's program, using the *Computer Associates* three-stage 'abstraction, filtration, comparison' test;
- Assess whether the amount of substantial copying is increased if non-substantial copying is added to it.

The American decision made clear that there had to be a literal comparison of the codes, this being the first level of abstraction at which the filtration and comparison exercises were to be carried out. This exercise Ferris J baulked at: the codes were immensely complicated and it seems that the plaintiff's expert failed to shed much light on it in the report he prepared for the trial.

The judge was satisfied that the plaintiff's program was entitled to the protection of copyright. In step two, he compared screen displays and key strokes, either together or separately, and the comments he made indicate that he was comparing the 'look and feel' of the programs.

The judge concluded that there had been no intention of copying the plaintiff's program, though the defendant had an intimate knowledge of it. There was the possibility that unconscious copying had taken place. However, he did not at that stage seek to decide whether copying had indeed taken place.

The judge found that three elements of the defendant's program were the result of copying of a substantial part of the plaintiff's program; that six further elements were the result of copying, but not of substantial parts; and two elements might have been the result of copying but even if they were the copying was not substantial. Six other similarities identified by the judge were not the result of copying at all.

Aggregating the second category of copying and putting them into the equation with the first, the approach outlined in the final step of the test set out by the judge, made no difference in this case. The judge therefore found that there had been some infringement of the plaintiff's copyright, but by no means as much as had been alleged originally.

Since the judge began his consideration with a decision that the plaintiff's program as a whole was protected by copyright, the results of the three part *Computer Associates* test were prejudged. Decisions about subsistence (and therefore infringement) of copyright can only be made after abstraction, and by failing to follow the logic of the American decision the judge has left English lawyers with a bigger problem than they had before.

### Conclusion

Nevertheless, the *Computer Associates* test has been endorsed by the English courts and is likely to consolidate its hold. It becomes particularly important with the amendments wrought by software directive; the courts are required to analyse programs to find what part of them may be protected, and the three step approach is a very useful tool.

## 22.3    Media

### 22.3.1    Introduction

The media rely extensively on intellectual property rights. Publishing of all types is concerned essentially with the exploitation of others' copyright works, whether by selling printed copies, making records or films, or broadcasting them. Some of these areas are dealt with below, in the section on entertainment.

Additionally, statute seeks to control ownership of the media. The power of the written and broadcast media make them important influences on public opinion, and too great a concentration of media power would be undesirable.

*Note*

There are arbitrary choices to be made between matters to be dealt with under the heading 'Media' and those to be considered as 'Entertainment' in the following section. You may disagree with the categorisation used, but for the sake of manageability of the sections it is appropriate to assign matters to one or the other; not too much should be read into where any particular topic appears.

### 22.3.2    Ownership

The Fair Trading Act 1973 (FTA) sets out rules for dealing with newspaper mergers designed to avoid excessive concentration in the hands of one person. The Broadcasting Act 1990 also contains restrictions on cross ownership of media outlets. In addition, ownership of television franchises is controlled to ensure that no one person has too much power.

**Newspaper mergers**

Sections 57–62, FTA effectively require the approval of the Secretary of State for a newspaper merger and that consent will not usually be given unless the Monopolies and Mergers Commission (MMC) has investigated the merger and considered its impact on the public interest.

A merger will be caught if the circulation of the newspapers owned by the newspaper proprietor will after the merger average 500,000 or more per day of publication. Daily, Sunday and local newspapers alone are involved, and only concentrations of press ownership are caught. So a takeover of a newspaper by a magazine publisher, or a non-media company, could be reviewed, if at all, only under the general provisions of the FTA.

The definition of a newspaper proprietor is central to these provisions. It includes not only the actual owner of a newspaper but also the owner of a controlling interest in a company which owns a newspaper, or a company in which a newspaper owner has a controlling interest. A controlling interest is one-quarter of the voting shares; it is unnecessary for one person to own all these shares, just to be able to control the way the votes are cast.

The Secretary of State's consent may be conditional or unconditional. Usually, it may not be given until the matter has been considered by the MMC, and the Secretary of State must refer it to the MMC within a month after being informed of the proposed merger. However, in three situations there is no need to refer it:

- Where the newspaper is not economic as a going concern and the case is urgent if the newspaper is to continue as a separate newspaper;
- The newspaper being transferred has an average circulation of 25,000 or less per day of publication; or
- The MMC has failed to report within the time limit.

If the Secretary of State is satisfied that the newspaper is not economic as a going concern and that there is no intention of continuing it as a separate newspaper, he must give consent without referring the matter to the MMC.

The MMC may have three months (now, usually, two, in an effort to speed things up) at most for its investigation. It may be extended for special reasons.

If the MMC considers that the merger will operate against the public interest, it must indicate what conditions (if any) it thinks should be attached to prevent this. In considering the public interest, the MMC must have regard to:

... all matters which appear in the circumstances to be relevant, and, in particular, the need for accurate presentation of news and free expression of opinion.

The Secretary of State is not bound by the MMC's recommendations, but is usually guided by them. Nothing in the Act says that the Secretary of State can only withhold consent after an adverse report. Transfers without consent are unlawful and void.

### Independent television franchises

**Restrictions on Channel 3 licences** The Broadcasting Act 1990 provides that no-one may hold more than two Channel 3 licences. It appears to be the government's intention that no person may hold two licences for areas which are contiguous. It also appears to be the government's intention that the holder of a licence for a large area (undefined) will not be allowed to have an additional one. These are matters which are not dealt with specifically in the Act but are left to ministerial discretion. In 1993, these restrictions were altered so one person could own two large licences and one small one. This relaxation led to the recent spate of mergers between ITV companies.

**Cross-ownership** Under the Broadcasting Act, national newspapers and satellite broadcasters are limited to a 20% holding in a Channel 3 or 5 service. Channel 3, Channel 5 and domestic satellite service licensees can only have a 20% interest in a licence for any other licensed service.

Holders of licences for non-domestic satellite services or foreign satellite services will not be allowed to own more than a 20% interest in holders of licences for Channel 3, Channel 5 or a domestic satellite service.

Rules restrict foreign ownership of licensed services, but do not apply to non-domestic satellite services. They do, however, apply to domestic satellite services. Domestic satellite services licences will not therefore be granted to non-EC individuals or non-EC companies which are non-EC controlled.

Schedule II, Part III sets out restrictions designed to prevent the accumulation of interests in licensed services. No one person may hold more than the number of licences specified for each category of service in paragraph 2(1) of that Part. Paragraph 10 of that Part enables the Secretary of State to provide further restrictions on participation by persons other than licence holders.

Paragraph 4, Schedule 2, Part III enables the Secretary of State to prescribe restrictions on the extent to which the holder of a licence to provide a relevant service from within a particular category, may be a participant in a body corporate which is the holder of another licence to provide a relevant service for them within the same category. Effectively, this is intended to control takeovers by licence holders of other licence holders.

The Act elaborates special rules on the participation by holders of television broadcasting licences in other holders of such licences. It divides television licences into three categories: regional Channel 3 services, national Channel 3 services and Channel 5. Where a person holds a licence to provide a service falling within one of those categories, they are not permitted to hold, or to participate with more than a 20% interest in any body corporate which is the holder of a licence to provide a service falling within either of the other two categories.

### TV listings

Copyright subsists in TV and radio programme listings, which in copyright terms are compilations. In *Independent Television Publications v Time Out* (1984) the High Court held that to reproduce listings information taken from *Radio Times* and *TV Times* was not fair dealing for purposes of criticism or review.

The MMC examined the licensing policies of the BBC and Independent Television Publications Ltd in 1985, concluding that the exercise of copyright to prevent the publication of alternative listings magazines was not an anti-competitive practice within the meaning of the Competition Act 1980.

Section 176, Broadcasting Act 1990 now provides that advance programme information must be made available to publishers who wish to use it: and in *RTE, BBC and ITP v Commission* (1991) respectively the Court of First Instance held that it was an abuse of a dominant position for the television companies to refuse to supply listings information to publishers except on very limited terms. In a decision which has a significant effect on the exercise of intellectual property rights, the Court sought to realise the consumer benefit that would flow from the production of a single guide.

*Note*

The judgment is being appealed to the European Court of Justice by RTE and ITP.

### Reprography

Reprographic reproduction has long been one of the most contentious matters in copyright law. Liberal use of the photocopier, a machine unknown when the Copyright Act 1956 came into operation, had driven a coach and horses through the provisions of that Act designed to protect the interests of copyright owners which also allowed users a fair crack of the whip.

The 1956 Act allowed certain acts to be performed for purposes of fair dealing. These included, *inter alia*, copying for research or private study. It was never clear why the adjective 'private' qualified only the second noun, nor the extent of copying which amounted to fair dealing. The British Copyright Council produced guidelines at one stage, but later withdrew them, and in 1988 there was a pressing need for the law to be reformed.

A further complication was that the Act permitted such dealings as far as the rights in literary works were concerned, but not as far as the rights of publishers in the typographical arrangement of a published edition was concerned.

The 1988 Act originally intended to change all that. It was going to permit fair dealing for private study and non-commercial research, and to ensure that publishers' rights were also within the permitted act. However, the government succumbed to the arguments of the user lobby and reinstated the wording of the 1956 Act.

The original idea had been to extend the scope of licensing schemes to cover a great deal of reprography. The Copyright Licensing Agency was set up in 1983 by the publishing industry and the authors, and negotiated agreements with some 116 education authorities. It expected that the 1988 Act would give it an enhanced role in the future, particularly in negotiating with industry.

Industry always argued that its copying was limited to purposes within the Act, or to its own copyright works, so no permission was needed. Unlike the education sector, multiple copying (or systematic single copying) was not indulged in. However, in 1993 agreement was finally reached between the CLA and the CBI (representing industrial users) to pay a licence fee for the continued use of photocopiers. Some industrial companies still hope to avoid the need to pay by ensuring that no copying for which a licence is needed is done in their businesses.

### 22.3.5 Publishing agreements

**The publishing bargain**

Publishers are in business to make money from the efforts of authors. Publishers take the risks and make the arrangements to produce sufficient copies of the author's work to meet anticipated demand for the work, in return for which they pay the author a royalty, commonly 10% of gross receipts.

Publishing agreements work either by taking an assignment or a licence of the necessary rights from the author. There is little agreement about which is the best approach, with different publishers choosing to operate by licence or assignment with little apparent rhyme or reason.

**Rights to be acquired**

The extent of the rights which the publisher must secure also differ. It is possible for the author to assign or licence the hardback rights to a book to one publisher and the paperback rights to another. Different publishers may well have the rights to the book in different countries. Translation rights may also be dealt with separately.

Then there are other rights, known as *subsidiary rights*. In an agreement which relates only to a hard-cover edition of the book, paperback rights will be numbered among these: so too will book club editions, serialisation rights, film rights, strip cartoon rights, and a multitude of other ways in which the author's work may be commercialised.

There may also be merchandising rights to take into account if the book spawns a plethora of T-shirts and other souvenirs (more likely if it is made into a film); electronic publishing rights, which are becoming more and more important; and separate rights in any accompanying illustrations and artwork.

Copyright in illustrations will probably belong to someone other than the author and will often be overlooked or dealt with by the publisher only indirectly, by getting the author to warrant that they own copyright in the entire work or has secured all the necessary permissions. This approach leaves the author at the mercy of the publisher; if it turns out that the illustrator has not given permission or assigned copyright, an action for breach of contract would lie against the author.

# Entertainment                                         22.4

### Introduction                                         22.4.1

Entertainment is also essentially about exploiting copyright works, whether musical, theatrical or cinematographic. The legal basis of what goes on in the entertainment world is therefore copyright, and there is no need to add to the commentary on copyright law found in Chapter 8.

The particular problems of copyright in cable and satellite broadcasting and in films are worthy of separate consideration, and it is also worth noting that performers do not enjoy *copyright* in their performances but a different right, governed by the law on rights in performances (Part II of the 1988 Act).

The area of greatest interest in the entertainment field is the competition implications of the agreements under which copyright works (especially music) are produced, recorded, and marketed. The copyright rules for satellite and cable broadcasts are also noteworthy. Finally, there is the role of collecting societies to be considered.

### Satellite and cableq                                  22.4.2

The problems for copyright in the satellite broadcasting and cable worlds are different. They are dealt with in a draft Directive produced by the EC Commission in 1993.

### Satellite

The difficulty here is knowing where permission to broadcast a copyright has to be obtained. Different national laws have come to different conclusions: permission may be required in the country where transmission starts, or where it finishes.

The draft Directive sets down a simple rule. Permission has to be obtained in the country where the transmission is made. This avoids the problem that the 'footprint' of a satellite transmission is difficult to control precisely.

Minimum standards of protection are also imposed by the Directive. This will avoid a country making itself a haven for satellite broadcasters, giving little protection for owners of rights in the material broadcast.

### Cable

The problem with cable is that it is primarily a means of retransmission. It frequently serves to convey material which has been broadcast, to people within the reception area of the broadcast. In that case, it is not a separate copyright 'event'.

When a cable transmission does need copyright clearance, it may be impossible to get in time. Cable retransmission is usually simultaneous, so there is no time to get the copyright owner's permission. The Directive deals with this by making obligatory compulsory licensing schemes under which cable operators can get all the permissions they need.

## 22.4.3     Films

Films are a type of copyright work. Protection is given to any recording from which moving images can be reproduced whether on celluloid, video tape, laser disc or computer diskette.

As we saw earlier, copyright consists of economic rights and moral rights.

### Ownership

Under the Copyright Act 1956 Act copyright in the soundtrack was assimilated to copyright in the cinematographic film. So a soundtrack album, though it was contained on a record and sold in a record shop, was, as far as copyright was concerned, a film. This is now no longer the case.

The first owner of the economic rights in a film is the producer. However, the director gets the *moral rights*. This is supposed to recognise the fact that it is the producer who makes the arrangements (especially the financial ones) for the film to be made while the director has the artistic input.

## Performers' rights

Part II, CDPA creates rights similar to copyright in performances. The basis of the right is that consent must be obtained to any exploitation of a performance. The consent will usually be the performer's, but any person who has recording rights in a performance also has rights under Part II of the Act over recordings made without consent.

The consent may be given by the owner of the recording rights or by the performer, who may however be constrained from doing so by the terms of the exclusive recording contract. These rights extend basically to persons who have performers under exclusive recording contracts.

Part II is retrospective to the extent that the rights which it gives attach to performances which took place before commencement, but nothing done before that time infringes those rights.

A performance only qualifies for protection if it is given by a qualifying individual or takes place in a qualifying country.

### Infringements

The *first* infringing act is making without consent, otherwise than for private and domestic use, a recording of, or the broadcasting of, the whole or any part of a qualifying performance. The *second* is the live broadcast or inclusion in a cable broadcast service, again without the consent of the performer, of the whole or any substantial part of a qualifying performance.

Section 183 provides that the use of a recording which was made without the performer's consent is a secondary infringement where it is used to show or play in public the whole or any substantial part of a qualifying performance, or to broadcast it or include it in a cable programme service. No infringement takes place unless the infringer knows or has reason to believe that the recording was made without consent. By s.184, importing, possessing and dealing with illicit recordings also constitute secondary infringements.

If the defendant can show that the illicit recording was acquired innocently by them or their predecessor in title – that is, the defendant did not know and had no reason to believe that it was an illicit recording – the plaintiff's only remedy is damages not exceeding a reasonable payment for the act complained of.

The effect of this section, which brings performers' rights into line with those of copyright owners, is that a trader who buys and then deals in a quantity of recordings believing them to be authorised cannot be sued for infringement. Generally, the trader will not be in a position to ascertain whether consent has been given. If, having sold half of them, the trader learns that the recording was made without the requisite consent, the protection of s.184(1) is lost, but s.184(2) limits the measure of damages which may be awarded.

### The rights of record companies

Record companies are given the right to take action on their own account against bootleggers. The person having the right must be a qualifying person and the recording contract must be exclusive. The performance itself does not, however, have to be a qualifying one.

Under s.186, the consent of the performer or any person who has recording rights is required for the recording of a performance which is subject to an exclusive contract, except where the recording is made for private and domestic use. This is the counterpart of s.182, but the restrictions on broadcasts and cable programmes are not applicable in the situation of a person having recording rights.

A person who has recording rights in a performance is bound by any consent given by a person, eg. the performer, through whom they derive their rights under the exclusive recording contract or licence. Once a recording is made, the consent of the performer is only relevant if there is no exclusive recording contract. If a person has the recording rights, only their consent is required because only their interests are affected by use of the recording.

The Act therefore provides that in the case of a qualifying performance the performer's consent to the use of the recording will suffice (it amounts to a retrospective consent to the making of it). In the case of a non-qualifying performance, the performer has no rights, only the person with recording rights, so the performer's consent here will not be sufficient to regularise the position.

### Broadcasting and cable

Section 187 provides that recording rights are infringed if a recording made without 'the appropriate consent' (or any substantial part of it) is used by being shown or played in public, or broadcast or included in a cable programme service, without the consent of the person having recording rights in relation to the performance or (in the case of a qualifying performance) the consent of the performer. There is no innocent infringement defence.

Similarly, importing (except for private and domestic use) or in the course of business selling, letting for hire, offering or exposing for sale or hire or distributing a record infringes recording rights unless the consent of the person who has those rights or (in the case of a qualifying performance) the performer is obtained. The defendant must know or have reason to believe that the recording is illicit, and if they acquired it innocently they will be liable only to damages not exceeding a reasonable payment in respect of the act complained of.

*Note*

There are statutory exceptions to performers' rights which correspond broadly to some of the statutory exceptions to copyright.

### The Tribunal's jurisdiction

The Copyright Tribunal is given jurisdiction to give consent on behalf of performers in certain circumstances. This power only extends to the making of copies of authorised recordings for purposes of 'repeat broadcasting, cable distribution, or perhaps for marketing to other broadcasters' and only applies where the performer has already authorised the making of one recording.

The Tribunal may only give consent to the making from the original recording of a further recording. However, the use of a recording for the purpose of making a broadcast or including a recording in a cable programme transmission is only an infringement of the performer's rights if the recording was made without consent. The Tribunal can, therefore, give all the necessary consents on behalf of the performer.

If someone wishes to make a recording from a previous recording of a performance, but the identity or whereabouts of the performer cannot be ascertained by reasonable enquiry, or the performer unreasonably withholds their consent, the Act permits that person to apply to the Tribunal which may give the necessary consent. This consent will have effect as if given by the performer for the purposes both of the performer's civil rights and criminal liability. The Tribunal may attach conditions to the consent, and may only give consent in the case of the unidentifiable performer after notices have been served or published.

Where the performer has refused to give consent, the Tribunal must be satisfied that their reasons do not include the protection of any legitimate interest which they may have. It is for the performer to show what their reasons are; if they offer no evidence the Tribunal may draw its own inferences.

The Tribunal is required in any case to take into account whether the original recording was made with the consent of the performer and is lawfully in the possession or control of the person proposing to make the further recording, and whether the making of the further recording is consistent with the obligations of the parties to the arrangement under which the original recording was made, or is otherwise consistent with its purposes.

If the parties fail to agree on the payment to be made for the consent, the Tribunal may make such order as it thinks fit concerning the consideration to be paid to the performer.

### The duration and transmission of performers' rights

Under s.191 rights in performances have a life of 50 years from the end of the calendar year in which the performance takes place, compared with the minimum provided for in the Rome Convention of 20 years.

Performers' rights may not be assigned and may only be transmitted on the death of the person entitled to them by testamentary disposition. If no such bequest is made, s.192 provides that the owner's personal representatives may exercise the rights. Any person thereby entitled to exercise the rights stands in the position of the performer for the purposes of Part II so the beneficiary of a specific bequest may in turn bequeath the rights. If there is more than one person entitled to exercise the rights they may exercise them independently. Assignments of the benefits of exclusive recording contracts are unaffected by any transmission of the performer's rights.

Where the rights have become exercisable by the performer's personal representatives, any damages which they recover in the event of an infringement are treated as part of the deceased's estate and will pass to the beneficiaries.

### What remedies are available?

Rights in performances are not full property rights like copyright, so (as with moral rights) infringement of any of the rights under Part II is actionable as a breach of statutory duty.

An action may be brought by the person entitled to the right which is infringed.

In addition to the usual remedies of damages and injunctions, orders for delivery up of illicit recordings may be made, and the rights owner has the right to seize illicit recordings. These remedies are closely related to those available in cases of copyright infringement.

### Offences

Sections 198–202 deal with criminal proceedings concerning performers' rights. Section 198(1) lists the acts which are criminal offences if committed without sufficient consent.

All in relation to an illicit recording, the offences are:

- Making for sale or hire;
- Importing into the UK otherwise than for the private or domestic use of the importer;
- Possessing in the course of a business with a view to committing any infringing act;
- Selling or letting for hire, offering or exposing for sale or hire, or distributing, all in the course of a business.

Liability requires that the defendant must have known or have had reason to believe that the recording in question was an illicit recording.

It is also an offence for a person to cause a recording of a performance to be shown or played in public, or broadcast or included in a cable programme service, thereby infringing any rights in the performance, if the person concerned knew or had reason to believe that such rights would be infringed.

The more *serious offences* of making, importing or distributing illicit recordings may be tried summarily or on indictment. The maximum penalties are respectively a fine not exceeding the statutory maximum or up to six months' imprisonment, or an unlimited fine or imprisonment for a period of up to two years or both. For any of the other offences under s.198 the penalty on summary conviction will be a fine not exceeding level 5 of the standard scale (currently £2,000) or imprisonment for a period not exceeding six months, or both.

It is also an offence for someone falsely to represent that they have authority to give consent to activities covered by Part II.

It is a defence for the accused to show that they believed on reasonable grounds that they were so authorised. This provision addresses the problem that no criminal liability attaches to activities of persons who thought they had consent because fraudulent consent had been given.

In criminal proceedings, a court may order that illicit recordings be delivered up to a person having performers' rights or recording rights in the performance or to such other person as the court may direct. This only applies where proceedings are brought against the person for an offence under s.198 and the court is satisfied that at the time of their arrest or charge they had in their possession, custody or control in the course of a business an illicit recording of a performance.

Search warrants may be issued authorising a constable to enter and search premises using such reasonable force as is necessary where a Justice of the Peace is satisfied that there are reasonable grounds for believing that an offence has been or is about to be committed in any premises, and that evidence that such an offence has been, or is about to be committed, is in those premises.

### 22.4.5  Artists' contracts

Publishers and promoters invest heavily in the authors and artists whom they sign up. This must be balanced against the freedom of the individual artist, which is invariably constrained by the terms of the contract.

The problem in the entertainment industry usually centres around long-term agreements. In two cases, restrictive agreements between managers and authors were struck down as being in unreasonable restraint of trade: *Davis (Clifford) Management Ltd v WEA Records Ltd* (1974) and *Schroeder Music Publishing Co Ltd v Macaulay* (1974). In each case the contract was for at least five years, copyright in all the songwriter's work was assigned to the management company, and there was no obligation on the management to promote the work.

The courts' objection was not so much to the advantage taken of an inexperienced artist but to the fact that the artist's ability to earn a living was placed entirely in the hands of the other party, who was under no compensating obligation.

The *Schroeder* case was followed in *Zang Tumb Tuum Records Ltd v Holly Johnson* (1990) – the 'Frankie Goes to Hollywood' case. The court objected there to the term of the agreement (nine years), the absolute assignment of copyright to the company, and the fact that the group was bound exclusively to the company. There was no obligation on the company to release records, it could terminate the agreement at certain points, and group members could not perform without its consent.

*Note*

At the time of writing, the George Michael litigation against Sony is in court. There the artist alleges that the company refrained from promoting his records because it disapproved of the direction in which he was taking his career. The agreement gave the record company freedom to decide whether to release his records. In addition to the usual points from the cases mentioned above, Michael is arguing that the agreement is restrictive of competition and is therefore void under Article 85 of the Treaty of Rome.

Undue influence can also lead to a similar result: see *O'Sullivan v Management Agency and Music* (1985).

### Collecting societies

Copyright owners cannot efficiently collect the royalties due for the use of their work. Composers could not find out every time their work was performed and levy a charge for the privilege. Performers could not sensibly charge for each use of a recording of their performances.

The only rational way to ensure that some remuneration gets back to the rights owners is to set up collecting societies to do the job for many rights owners. Rights are assigned to these societies (of which in the UK examples are the Performing Rights Society, Phonographic Performance Limited and the Mechanical Copyright Protection Society).

Collective licensing raises significant potential problems for competition law. Indeed, much of the case law of the EC is concerned with the activities of collecting societies. They were considered by the MMC in 1988 which found that:

... collective licensing bodies are the best available mechanism for licensing sound recordings provided they can be restrained from using their monopoly unfairly.

This need underlay the establishment in 1956 of the Performing Right Tribunal, now reconstituted as the Copyright Tribunal. Initially given jurisdiction over licences for public performance, broadcasting and inclusion of works in cable programmes, it now (since the 1988 Act) also covers disputes over licensing schemes operated (or proposed to be operated) by collecting societies in all areas of copyright.

Schemes and licences may be referred to the Tribunal for determination of the reasonableness of their terms. Orders can also be made relating to the works covered by the schemes (and in certain circumstances works not covered by them). Licensing schemes may also be licensed by the Secretary of State, which has the effect of cancelling rights given to users under some of the permitted provisions of the Act.

## Spare parts

### Introduction

Control over spare parts gives manufacturers the chance to make enhanced profits from which they can subsidise the price of the original article. Robert M Pirsig describes the problem in *Zen and the Art of Motorcycle Maintenance*:

It's a well-known industrial policy to price the original equipment competitively, because the customer can always go somewhere else, but on parts to overprice and clean up.

*Note*

The problem has been particularly conspicuous in the motor industry. *See the MMC Report on Car Parts* (1982), HC 318.

A further consideration is that spare parts are often manufactured at the same time as the parts which go into the product in the first place (original equipment) and may be made by subcontractors either to the manufacturer's design or to their own. Parts may then have to be held in stock for many years before there is any demand for them.

### 22.5.2    The *Hugin* decision

In *Hugin v Commission* (1979) the ECJ considered whether it was abuse of a dominant position not to supply spare parts to non-authorised repairers. The Court upheld the Commission's view that the relevant market was that for spare parts for cash registers, not the market for cash registers. There was no interchangeability between spares for different types of cash register and Hugin's copyright would enable it to stop others making spares. (There was, however, no effect on trade between Member States, so Hugin was not in breach of Article 86.)

### 22.5.3    The *Volvo* and *Renault* cases

In *Volvo v Veng* (1988) and *Renault v CICRA and Maxicar* (1988) the ECJ held that there was no abuse of a dominant position if the owners of national IP rights used them to prevent others making replacement parts. If national laws wanted to give such rights that was a matter for them, unless the EC was harmonising the area. At that time it was not, although the introduction of EC design legislation will make a difference.

*Note*

Whether UK law ever gave such rights is now in doubt following the Registered Design Appeal Tribunal decision in *Re Ford and Iveco's Applications* (1993) that designs for, *inter alia*, body panels were not designs for 'articles' within the 1949 Act's meaning.

### 22.5.4    Copyright Act 1956: *BL v Armstrong*

The Copyright Act 1956 protected drawings against anyone making three-dimensional articles resembling the drawings. Functional articles therefore received protection under copyright law.

This situation was heavily criticised – why should functional designs get the full copyright term when aesthetic designs only had 15 years under the Registered Designs Act 1949?

Matters came to a head in the House of Lords in *BL v Armstrong* (1986). Their Lordships created a *spare parts exception* to allow them to reach a decision which they clearly considered just.

The Lords held that the manufacturer of complex products such as motor cars sells not just the physical goods but also the right to keep them maintained economically. From this proposition it is relatively easy to conclude that using intellectual property rights to prevent the manufacture of replacement parts amounts to a derogation from the grant of that right. Their Lordships decided that a spare parts exception (they did not define a spare part) was needed to avoid this consequence, and so limited the exercise of intellectual property rights.

The effect was to leave little of copyright protection. However, the importance of the decision was reduced somewhat by the reform of the law which then proceeded quite rapidly, although, as we saw in Chapter 8, the *BL v Armstrong* decision remains current for designs still reliant on copyright for their protection.

### MMC Report on *Ford*                                           22.5.5

The MMC's *Ford* report (Cmnd 9437, February 1985), under the Competition Act 1980, found that there was an anti-competitive practice being pursued by the Ford Motor Company, consisting in not granting licences to allow others to make repair or replacement panels for its products. In particular, repair panels were not at that time made by Ford itself.

### Copyright, Designs and Patents Act 1988                         22.5.6

The Act addresses the spare parts problem by excluding *mandatory design features* from both registered and unregistered protection. As we saw (see Chapter 9, para. 9.3.2) the 'must fit' exception excludes features of designs for parts which have to be the way they are to fit into something else: and the 'must match' exception addresses the problem of body panels.

The monopoly created by IP protection for designs is also diluted by the licensing of right provisions, which apply in different ways to unregistered design right (*see* Chapter 18, para. 18.4) and to registered designs (*see* Chapter 18, para. 18.6.3).

### EC Green Paper on Designs                                        22.5.7

The EC Commission produced proposals for a Community-wide design system and harmonisation of national design laws in 1991 (*see* Chapter 13). The proposal was published in mid-1993, with some significant changes.

The Commission's proposal had originally included a 'must fit' but not a 'must match' exception. After hearings on the subject, the Commission refined the proposed legislation in mid-1992. At this stage it decided that functional designs should be protected as much as aesthetic ones, thus provoking an outcry from the panel manufacturing lobby. Without a 'must match' exception, or a repair clause (an idea borrowed from US law) they would be seriously prejudiced.

When the proposal finally came to be published, it contained what the spares lobby had been after: a provision which limited to a mere three years the protection given to parts whose shape was necessary to restore the appearance of another object. However, the principle of this amendment has been accepted (it is reported) only with great reluctance by the officials of the Commission whose job it is to draft the legislation, and the chances of its being changed in the Parliament (the proposal is proceeding under Article 100A, which gives the Parliament two readings) are considered high.

*Note* _____

On EC design legislation, *see* also Chapter 12, para. 12.5.
_____

## Self-assessment questions

1  Describe the system of protection for plant varieties.

2  What will be the effect of the EC Biotechnology Directive?

3  What changes in UK law are made by the Software Directive?

4  What is the look and feel of a computer program?

5  Describe the three-step approach defined in *Computer Associates.*

6  What controls does the Fair Trading Act impose on newspaper mergers?

7  What is the function of the Copyright Licensing Agency?

8  Describe the effect of the draft EC Directive on satellite and cable.

9  What problems are involved in drafting long-term recording agreements?

10  How is the problem of monopolisation of designs for spare parts dealt with in:

(a) the 1988 Act;

(b) the proposed EC legislation on designs?